Praise for
A People's History of Christianity

"The curious but hesitant reader who wonders whether Christianity just might have something in it for them will find that the answer is YES."

—Daniel Walker Howe, Pulitzer-Prize-winning author of *What Hath God Wrought*

"It would be difficult to imagine anyone reading this book without finding some new insight or inspiration, some new and unexpected testimony to the astonishing breadth of Christianity through the centuries."

—Philip Jenkins, author of *The Lost History of Christianity*

"In this beautifully written history, Bass reveals the living, beating heart of love at the core of Christian faith."

—Sara Miles, author of *Take This Bread*

"Bass offers just what is needed for a church (alongside a society) that is into deep amnesia with little self-awareness. . . . This presentation includes lots of folk along the way who never made the 'power lists.' Readers will resonate with this inclusivene[illegible] grateful."

—Walter Bruegge[illegible] Seminary

"It was a delight to read this book. [illegible]tianity raises new kinds of questions, illumin[illegible]glected themes, prompts reassessments of familiar topics, and draws the reader into fresh forms of engagement with the history. The prose is sparkling and the insights are manifold."

—E. Brooks Holifield, professor of American church history, Emory University

"Intelligent and sassy, honest and redemptive. Bass celebrates a God who is big enough to survive the embarrassing mistakes of Christendom. This book is an invitation to participate in the next beautiful chapter of what it means to be the church in this broken world."

—Shane Claiborne, author of *The Irresistible Revolution*

"Diana Butler Bass has a gift when it comes to teaching church history. *A People's History of Christianity* is also a joyful apologetic for a 'new kind of Christianity,' one caught up in the current and flow of loving God and neighbor. I already gave away my copy, because I knew it would help salvage the faltering faith of a disillusioned friend."

—Brian McLaren, author of *Everything Must Change* and *A New Kind of Christian*

"Interesting, insightful, illuminating, and remarkably relevant."

—Marcus Borg, author of *The Heart of Christianity*

"An excellent introduction to grassroots renewal movements as well as to the various shapes that Christian spirituality has taken through the ages. As it builds insightful bridges between the past and the present, this book is necessary reading for any who may have thought that history is irrelevant to present-day living."

—Justo L. Gonzalez, author of *The Story of Christianity*

"Bass brings to the forefront forgotten voices who have had untold effect upon the Church. Her writing gives a depth and context to what devotion to Christ and mission for the world should be. She makes the case that it is our ability to learn from yesterday that gives us the possibility for progress tomorrow."

—Jim Wallis, author of *The Great Awakening*

"With her customary lucidity and charm, this time in the mode of Howard Zinn's historical populism, Diana Butler Bass gives us this splendid account of the grassroots movements that have kept alive the spirit and way of Jesus for two thousand years. *A People's History of Christianity* is enjoyable and illuminating."

—Gary Dorrien, Reinhold Niebuhr Professor of Social Ethics, Union Theological Seminary Professor of Religion, Columbia University

"Bass invites us into a deep conversation with the past, which thrusts us into the future with hope. A must for Christians and seekers of all stripes—a book that will ground the 'liberals' in a lively tradition and challenge the 'conservatives' with the fact that God is always doing something new."

—Alan Jones, former dean of Grace Cathedral and author of *Reimagining Christianity*

"Bass has created a perfect armchair companion for contemporary Christians. . . . *A People's History of Christianity* is our story retold with both clear-eyed affection and a scholar's acumen."

—Phyllis Tickle, author of *The Great Emergence*

"*A People's History of Christianity* is just that—a people's history, describing the diversity of Christian thinking, ethics, and practices over the centuries, and so important to the renewal of religious imagination today."

—Wade Clark Roof, University of California at Santa Barbara and author of *Spiritual Marketplace*

"Bass reacquaints the reader with two thousand years of Christian voices whose faith called for social justice and radical love. By rendering their wisdom accessible, the author encourages the reader to a devotional and ethical renewal that is exhilarating and challenging."

—Paul Brandeis Raushenbush, ed., *Christianity and the Social Crisis for the 21st Century*

A PEOPLE'S HISTORY – OF – CHRISTIANITY

The Other Side of the Story

DIANA BUTLER BASS

HarperOne
An Imprint of HarperCollins*Publishers*

Bible quotations, unless otherwise noted, are from the New Revised Standard Version of the Bible, copyright © 1989 by the Division of Christian Education of the National Council of Churches of Christ in the U.S.A.

FIRST HARPERCOLLINS PAPERBACK EDITION PUBLISHED IN 2010

Designed by Level C

Library of Congress Cataloging-in-Publication Data
Bass, Diana Butler.
A people's history of Christianity : the other side of the story /
Diana Butler Bass.
p. cm.
Includes bibliographical references.
ISBN 978-0-06-144871-3
1. Church history. 2. Liberalism—Religious aspects—
Christianity—History. I. Title.
BR148.B37 2009
270—dc22 2008051764

17 18 RRD (C) 10 9 8 7

To Emma Katherine Bass

Contents

PART V
THE RIVER
Contemporary Christianity, 1945–Now

INTRODUCTION

After Jesus

In the mid–1990s I was having dinner with a friend. Although she studies religion professionally, she claims no personal faith. Somehow the conversation turned to my Christian commitment, part of my life that has perplexed her.

"I don't understand how you still can be a Christian," she stated.

"I know, it isn't the easiest thing to be these days," I lamented, feeling a little foolish. "But I just can't get away from Jesus. I actually love Jesus and his teachings."

"Jesus?" she questioned. "I don't have any trouble with Jesus. It's all the stuff that happened *after* Jesus that makes me mad."

For more than a decade now her comment has remained with me, mostly because I have heard many others say similar things. Jesus fascinates millions, but Christianity, the religion that began with Jesus, leaves countless people cold. What happened after Jesus—oppression, heresy trials, schisms, inquisitions, witch hunts, pogroms, and religious wars—witnesses to much human ambition and cruelty. The things people do in Jesus's name often contradict his teachings. From Constantine to Christendom to the Christian Right, "after Jesus" can be remarkably depressing for thoughtful and sensitive souls. This dismal historical record surely was not what Jesus intended as he preached a merciful kingdom based on the transformative power of God's love.

Although I tried to deflect her criticism that night, I share my friend's concerns. She was asking moral and theological questions of history. Where is God in the midst of this? Shouldn't a faith be judged on the actions of its followers? Does God act in human history? She had concluded, as many people do, that if God is in the Christian story, then God must be indifferent or evil. If God is not in the story, then why bother? For spiritual searchers and secular people alike, the Christian God is not worth the trouble of the questions that history raises.

Christians, of course, have engaged with these questions, hoping to win over doubters and justify their faith. Not wanting to reject God on the basis of these criticisms, liberal Christians claim that human history is not God's fault. People in the past failed to live up to Jesus's ideals; therefore history is essentially a litany of Christian mistakes. So they reject tradition in favor of the hope of doing better in the future. Other, more conservative, Christians see God everywhere. From their perspective, God controls history, with a divine finger moving every actor and action. Natural and human evils are then God's judgments on sin. History serves as a moral lesson for individuals to submit to the saving work of Jesus or face the consequences in this life and beyond.

I accept none of these conclusions regarding the history of Christianity. Since I was eighteen, during my first year in college, the history of Christianity has fascinated me. Amid the chronicle of popes, schisms, and doctrinal fights, I discovered stories of interesting people whose lives were transformed through faith—people like John Newton (1725–1807), the author of the hymn "Amazing Grace," a slave trader who repented and became a minister, or Monica (331–387), the faithful Roman mother who prayed without ceasing that her brilliant but pagan son, Augustine, might convert to Christianity. I loved the stories of the unexpected mercy of God in their lives; they were people who were to be admired and whose experiences held insights for living faithfully today. Encountering them led me to the academic study of church history in seminary and graduate school. For a decade I worked as a college professor, introducing undergraduates to two thousand years of Christian history in fourteen weeks or less—a challenging pedagogical task if ever there was one.

Delving into the story of what happened after Jesus involved more, however, than intellectual curiosity. The Christian past raises meaningful contemporary issues. In the classroom I discovered that this crucible of questions resonated with my students and brought history to life. Exploring the past, we understood our actions anew; we discovered unexpected spiritual possibilities for our lives. As Archbishop of Canterbury Rowan Williams says, "History will not tell us then what to do, but will at least start us on the road to action of a different and more self-aware kind, action that is moral in a way it can't be if we have no points of reference beyond what we have come to take for granted."[1] I found this to be true.

Embarking on a spiritual journey through history is unsettling as it opens us up to stories we may not know—for many Christian stories have been overlooked or misunderstood by even the faithful themselves. By discovering the other side of the story, God's spirit might be discerned in Christian history. What happened after Jesus may well surprise us.

The Usual Story

Christians assume they know their story, but in reality they have only vague notions of what happened after Jesus. Over the years student papers revealed a popular understanding of church history, admittedly not very sophisticated, but a story that still possesses some cultural resonance. The usual story is that of "Big-C" Christianity—Christ, Constantine, Christendom, Calvin, and Christian America.

The tale runs thus:

> Jesus came to the earth to save us, but he founded the church instead. That church suffered under Roman persecution until the emperor Constantine made Christianity legal. With its new status, the Christian religion spread throughout Europe, where popes and kings formed a society they called Christendom, which was run by the Catholic Church and was constantly threatened by Muslims, witches, and heretics. There were wars and inquisitions. When people had had enough, they rebelled and became Protestants, their main leader being John Calvin, who was a great theologian but a killjoy. Eventually Calvin's heirs, the Puritans, left Europe to set up a Christian society in the New World. The United States

of America then became the most important Christian nation in the world, a beacon of faith and democracy.

Big-C Christianity is militant Christianity. It is not necessary conservative religion, for there exist liberal versions of it as well.[2] Rather, it is a theological disposition that interprets Christianity as an us-against-them morality tale of a suffering church that is vindicated by God through its global victory over other worldviews, religions, or political systems. Militant Christianity tolerates (and often encourages) schisms, crusades, inquisitions, and warfare as means—metaphorical if not actual—to the righteous end of establishing God's will on earth.

Elements of this story form American public discourse; politicians and preachers regularly refer to it. It is, of course, a bastardization of an old story line, a triumphal tale of Protestant superiority and Christian manifest destiny. Journalist Jeff Sharlet refers to this story as "providential history."[3] As far as I can discover, Cotton Mather composed the first version of it in 1702 as the *Magnalia Christi Americana*, or "The Great Deeds of Christ in America." From then until now some form of this church history has informed American culture. Atheist Sam Harris and evangelical activist James Dobson both believe it, and they attack or defend Christianity on the basis of it. Many people have doubted and rejected Christianity on the basis of this story. In a very real way, the Big-C story has been Christian history.

Having learned a softer, more sophisticated version of it in seminary, I believed it too. So did my friend. As she challenged me, I began to wonder if there was a different story to tell. If I could have admitted it to her at the time, I would have said that the Big-C story angered me too. Was there another side to the story? What would Christianity look like from another perspective?

As I ruminated on this I realized that believing the usual story is one thing. In recent years, however, something else has happened. Many no longer remember. For vast numbers of people, including Christians, history has ceased to exist.

Spiritual Amnesia

During my first year as a professor I taught at a Christian college, a place where all students claimed personal faith. In other words, they were serious young Christians. One day, lecturing on the medieval church and the Crusades, I explained how in 1095 Pope Urban II launched a holy war against Muslims. Most of the students took notes. But one young woman, looking very worried by the idea of Christians starting a war, shot up her hand. "Professor," she began, clearly wanting to blame Roman Catholics for the affair, "what did the Protestants say about this?"

"Well," I answered slowly, "there were no Protestants in 1095." I did not have the heart to tell her that Protestantism would not exist until more than four hundred years later.

Puzzled, she blurted out, "But where were they?"

At the present juncture of history, Western Christianity is suffering from a bad case of spiritual amnesia. Our loss of memory began more than two centuries ago, at the high tide of Enlightenment thought around 1800. The diminishment of tradition did not escape notice. As early as 1815 the poet Shelley reflected on the experience of religious amnesia:

Like broken memories of many a heart
Woven into one; to which no firm assurance,
So wild were they, could her own faith impart.[4]

As modern society developed, the condition of "broken memories" became more widespread. Indeed, in the words of one French Catholic thinker, the primary spiritual dilemma of contemporary religion is the "loss *and* reconstruction" of memory.[5]

Understanding the loss is easy. Unlike Shelley, who identified the brokenness of memories as problematic, other modern thinkers wanted to forget. To them, European Christianity was a trash heap of magic, superstition, and repressive tradition, a faith needing to be enlightened by Reason and Science. The medieval world was like a stained-glass window in one of Christendom's ancient cathedrals—pretty, perhaps, but you cannot see through it. As the Middle Ages ended, rationalists and revolutionaries smashed the cathedral windows to let in the clear light of human progress.

In the case of Western Christianity, people shattered memory because the past was too painful, too oppressive, and too violent for emerging sensibilities of tolerance and equality. Better forget than remember. Many Western people, even a good number of Christians, I suspect, secretly agree with the atheist Christopher Hitchens when he claims, "Religion poisons everything."[6]

Thus we inhabit a posttraditional world—a world of broken memory—in which some tell history badly, others do not know it at all, and still others use history to manipulate society to their own ends. All contemporary faiths struggle with lost memory. Some may protest that certain religious groups, such as various conservative, evangelical, fundamentalist, or Roman Catholic communities, possess a strong sense of tradition. One need only listen, however, to the jeremiads from evangelical leaders or cries from the Vatican bemoaning the biblical illiteracy and ahistorical sensibilities of their young people to know that all is not well among even those groups claiming, with faith-filled assurance, that they will never forget.[7]

Moderate and liberal religious people have suffered most dramatically, perhaps, from spiritual amnesia. Unlike Enlightenment window smashers or those asserting certainty, these people, like Reform Jews, mainline Protestants,[8] and liberal Roman Catholics took up the challenge of trying to reconstruct memories of faith in a changing world. Attacked by both secular humanists and their self-assured religious cousins, these groups wondered if trying was worth the effort, often vacillating between rejecting the past and bearing its weight. What to remember? What traditions can be retained? What should we teach our children?

At the center of the attempt to remember stands a startling question: Is spiritual amnesia a precursor to religious Alzheimer's, a fatal loss of memory for which there is no cure?

A Community of Memory

I am a Christian, an Episcopalian, a member of one of those much-maligned mainline churches struggling with these cultural tensions. Sociologists claim that "the history of Protestantism has been, and continues to be, an ongoing struggle to shape a meaningful narrative about life in the modern Western world."[9] Being a Christian should involve memory, history, and story.

My childhood church did not, sadly enough, provide a meaningful narrative of life. I was born in 1959 in Baltimore, Maryland, and baptized in a Methodist congregation that my ancestors helped found. It appears that such a church would be rich in memory, but it was not. Throughout the 1960s it retreated from tradition. This made sense since much of the tradition Methodists inherited was unjust. In those days Methodists had separate churches for black and white people, had few female pastors, and lent unquestioned support to the state in all that it did. By jettisoning these things, many churchgoers turned away from the past in favor of becoming, as one of my Sunday school teachers said, "modern Methodists."

In the process, Christians enacted the habits of church but lost the deeper stories of tradition. Churchgoers learned to make sock puppets for Bible school and to prepare casseroles for a potluck, but they rarely learned about John Wesley, the founder of Methodism, or much of anything about the Bible. Members knew much about contemporary political issues, but the church forgot devotion. They did not learn how to pray, the meaning of worship, or how to reflect on life theologically. When Christians broke with misguided traditions, they succumbed to the "baby out with the bathwater" syndrome, ridding themselves of the past—a scenario repeated in thousands of mainstream churches.

Later, when I was a teenager, I joined a conservative nondenominational church. I joined, not because I believed their ideas about hell and salvation, but because they opened scripture, taught Christian history, and engaged people in prayer. They taught that Christianity was, among other things, a tradition to be embraced and experienced. However, they too had lost memory. Although they retained a rich history of devotion, they had rejected the history of Christian social justice. They did this apparently because liberal Protestants believed in social justice, and they wanted to make the point that they were not liberal. So they cut themselves off from history as well and, in the process, lost Christianity's moral memory.

One community had lost its devotional memory, the other its ethical memory. Between them, they had severed Christian history in two, cutting the threads of a cohesive story in which piety and ethics once created a whole cloth. This proved bad for both. As sociologist Robert Bellah points out, communities "have a history—in an important sense they are constituted by their past." He claims that "real community" is a "community of memory, one that does not forget its past."[10] If Bellah is correct—and I believe that he is—then the primary calling of the faith community is to remember.

The Not-So-Usual Story

This book is not about lost memory. Rather, it is about memory found and the ways in which Christian history tethers contemporary faith to ancient wisdom. However cloudy their memory, posttraditional people still hanker for spiritual inspiration; wanting to hear stories that strengthen our connection with God and with our neighbors.

The Big-C story, the tale of Western Christianity's triumphal spread, has largely failed to speak to these contemporary longings. But that does not mean Christian faith has failed. There exists a different story—one that people want to hear—of folks like themselves who struggled to live as Jesus told them to, loving God and doing right. It is not a militant story. Rather, it is a story of generative Christianity, a kind of faith that births new possibilities of God's love into the world. Whereas militant Christianity triumphs over all, generative Christianity transforms the world through humble service to all. It is not about victory; it is about following Christ in order to seed human community with grace.

I think of this generative story as Great Command Christianity. In Luke 10:25–27, a lawyer approached Jesus and asked him, "Teacher, what must I do to inherit eternal life?" Jesus responded, "Love the Lord your God with all your heart . . . and love your neighbor as yourself." Immediately following this command, Jesus told the story of the Good Samaritan, the parable of a wounded man's rescue by a stranger, as an example of saving faith. "Go and do likewise," Jesus told the lawyer.

In these words from the Gospel of Luke begins *A People's History of Christianity*. Jesus's story is not only a good story, it is also the first step on a journey through Christian tradition, the history of Christian people who embrace the Great Command and follow Jesus's instruction to "go and do likewise." Unlike formalized church tradition, something that often appears as an approved list of what to believe and how to act, this is open-ended history. Great Command Christianity invites us to participate in a living tradition, to reconsider faith as a community of people who practice God's love and mercy through time.

As such, *A People's History of Christianity* makes two interrelated claims. First, lived Christianity cannot be understood in terms of the Big-C story; rather, it is best experienced as a community that remembers the ways in which Christian people have enacted the Great Command in different times and places. This history is less a magisterial narrative and more like a collection of campfire tales—discrete stories that embody Christian character, virtue, suffering, and commitment as people "go and do likewise." Friends swapping stories.

The second, and maybe more surprising, claim is that after decades of struggle, moderate and liberal Christianity is experiencing an unexpected renewal in North America. Many people now refer to this energized cluster as "progressive" or "emerging" Christianity. I have come to think of it as beyond existing categories of conservative-moderate-liberal. Instead, I refer to it as generative Christianity. In congregations and as individuals, people have stumbled into meaningful spiritual practices and a renewed sense of social justice without knowing, perhaps, that these new discoveries have long histories in the Christian tradition.[11] Without a sense of history, progressive Christianity remains unmoored, lacking the deep confidence that comes from being part of a community over time. What progressive Christians need to understand is that "emerging" Christianity has a story. Their faith is not new; the generative faith of Great Command Christianity is a reemerging tradition that has always been the beating heart of Christian history.

For this rebirth to be sustained, progressive Christians must not fear tradition. Rather, they should fear ignorance of history because ignorance allows others to use static interpretations of tradition against renewing forms of faith. Tradition is essentially the process of making connections through time, a reflective practice that makes history speak in new settings. Generative forms of Christianity must be grounded in history and claim their rightful place in the long story of faith.

The past has not been progressive Christianity's strongest suit. The very word *progressive* implies shunning tradition in favor of an unfolding future. Yet generative Christians maintain that present, past, and future—the living, the dead, and the yet to be born—are intimately related in God. In less theological language, Bellah insists that remembering leads to what is ahead: "Communities of memory that tie us to the past also turn us toward the future as communities of hope." Tradition is a lifeline to hope. Without it, progressive Christianity easily devolves into yet another political or social agenda, a largely secular worldview dressed up in religious language or blessed by a passing prayer.

Even though some of my colleagues wonder if I have embarked on a fool's errand to encourage progressives and post-traditional Christians to reclaim history, I can only point out that in recent years spiritual searchers have taken a new interest in old stories. That interest has been most noticeable in Jesus scholarship and in early Christianity. Scholars have been scouring the earliest decades of church history, looking for Jesus, searching for liturgical and ethical practices, and trying to understand the politics of early Christian communities. Through their work many Christians—as well as many postreligious people—are finding new memories of Jesus, linking their lives today with the most ancient traditions of faith. The quest to remember has already begun.

The Jesus who captures the imagination of generative Christians is Jesus the religious revolutionary, the one who teaches wisdom and resists the world's domination system to preach the kingdom of God. His is not a revolution of militant victory, rather of humility, hospitality, and love. Emerging Christianity deemphasizes Jesus the Warrior in favor of Jesus the Prophet.[12] But what, as my friend asked, of *after* Jesus? Shouldn't we expect in some way or another to see this Jesus in the community he founded? *A People's History of Christianity* looks for Jesus in the history of church, the spirit-enlivened community that he called his "body." Given these theological ideas, I assume that Jesus may be discovered in the later centuries of Christian experience as well as in early faith communities. The alternative history finds God in the people who took Jesus the Prophet seriously, those who tried to live what he taught and embody the kingdom he proclaimed. As such, Great Command Christianity is a history of holy and humble rebellion—of those who opposed the church when it was too rich, too comfortable, too cozy with the "principalities and powers of this world," or too full of its own glory.

This book draws from new scholarship in religious studies, theology, and history. The title, *A People's History of Christianity*, evokes Howard Zinn's magisterial essay on American history, *A People's History of the United States*. Published in 1980, Zinn's book wove a history of social activism by telling history from the perspective of women, outsiders, and working people. He did so to help Americans better understand their identity as revolutionaries and to take action on behalf of the poor, peace, and the planet. Eschewing historical orthodoxy, he confessed, "I had no illusions about 'objectivity,' if that meant avoiding a point of view. I knew that a historian was forced to choose, out of an infinite number of facts, what to present, what to omit."[13] This book has much the same purpose from a Christian point of view.

To discover how Christians imitated the life of Jesus the Prophet, I have focused on people, the known and the not so well known. Like Zinn, I sidestep issues of orthodoxy and instead focus on the moments when Christian people really acted like Christians, when they took seriously the call of Jesus to love God and love their neighbors as themselves. Historian Mary F. Bednarowski notes that "people's histories" are naturally "subversive," as they open space for little-heard voices to speak.[14] Roman Catholic theology actually has a name for the insights of regular people, the *sensus fidelium*—that God's people, filled with the Holy Spirit, possess a natural wisdom regarding justice, truth, and goodness.

Unlike Zinn, however, I have included many well-known people, those who might count as elite Christians—authors, pastors, and theologians. I did so on purpose, assuming that in a time of spiritual amnesia, many readers need to know major characters in church history as well as newly included ones. In each case I emphasized aspects of major figures' work that have not received the greatest attention, ideas that could or should have a broader impact on the practice of Christian faith.

Keen readers will know that none of these people are perfect. To use the language of prayer, they did things they "ought not to have done." At its most realistic, Christian theology insists that all human beings are simultaneously sinners and saints. Thus the early theologian John Chrysostom can offer a scorching and important critique of materialism while at the same time saying deeply offensive things about Jews. Such ugly inconsistencies teach us that Christians can and must do better. And, not to excuse Chrysostom, they also should remind us to practice historical generosity. One day we too shall be held accountable for what our great-great-grandchildren deem hypocritical, stupid, or wrong. Jesus's teaching to "judge not, lest you be judged" seems particularly apt in studying Christian history. As for the faithful, we must do our best while striving to go beyond even that.

And, also unlike Zinn's, my history is not neat. He created a tight chronological narrative of America's populist spirit. In recent years scholars have questioned the idea that some sort of grand narrative, a metanarrative, links history in a seamless, linear story. I agree with them. Here, bits of history illuminate larger spiritual and social questions, in order to find the radical Jesus through the church. It is more a mosaic than a systematic analysis; it makes sense artistically and from a distance rather than up close. It is suggestive, not comprehensive. In choosing this style, I have followed the advice of Archbishop Rowan Williams, himself a historian, who says that emerging Christianity is a "plotless narrative" and that it is untidy, decentered, paradoxical, and full of questions. He claims that history is not a story to justify the present; rather, history seeks to ground the present in the "strangeness" of the past.[15]

A People's History is a scrapbook of traditions that may have been forgotten, mislaid, or misinterpreted, rearranged on a page to evoke memories of the Christian God. It is an attempt to find the history of the prophetic Jesus in the church, the Jesus who spoke for the poor and oppressed, who broke bread with sinners, who wanted his followers to know life fully, who inspired people to give up all and follow him, and who believed—even when dying on a cross—in a world of justice, beauty, and love.

I am first to admit that this Jesus has often been elusive in Christian history. But he is there. *A People's History* is not intended as a nostalgia trip to some halcyon faith-filled days of old when the church got it right. The church has never gotten it completely right. But it has not gotten it completely wrong either. Throughout the whole of church history, people have made some pretty valiant attempts to make it better. This book seeks to create a realistic sense of what Christianity can be—because it has, at some times, managed to embody the heart of its founder. The narratives presented here are those of usable history, stories told for the purpose of strengthening community by deepening its spiritual practices and renewing its vision of social justice. To go back and tell the stories of generative Christianity is to find a way forward in a confusing, painful world.

With the exception of the final part on contemporary Christianity, the sections that follow are structured in the same way. The spine of the story remains located in Western Christianity, not to exclude anyone's story or hurt anyone's feelings, but because I am trying to help Western Christians move away from their triumphal Big-*C* history toward a more humble reading of their story. Each part introduces the main historical periods of Western Christianity: Early Christianity, 100–500; Medieval Christianity, 500–1450; Reformation

Christianity, 1450–1650; Modern Christianity, 1650–1945; and Contemporary Christianity, 1945–now. Individual chapters explore the ways in which Christians struggled with Jesus's Great Command to love God (devotion) and love their neighbor (ethics). By focusing on these two aspects, I hope that Christians can locate themselves in a past of spirituality and social justice, that emerging communities of faith might remember never to sever the connection between attending to the inner life and doing good in the world.

Fool's errand or not, these pages search the Christian tradition for a path to a vital, hopeful, hospitable, and open faith—a faith that can heal, reconcile, and bring peace. Maybe I was right to feel a little foolish with my friend so many years ago. She was, after all, correct. If Christianity offers spiritual insight, people should be able to see Jesus in church history. Her blunt assessment pushed me to look for a different story, a story that was part of the tradition all the time but that even I had overlooked.

People sometimes accuse me of being optimistic. To that charge, I plead guilty. Being a generative Christian myself, I always hold to the possibility of new life arising from darkness and death (generative Christians call such optimism "resurrection"). I actually trust that individual Christians can remember and that Christianity can be the kind of faith I have described here, a community of memory that offers hope for the future. So if your spirituality is either curious or quixotic like mine, come along on this fool's journey. After all, in medieval Christianity, the fool was the most truthful storyteller at court.

PART I

THE WAY

Early Christianity 100–500

ONE

Christianity as a Way of Life

During the first round of research for my recent study of vital mainline Protestant churches, I sent my project associate, Joseph Stewart-Sicking, to Calvin Presbyterian Church in the small working-class town of Zelienople, Pennsylvania. Joe grew up Roman Catholic and became an Episcopalian as a student. He had never attended a Presbyterian service, much less spent a week observing the life of a Presbyterian congregation. Throughout the week he called in reports of how the people of Calvin Church—their lives and their spirituality—intrigued him.

When Joe returned to the office, I asked him, "What surprised you the most? What did you see or hear that you did not particularly expect?"

Joe thought for a moment and replied, "Gregory of Nyssa."

"What?" I asked.

"Gregory of Nyssa. Other early Christian theologians. And the desert fathers and mothers. Every time I asked them about their spiritual practices, they told me about church history."

Joe's response startled me. Not all Presbyterians are familiar with the fourth-century theologian Gregory of Nyssa. But there, in a modest church in a small western Pennsylvania town, folks had found spiritual friends from the early church, people whose ancient wisdom they embraced for today. Across the country renewing congregations like Calvin Church are becoming conversant with ancient Christian theologians, practices, and texts. From Jesus to St. Benedict in the sixth century, people are discovering the distant Christian past anew.

Back for the Future

Few periods of church history have captured as much popular attention as early Christianity. At my local bookstore the Christianity section is full of dozens of books about Jesus, the Gospels, Christianity and the Roman Empire, and ancient churches. I recently counted: other than contemporary issues, fewer than twenty books on those same shelves cover topics beyond Christianity's first four centuries. In addition, three shelves are devoted solely to what the bookstore manager tags as Hidden Histories: Gnosticism, the Gospel of Judas, and Mary Magdalene. Early Christianity is a publishing sensation.

Popular interest in ancient Christianity did not begin, however, with the current trend. Since Albert Schweitzer's *Quest of the Historical Jesus* appeared in English in 1910, Protestants have actively pursued the question of who Jesus really was and what Jesus actually taught. Although a German theologian, Schweitzer introduced the notion to mainstream North American Protestants that somehow the original message of Jesus had been corrupted by later interpretations and that Christians must strip away the historical accretions to find the real Jesus.[1]

This notion meshed with romantic ideals of the day. Many people hoped that they could somehow recover the original purity and simplicity of the gospel and, by doing so, reform or recreate their churches.[2] For a century scholarly Christianity has embarked on a quest backward. The ancient faith may be the best source to renew the present. During much of the last century the focus has been on Jesus and the first decades of the Christian movement, as in Schweitzer's *Quest* or more recently in the Jesus Seminar, with writers such as John Dominic Crossan and Marcus Borg. Parallel to the interest in Jesus, a new fascination with ancient worship and liturgy took shape, and the emphasis on the primitive church widened to include the first five centuries of Christianity, not only Jesus and his immediate followers.

Will the Real Rome Please Stand Up?

In many churches today Christians can be heard to remark that our world—the world of the twenty-first century—resembles the period of the early church more than any other time in history. Typically, they mean that Christianity is no longer the dominant way of organizing life in an increasingly secular and pluralistic West, that in most Western countries Christianity is institutionally on the wane and does not command the influence and privilege once accorded it.[3] With some regularity many Western believers now speak of living in a post-Christian society. As a result Christians now find themselves members of one religion among many: Christians can no longer assume that their faith is the birthright religion of the majority, and that the faithful need to adopt a missionary vision in order for their churches to survive in religiously and culturally diverse societies.

Although many Christians think such comparisons are recent, thoughtful observers noted this change around the turn of the *last* century. "It is unlikely that Christianity will retain so nominally exclusive a sway as it has hitherto done in Western Europe," predicted Wellesley College professor Vida Scudder in 1912. "In all probability, the day of its conventional control is passing and will soon be forgotten." She continued:

> The time will come when the Christian faith will have to fight for right of way among crowding antagonists as vigorously as in the times of Athanasius and Augustine. And in thoughts like these all genuine Christians must rejoice. Without the call to high adventure, the faith has never flourished.[4]

By comparing the situation to that of the early church, modern Christians remember the religious status of their ancient ancestors as outsiders in non-Christian Rome. Because they faced issues similar to those we face, they serve as guides for us.

This kind of thinking, no matter how helpful the comparison, may tempt Christians toward historical romanticism, the belief that if they could only recreate some pristine age everything would be well. As much as contemporary believers might find similarities between our time and that of Christianity in ancient Rome, the two are not the same. The ancient Mediterranean world that Rome once ruled was a vast, culturally diverse set of societies, unrelated by languages, economics, religions, and histories, all forced into political unity by a brutal military. Vast numbers of people who inhabited the Roman Empire resented or hated Roman rule and experienced few, if any, benefits from its social and economic structures. The empire was not in any modern way even vaguely democratic or inclusive; instead, it was a rigidly hierarchical and status-based world of haves and have-nots, of masters and slaves. Unlike a Hollywood sword-and-sandal film, the ancient world was not a pleasant place absent conveniences such as sewer systems and running water. As sociologist Rodney Stark describes, "Greco-Roman cities were small, extremely crowded, filthy beyond imagining, disorderly, filled with strangers, and afflicted with frequent catastrophes—fires, plagues, conquests, and earthquakes." Unlike Western urban life today, where even the poor have access to marginally acceptable services, "life in antiquity abounded in anxiety and misery" for nearly everyone.[5]

Not only was the ancient world entirely different from our own, the time period dubbed "the early church" lasted five hundred years, a half millennium. In the fifth century the great theologian St. Augustine was almost as far removed in time from Jesus as we are from the Protestant reformer Martin Luther. In those five centuries the ancient Mediterranean world underwent huge political, cultural, and economic changes; these massive transformations influenced Christian practices and theology, creating and recreating congregations that adapted and readapted to the changes around them. "Early Christianity" and "ancient church" were not monolithic realities. Instead, if we are thinking about them rightly, we will understand that these five centuries were messy, chaotic, violent, and foreign to our understandings and imaginations. Ancient Christianity grew up in a vast geographic space, in many cultures, and over a long period of time, developing through diverse spaces, peoples, and centuries. Romanticism fails us; post-Christian Christianity is not that of the early church. If we are honest, we can barely understand those centuries and the people who inhabited them. Our ancestors are strangers to us; they lived in an alien world.

Christianity as a Way

If the Roman world was so completely different from our own, what can be said of early Christianity that has any meaning to us today? What "high adventure," as Vida Scudder suggested, does ancient faith hold for contemporary people?

For all the differences between our world and theirs, for all the complexity of primitive Christianity, a startling idea runs through early records of faith: Christianity seems to have succeeded because it transformed the lives of people in a chaotic world. Indeed, in his study of the growth of Christianity in the ancient world, Rodney Stark suggests that

> The power of Christianity lay not in its promise of other worldly compensations for suffering in this life, as has so often been proposed. No, the crucial change that took place . . . was the rapidly spreading awareness of a faith

that delivered potent antidotes to life's miseries here and now![6]

Throughout the first five centuries people understood Christianity primarily as a *way of life* in the present, not as a doctrinal system, esoteric belief, or promise of eternal salvation. By followers enacting Jesus's teachings, Christianity changed and improved the lives of its adherents and served as a practical spiritual pathway. This way—and earliest Christians were called "the People of the Way"—bettered existence for countless ancient believers.

The way, with its transformative power, challenged the status quo and infuriated ancient defenders of Roman religions, many of whom argued that the new Christian religion was an immoral sect, with secretive rites and rituals that undermined traditional Roman values of loyalty and family. Indeed, early commentators scarcely attacked Christian doctrines, but they consistently portrayed Christian devotional practices as radical and socially divisive. Christianity had effectively "created a social group that promoted its own laws and its own patterns of behavior."[7] These behaviors, at odds with Roman custom, earned Christians the reputation of being revolutionaries and traitors to the good order of the state.

Christian defenders, such as Justin Martyr (ca. 100–ca. 165), used the example of Christian practice to make the case that Jesus's way "mended lives":

> We who formerly . . . valued above all things the acquisition of wealth and possession, now bring what we have into a common stock, and communicate to everyone in

> need; we who hated and destroyed one another, and on account of their different manners would not live with men of a different tribe, now, since the coming of Christ, live familiarly with them, and pray for our enemies.[8]

To Justin, the old ways had passed; a new way opened in Jesus. Far from being divisive, Christianity was an inclusive faith that might bring diverse peoples together. However one interpreted the effects of the new faith, both enemies and defenders of Christianity understood that the new religion transformed people, giving even women, peasants, and slaves a meaningful ability to reorder their lives.

The way was based on Jesus's teaching recorded in Mark 12:28–34.[9] An unnamed questioner asked Jesus, "Which commandment is the first of all?" And Jesus replied with what is now called the Great Command: "'You shall love the Lord your God with all your heart, and with all your soul, and with all your mind, and with all your strength.' The second is this, 'You shall love your neighbor as yourself.' There is no other commandment greater than these." Loving God and neighbor was, according to Jesus, the way of the Kingdom of God and the path of salvation. In the account of this teaching in the Gospel of Luke, Jesus adds, "Do this, and you will live" (Luke 10:28).

Early Christians understood the centrality of Jesus's teaching. The *Didache* (ca. 100/120 CE), an ancient Christian instructional manual, opens with these words: "There are two ways, one of life and one of death, but a great difference between the two ways. The way of life, then, is this: First, you shall love

God who made you; second, love your neighbor as yourself, and do not do to another what you would not want done to you."[10]

Jesus's followers took these words seriously. In many cases, and unlike contemporary practice, the process of becoming a Christian took several years, an extended time of teaching spiritual inquirers the way on which they were embarking. Christianity was considered a deliberate choice with serious consequences, a process of spiritual formation and discipline that took time, a way of life that had to be learned in community. Many early Christian communities frowned upon instantaneous conversion. Manuals like the *Didache* served as textbooks for converts. To drive home the point, early church architects built baptismal fonts to resemble sarcophagi, symbolizing death to the old way of life or, more erotically perhaps, as a vulva to indicate the birth of a new life.[11] Thus, in the context of their world of suffering, Christians were taught that the faith as a radical way of life comprised the two loves, and it was these two loves that they strove to enact in their own souls and in their communities.

It is upon the Great Command that we find common ground with ancient Christians, not because our world is like theirs or because they somehow knew how to be better Christians than we do. Many of them, to be sure, did not follow very well; they, like us, struggled, doubted, and failed to walk the way. Yet even in our shortcomings (or perhaps because of them), we stand with them in the way. Generative Christians, like them, seek a life organized around love for God and neighbor. We recognize their longing for change. And in many quarters Christian communities are once again embracing the ancient insight that the faith is a spiritual pathway, a life built on transformative practices of love rather than doctrinal belief.[12] We are, beyond mere romanticism, recapturing wisdom from ancient Christianity. How our ancestors interpreted and practiced the way, however, holds some surprises and challenges for us today.

TWO

Devotion: The Love of God

More than anything else, Christianity is a love song. People shy away from saying that out loud, though. Maybe it seems too sentimental, a little embarrassing. Perhaps Christians fear that they themselves barely understand the radical implications of a way of life based on the love of God. Maybe they think no one will believe them. Certainly, in the eyes of many contemporary critics, Christianity does not seem very loving. In a recent survey, for example, more than three-quarters of young churchgoers (those inside the faith!) identified Christianity as judgmental, hypocritical, out of touch, insensitive, boring, and exclusive—the antithesis of love. Only 16 percent of young adults outside the faith said that Christianity "consistently shows love for other people."[1]

Yet love is what Jesus preached—and what he embodied. In the early church devout Christians tried to embody God's love and to experience God in such a way that love reshaped their lives. "Love for God is ecstatic, making us go out from ourselves," wrote Dionysios the Areopagite around 500; "it does not allow the lover to belong any more to himself, but he belongs only to the Beloved." Not all Christians achieved this; they too struggled with loving God. But Romans frequently criticized the Christian emphasis on love as somehow a little deluded and perhaps prurient, suggesting that followers of the Jesus Way made it known that theirs was a path of love. Early Christians insisted that love—not rationality or politics or even virtue—was the primary bond between God and human beings. Love was God's symphony, the perfect beauty that human beings experienced through the practices of faith—by imitating Christ and following his way.

The Imitation of Christ

"Young Mother Martyr Video" flashed a headline on FOX news. Another suicide bombing in the Middle East, stated the anchor, this time the Palestinian mother of two small children. On the video, a youthful woman happily proclaimed her faith in Allah and looked forward to being welcomed into paradise. "It is just terrible," said the indignant co-anchor. "What kind of religion would encourage a mother to die?"

Although it is not a precise moral equivalent, the answer to the co-anchor's question may surprise her: Christianity, for one.[2] In 203, Roman authorities arrested Vibia Perpetua (d. 203), a North African believer and a young mother of good family, for being a Christian. Unlike the contemporary woman on FOX news, Perpetua did not seek martyrdom (nor did she kill to achieve it), but she welcomed her impending death as a sign of her faithfulness to Christ.

At first she found prison terrifying "because never before had I experienced such darkness." Anxiety tore at her heart—mostly for the child she had left behind. But the officials, feeling some sympathy for the nursing mother, allowed the infant to join her in jail. "Suddenly the prison became my palace," she wrote, "and I loved being there rather than any other place."[3]

Although Perpetua's family worked for her release, the noblewoman refused to leave the jail. Her prison diary, one of the few published works by an ancient Christian woman, recounts her struggle between her love for her father, her desire to raise her son, and her loyalty to Christ. Empowered by visions of paradise, she chose the path of martyrdom. "I thank God," she said to an angel in a dream, "for although I was happy on earth, I am much happier here right now." Perpetua's final joy would have to wait, however, since she and the slave Felicitas, who was pregnant, wanted to die together. Even Roman authorities were loath to kill a woman with child. So the two imprisoned women anticipated both the impending birth and their coming deaths.

When Felicitas delivered her daughter, the women were sent to the arena for the games:

> Perpetua followed with quick step as a true spouse of Christ, the darling of God, her brightly flashing eyes quelling the gaze of the crowd. Felicitas too, joyful because she had safely survived child-birth and was now able to participate in the contest with the wild animals, passed from one shedding of blood to another; from midwife to gladiator, about to be purified after child-birth by a second baptism.

Given a final chance to recant, Perpetua shouted back to her tormenters, "You condemned us; God condemns you!" Thrown to the bulls, and in a particularly gory contest that Christian onlookers attributed to evil spirits, the women suffered injury, only to have the gladiators finish the deed. Perpetua, groaning from broken ribs, seized the executioner's trembling hand and guided the sword to her throat. The editor of her prison journal opined, "Perhaps it was that so great a woman, feared as she was by the unclean spirit, could not have been slain had she not herself willed it."

What made these two young mothers so willingly embrace death instead of fearing it? Few ancient practices are as difficult for modern Christians to comprehend as martyrdom. The word *martyr* implies fanatical faith, a sort of self-loathing that leads to insanity and violence. Yet in the public arenas and dark prisons of the Roman Empire, early believers expressed their love of God by giving up their lives for Christ. As the ancient theologian Tertullian (ca. 160–ca. 225) remarked, "The blood of the martyrs is the seed of the Church." Although no one knows the exact number of martyrs, there were not as many as popularly imagined. Not every Christian faced martyrdom in the ten great persecutions of the early church, but enough did that their stories fueled the devotional lives of even those who lived quietly. Perpetua's diary, for example, was read as part of the Sunday liturgy in many communities. Her martyrdom day was marked by special devotion, and decades later a church was dedicated to her in Carthage.[4]

Martyrdom, or the willingness to be martyred should occasion arise, testified to the soul's love of God and fidelity to Christ. As Polycarp, the bishop of Smyrna, stated so elegantly at his trial (ca. 156 CE), "I have served Christ for eighty-six years and he has done me no wrong. How shall I abandon my king who has saved me?" Early Christians believed that martyrdom was the ultimate imitation of Jesus. As Christ had died for the love of humanity, so they too were called to die for a greater love than their earthly loves. Those who faced the trial with resolve, who remained steadfast in love, entered into eternal bliss.

Few Christian women were called, like Perpetua, to face gladiators in the arena, and, in some ways, death was not really the point of the story. Most ancient Christians were called to make difficult choices because of their faith, choices that often involved conflicting loyalties between family and church that entailed "dying" to their former way of life. To ancient believers, Perpetua and Felicitas were women whose faith forced them to make the most terrible choice—to follow their earthly fathers' wishes or to imitate their Heavenly Father through Jesus Christ. Ultimately, the women choose Christ, a painful and difficult choice, but as Perpetua testified, it was a way of true freedom. Martyrs like Perpetua became quite popular, but most people knew that they would not face such a stark conflict in their own lives. As hard as the way of imitation may be, it would rarely be as demanding as that of Perpetua. Martyr stories comforted and challenged those who lived more mundane lives.

Thus, while the martyrs provided the ultimate example of Christlike imitation, the everyday practice of imitating Jesus in making hard choices became the cornerstone for ordinary Christian life. Early on, Romans scornfully tagged the Jesus followers with the name "Christian," meaning "little Christ."

Being a Christian meant being like Jesus; following his way meant imitating the life of its guide and founder, even to the cross.

Honoring the Body

In 1993 on a warm day in Santa Barbara, California, I drove up the hills behind the city to Mount Calvary Monastery for a retreat. As I perused the bookstore for something to read, some calligraphy artwork caught my attention. Drawn by a brother, one image bore a saying attributed to Irenaeus of Lyon (ca. 115–202): "The glory of God is the human person fully alive." I had never heard those words before, and I stared at them for a long time. Irenaeus? I raked my memory. Oh, yes. He was the second-century bishop of Lyon who wrote a book with the off-putting title *Against Heresies.* I avoided that treatise in graduate school. But I liked these words. What did Irenaeus mean? What occasioned them? I bought the picture and meditated on the words. It still hangs above my desk.

Irenaeus was born in Asia Minor (Turkey) and as a young man became a disciple of Polycarp, the bishop who was later martyred. Not much is known about Irenaeus except that he served as a missionary in France. When the local bishop was killed in a persecution, Irenaeus was chosen to fill the vacancy. His theology grew from his responsibilities as a pastor. He was not a philosopher; instead, he sought to strengthen the church by helping new Christians experience the love of God through the practice of faith.

In Lyon at that time, however, there existed a problem in the Christian community. An ancient religion called Gnosticism (in many instances, Gnosticism had blended into a form of Christian Gnosticism that offered an alternative reading of faith than mainstream Christianity) attracted some Christians away from the churches under the bishop's care. Contemporary Christians often have an acquaintance with Gnosticism through popular scholarship. In recent years books like Elaine Pagels's *The Gnostic Gospels* introduced early Gnostic texts to the general public, giving the old rival of orthodox Christianity a sympathetic hearing while posing a challenge to traditional churches.

The situation in Irenaeus's time was perhaps not that different from popular interest in Gnosticism today. From Irenaeus's perspective, this was a dangerous development for Christianity. For all its attractiveness, both to ancient Romans and to us, most forms of Gnosticism were based on the idea of dualism: spirit is good and matter is evil. Thus creation is, at best, a kind of illusion and, at worst, demonic. The enlightened soul must, through the means of some secret knowledge (or *gnosis*), escape this world and find its true home in the spiritual realm. It is easy to understand how well Gnosticism would mesh with Christianity and that many would find a Gnostic interpretation of the Gospels appealing.

It is tempting to think that Bishop Irenaeus was simply protecting his theological turf and ecclesiastical power by arguing against Gnosticism in *Against Heresies.* However, Irenaeus appeared most concerned with the negative way that Gnostics interpreted creation. In his mind the love of God was bound up with the world that God had made; there existed an intimate relationship between matter and spirit, especially demonstrated in the Christian idea that Jesus was born as a human being. As a result Irenaeus developed the concept of deification, that "God became man, so man could become like God." He further explained, "Christ became what we are, so that He might bring us to be what He Himself is."[5]

Creation is good, therefore, since God could never become evil. And salvation is a kind of dance, a process of growing ever more to be like God. God made humans in God's image, yet humans backed away from God. Jesus came as a human being to be with us; in his death and resurrection Christ went back to God, taking our common humanity with him to be reunited with divinity. Irenaeus's vision is one of cosmic unity, in which heaven and earth, spirit and matter, divine and mundane, intertwined in the beauty of universal love.

Not only did Irenaeus affirm an innate spirituality of creation, but he also emerged as a Christian humanist. Because human beings participate in the journey of becoming like God, the divine presence infuses human activity. As one historian notes, "Human nature, and so human actions, can no longer transpire without the divine nature."[6] Irenaeus's view is mystical, spiritual, and cosmic—very like Gnosticism. But unlike the view of the Gnostics, it is holistic, not dualistic. Salvation is not a secret reserved for an enlightened few; rather, the love of God is visible to "all living on earth." Deification affirmed human capacities rather than consigning humanity to an endless cycle of evil that can only be escaped.

Irenaeus was probably the first Christian theologian to teach deification, but he was by no means the only. One of his contemporaries, Clement of Alexandria, said, "The Logos of God had become man so that you might learn how a man may become God."[7] At first it may seem difficult to understand how deification is a practice: how do Christians do it? Harvard professor Stephanie Paulsell suggests that the emphasis on the goodness of creation emerges in the practice of honoring the body, "the difficult friendship with our bodies." She describes this practice as part of "a way that bears witness to God" because "the body reflects God's own goodness."[8] Early Christians, like Irenaeus, believed in deification because they believed that God had become *incarnate*—that he was actual flesh and blood in the exact same way we are—in Jesus Christ. Honoring the body, therefore, signals human connection with God through Christ. Intrinsic to salvation is befriending creation. In some ways deification, this honoring the body, is the flip side of imitating Christ. We imitate Jesus because he first imitated us; we are woven of the same spiritual cloth.

"The glory of God," Irenaeus wrote, "is the human person fully alive." Irenaeus was not simply being cranky, attacking Gnostics because they interfered with his authority. No, he tried to articulate a very difficult part of the Christian way of life: to remember in all things that, beginning with Jesus's humanity, the "body is a sacred gift."[9] Salvation works itself out within the context of this world; it is a process of honoring creation, of acting humanly toward God, ourselves, and our neighbors. I would later learn the rest of Irenaeus's quote:

> For the glory of God is the human person fully alive; and life consists in beholding God. For if the vision of God which is made by means of the creation, gives life to all living in the earth, much more does that revelation of the Father which comes through the Word, give life to those who see God.[10]

A life-affirming, universal vision of God's cosmic love where everything is sacred.

Reading Scripture

In June 2008 evangelical leader James Dobson attacked Barack Obama on the basis of a speech that the candidate had given about religion and politics. In it Obama defended the role of religion in public life while pointing out the difficulty of discerning specific policies:

> Which passages of Scripture should guide our public policy? Should we go with Leviticus, which suggests slavery is ok and that eating shellfish is abomination? How about Deuteronomy, which suggests stoning your child if he strays from the faith? Or should we just stick to the Sermon on the Mount—a passage that is so radical that it's doubtful that our own Defense Department would survive its application? So before we get carried away, let's read our Bibles. Folks haven't been reading their Bibles.[11]

For Obama, the literal reading of the Bible proves troublesome, yet he, as a serious progressive Chistian, still believes that larger, universal principles of faith should be brought to bear in politics. Dobson attacked the speech, saying that Obama had "distorted" the "traditional" way of understanding the Bible and accused him of a "fruitcake interpretation" of religion and politics.

Across the river from Washington, DC, sits the colonial town of Alexandria, Virginia, the city where I live. In my

Alexandria there are political organizations and a theological seminary, government offices and myriad churches. Concerns over public life and faith are part of everyday life. The city in Virginia bears the name of Alexandria, Egypt, the ancient second city of the Roman Empire, where questions of sacred scripture and political life were as vexing as they are today.

Almost rivaling Rome itself in size and importance, ancient Alexandria was more cosmopolitan than Rome. Located at the mouth of the Nile River, its massive port, with two harbors and a legendary lighthouse, served as a crossroads of the ancient world. Not only an economic power, Alexandria acted as a cultural and intellectual hothouse and was home to the Museum, the largest university in the ancient world with a 700,000-volume library. Prominent scholars from across the empire gathered in Alexandria to work and study at the great library.

In this environment Greek culture (Hellenism) flourished under Roman occupation. The same was true for Semitic culture; Alexandria was home to the largest community of Jews in the ancient world. Babylonians and Persians also lived in the Egyptian port, bringing their philosophies and religions into this pluralistic montage.

No one knows when Christianity first came to Alexandria. Oddly enough, the Apostle Paul never visited the city on his missionary journeys. In Acts 18:24–25, however, Luke describes Apollos, a native of Alexandria: "He was an eloquent man, well-versed in the scriptures. He had been instructed in the Way of the Lord; and he spoke with burning enthusiasm and taught accurately the things concerning Jesus." Perhaps unsurprisingly, the first biblical mention of Alexandrian Christianity referred to the intellectual life.

Alexandria's first Christians started an academy called the Catechetical School.[12] It quickly became the most famous center for Christian learning in the Roman world. Not a university in the modern sense, the school admitted candidates to study the Christian faith to prepare for baptism. They met with a philosopher—a teacher of practical wisdom—to learn the way. The school taught both intellectual content and spiritual practices; as its master Origen said, "If you want to receive Baptism, you must first learn about God's Word, cut away the roots of your vices, correct your barbarous wild lives and practice meekness and humility."[13] Learning the Christian way prepared inquirers for the rite of new birth.

Several remarkable masters headed the school, including the great mystical teacher Clement of Alexandria (c. 150–211/216). But Origen, one of Clement's pupils, who served the school from 202 to 231 CE, emerged as the most prominent Christian intellectual of the third century. Born to a Christian family in Alexandria in 185, Origen had a classical Greek education, with the addition of scripture study, fasting, and a thrice-daily prayer discipline. And when he was barely a teenager, his father was martyred. Origen almost experienced the same fate—except for the fact that his mother hid all his clothes and confined him to their house. Not to be outdone by his father's sacrifice, Origen heeded his own advice—as well as the literal instruction in Matthew 19:12—to "cut away" the roots of vice by castrating himself for Jesus. Known for both his genius and piety, Origen became a teacher at the Catechetical School while still in his teens (although, to be fair, all the other qualified teachers had been recently martyred). Throughout his life Origen maintained rigorous intellectual pursuits while engaging in practices such as almsgiving and visiting prisoners in jail. He died around 251 CE, finally following his father in martyrdom.

Origen, a complex character, inspired his students and infuriated his enemies. Of him one scholar remarked, "There are many Origens: philosopher and scholar, mystic, systematician, proponent of an esoteric system, exegete and allegorist, saint (even martyr), true Gnostic, one for who mystical knowledge is the way to salvation, Hellenist, Platonist, moralist, ascetic, eunuch, syncretist, and man of the church."[14] Threading through his multiple identities are Origen's early loves: the scriptures as the Word of God and prayer. For him, studying scripture and devotion in prayer were not two separate exercises. Rather, he practiced both at the same time in the form of biblical interpretation he both developed and employed: allegorical, or spiritual, reading.

Many early theologians—including Irenaeus of Lyon—used allegorical methods, but Origen deepened both their theory and practice. He acknowledged that scripture possessed a literal and historical meaning but that this interpretation was only for "simple believers of simple mind," those whose spiritual maturity could not grasp the Word's deeper dimensions.[15] The deeper dimension was allegory, a form borrowed from Greek literary theory, of "speaking one thing and signifying something other than what is said."[16] At the Catechetical School serious followers of Jesus's way learned to push beyond literal interpretation and mine scriptures for their spiritual meanings.

Origen believed that literal reading, while acceptable for ordinary Christians, posed a problem for the church: skeptics and intellectuals would easily see the contradictions of scripture, thus causing them to reject the gospel or fall into heresy. Literalism, far from making Christ plainly visible, acted as an obstacle to Christianity by raising unnecessary questions about God's veracity. The problem with literalism began, according to Origen, in Genesis:

> Who is found so ignorant as to suppose that God, as if He had been a husbandman, planted trees in paradise, in Eden towards the east, and a tree of life in it, i.e., a visible and palpable tree of wood, so that anyone eating of it with bodily teeth should obtain life, and, eating again of another tree, should come to the knowledge of good and evil? No one, I think, can doubt that the statement that God walked in the afternoon in paradise, and that Adam lay hid under a tree, is related figuratively in Scripture, that some mystical meaning may be indicated by it.[17]

The mystical meaning entailed seeking out "the heavenly things of which these serve as a pattern or shadow" in the text. For Origen, reading scripture was a search for the "wisdom hidden" under the literal words. In his book *On First Principles* Origen pointed out scriptural contradictions from Genesis through the Gospels. Not intending to ridicule God's Word, Origen claimed,

> The object of all these statements on our part, is to show that it was the design of the Holy Spirit, who deigned to bestow upon us the sacred Scriptures, to show that we were not to be edified by the letter alone, or by ev-

> erything in it—a thing which we see to be frequently impossible and inconsistent; for in that way not only absurdities, but impossibilities, would be the result; but that we are to understand that certain occurrences were interwoven in this "visible" history which, when considered and understood in the inner meaning, give forth a law which is advantageous to men and worthy of God.[18]

The Christian allegorist looks for the truth behind the text, always seeking Christ, the living word, breathing through scripture. To Origen, the Word was more than mere words.

I confess that I have always wondered if Origen's teenage enthusiasm for literal reading—the one demonstrated by self-mutilation—inspired him to seek an alternative way of reading scripture! He knew the dangers of literalism firsthand and "deplored such rigorous fanaticism."[19] Whatever his personal struggle, reading the Word remained Origen's primary devotional practice. He directed his attention toward finding Christ in scripture, developing spiritual reading to a high art, eventually writing commentaries on numerous biblical books. Of all his commentaries, the one on Song of Songs stands as a masterwork on love. In it Origen interpreted the erotic narrative as the relationship between Christ and the soul, carefully drawing out the spiritual implications of the book's sexual imagery as a way of wisdom.[20] Because of its power to arouse both sexually and spiritually, the Song of Songs, Origen believed, should not be read by young Christians; it should be "reserved for study till the last."[21] Scripture, Origen knew, in the wrong hands could be a dangerous thing. He learned how to read biblical texts seriously but not literally, a way of reading that is deeply ingrained in Christian tradition.

"Come Follow Me"

Around the year 270 a young Christian named Anthony (ca. 250–356), recently orphaned and made wealthy by his parents' estate, walked into a church. That day the leader of the gathering preached on the story of the rich young ruler, a man who came to Jesus and asked how he might be saved. Jesus replied, "If you wish to be perfect, go, sell your possessions, and give the money to the poor, and you will have treasure in heaven; then come, follow me" (Matt. 19:21).[22]

Struck to the heart, young Anthony—having no acquaintance with allegorical reading, I suspect—gave away everything he owned, embraced an ascetic life, and went to live out in the Egyptian desert to do battle with his inner demons and the devil himself (ancient people generally believed that the devil lived in the desert). Anthony's quest for solitude, in imitation of Jesus's withdrawal into the desert, was an innovation. Although there had been monks and hermits before Anthony, he was the first to join the geography of the land and its struggle of isolation with the spiritual struggle of the soul. For him, the way to follow Christ was physical relocation—to remove oneself from the familiar and travel to a desolate place to find holiness. "Come follow me" became a literal practice of devotion, an act of leaving behind the known world for the unknown journey to God.

Anthony lived an extraordinarily long life (he was finally martyred in Alexandria when more than one hundred years old—one wonders why the Romans even bothered!) and attracted tens of thousands of followers to the desert, thus inventing a new way of life for committed Christians. Indeed, in the fourth century it appeared almost the religious fashion to flee the cities for the desert in pursuit of holiness. What began as a solitary act quickly became a movement, one that eventually organized spiritual seekers into communal life in the wilderness. These Christians surrendered comfort and wealth, following Anthony—and, of course, Jesus—to this harsh geography, making famous the quip of the day, "There are as many monks in the desert as there are laymen in the rest of the world."[23] And it was not only men: one convent outside Cairo was reported to have been home to twenty thousand women.[24] Many less formalized communities gathered around spiritual teachers, called *abbas* and *ammas*, to learn a Christian way of life.[25]

Collectively, we call these people the desert fathers and mothers, and some of their wisdom has been preserved in short stories and teachings. Escaping cities and seeking solitude did not mean abandoning others. Indeed, the desert wise ones found that encountering God and oneself in silence led to a greater understanding of the "sacredness of our neighbor and all that has been created."[26] Of this principle, Dorotheus of Gaza said, "Each one according to his means should take care to be at one with everyone else, for the more one is united to his neighbor, the more he is united with God."[27] Thus solitude acted as the first step of recreating community along the lines suggested by Jesus. Amma Syncletica summed up the desert vision: "Salvation is exactly this—the two-fold love of God and of our neighbor."[28]

For those who went to the desert, "come follow me" was not an escape; rather, it served as an alternative practice of engagement—the first step on the way toward becoming a new people, a universal community of God's love.

"Come follow me" was intimately bound up with the practice of prayer. For prayer connects us with God and others, "part of this enterprise of learning to love." Prayer is much more than a technique, and early Christians left us no definitive how-to manual on prayer. Rather, the desert fathers and mothers believed that prayer was a disposition of wholeness, so that "prayer and our life must be all of a piece." They approached prayer, as early church scholar Roberta Bondi notes, as a practical twofold process: first, of "thinking and reflecting," or "pondering" what it means to love others; and second, as the "development and practice of loving ways of being."[29] In other words, these ancients taught that prayer was participation in God's love, the activity that takes us out of ourselves, away from the familiar, and conforms us to the path of Christ.

But prayer was not reserved for those who moved to the desert, as desert spirituality moved back to Egyptian cities, especially Alexandria. The monastic practice of ceaseless prayer exemplified the goal of the love-drenched life for regular people as well. Although we do not know the names of such people, their memory is captured in an icon at St. Gregory of Nyssa Episcopal Church in San Francisco. There, in the spectacular mural of *The Dancing Saints*, an Alexandrian washerwoman, no doubt influenced by the devotion of the desert dwellers, represents "the holiness of all that is ordinary and routine" in the unity of prayer and work.[30] From ancient wilderness to contemporary California, Jesus's call to "come follow me" invites all to abandon worldly riches to find the love of God in unexpected places and simple acts.

Hallowing Time

At a conference where I was speaking in Vancouver, British Columbia, in 2008, Pastor Ed Searcy welcomed the audience gathered at University Hill United Church. "Please take a calendar as a gift," he told the congregation, pointing to a table in the back of the room. "It isn't a regular calendar; it is a church year calendar." He went on to explain that the pages were not arranged by month. Rather, they were organized by season—Advent, Christmas, Epiphany, Lent, Easter, Pentecost, and Ordinary Time. The congregation had used the calendar in creative ways to experience the flow of Christian time. "Some people have hung it in their offices," Pastor Ed related. In secular Vancouver, he laughed, "That has started a few conversations!"

Along with the calendar came an explanatory handout. "The way we mark time, starting from when we are children, powerfully shapes our identity," it stated. "Our identity guides our way of being and doing in the world. As Christians, the story of the Way of Christ is our calendar, our identity and our call to be a salty, yeasty community for the sake of the world and glory of God." No secular holidays were listed on the calendar's beautifully decorated pages—no Mother's Day, no Canada Day, no Thanksgiving. Only feast days and scripture readings for Sundays: Ash Wednesday is February 6; All Saints Day is marked on November 1; and Christian New

Year's Eve falls on November 29. The University Hill Church publishes the calendar "to enable the re-telling of the life and story of Jesus Christ. It encourages people to live differently from the dominant culture." They see "living in God's time" as an act of subversion.[31]

In the earliest years of the church Christians began to celebrate time in a different manner than did their neighbors. Just as in Vancouver, having a cycle of their own time marked the Jesus community in a unique way, providing their festivals and spirituality with alternative rhythms to those of both Judaism and pagan religions. The Roman calendar too proved a formidable challenge to living according to Jesus's way. Although converts embraced a new life, much political and religious life still revolved around the old Roman sense of time. Well into the sixth century, Bishop Martin of Braga chastised Christians for "observing days for idols . . . for observing Vulcan's day . . . and for observing Venus's day at weddings."[32] This would be akin to rebuking Americans for celebrating the Fourth of July and Halloween.

Wanting to practice time in a distinctly Christian way, early believers developed a year based on Sunday worship and the feast of Easter. They moved their Sabbath from the last day of the week to the first. "We assemble on the day of the sun because it is the first day," wrote Justin Martyr, "that on which God transformed the darkness and matter to create the world, and also because Jesus Christ our Savior rose from the dead on the same day."[33] By the second century the Christian year centered on the Pascal feast, the great commemoration of the death and resurrection of Jesus. The Easter cycle unfolded over three days, beginning with Good Friday, called the *triduum*, which Ambrose of Milan referred to as "the three most sacred days" of Christian time. In those three days Christians grounded their spiritual identity.

Sometime around the year 400, Egeria, a Spanish woman, embarked on a multiyear pilgrimage to the Holy Land. We know little about her; she may or may not have been a nun, but she appears to have possessed considerable resources to make such a lengthy journey. She kept a journal of her travels, written in the form of letters to her "sisters" at home. Her diary traces Christian time as she visits distinctly Christian sites, paying scant attention to anything Roman. She moved in an alternative universe, one in the world but defined by an entirely different set of concerns and practices. In her pilgrimage, writes historian Robert Bruce Mullin, "the whole year was invested with symbolism," the center of which was Easter.[34]

Egeria reported on the "Great Week," the week before Easter, which Christians now refer to as Holy Week, as a special time of worship both in churches and at various holy sites around Jerusalem. She described Palm Sunday:

> All the people walk before the bishop singing hymns and antiphons, always responding: "Blessed is he who comes in the name of the Lord." And whatever children in this place, even those not able to walk, are carried on their parents' shoulders, all holding branches, some of palm, some of olive; [they walk] through the whole city, all go on foot, the matrons as well as the noble men . . . singing responses, going slowly so that the people may not tire.

Each day was marked with worship and processions, gathering large congregations of people from every station of life. She wrote on Good Friday at the service commemorating the crucifixion of a crowd so great "one cannot even open a door." From noon to three, people listened to the Gospel accounts of the Passion; there was no music, only the sound of people crying. "At each reading," she reported, "there is such emotion and weeping by all the people that it is a wonder; for there is no one, old or young, who does not on this day weep for these three hours more than can be imagined because the Lord has suffered for us." An all-night prayer vigil followed the service.[35]

Holy Week led up to the Saturday night vigil, when the faithful walked, their way illuminated by hundreds of candles, to the church where new Christians were baptized. There the whole congregation sang and celebrated the first Eucharist of Easter in a feast. Her delight in the Great Week is obvious, as she carefully recounted all she observed. "Journeys are not hard when they are the fulfillment of hopes," she wrote.[36]

Christian time unfolds from the locus of these three days and in no way may be considered a morbid experience. Egeria pointed out that the crucifixion was commemorated on one day—Good Friday—whose meaning could not be understood separate from the Easter feast that followed. She duly reported weeping, not because Christianity was a gloomy faith, but because it so startled her. She had never seen such great spiritual lamentation before. It was precisely because Christian time was hopeful, a celebration of God's restoration of paradise here and now, that Egeria underscored mourning over Christ's death on the cross so specifically. The full *triduum*, the three central days of Christian alternative time, forcefully made the point that God was with humanity to transform suffering into a joy-filled feast as the days move from crucifixion to celebration. Early Christians did not wait for God to fix time or to rescue them from time; instead, they believed that God had hallowed time by acting out Christ's love in time. So they redeemed earthly time. As Irenaeus of Lyon said, "The church has been planted as a paradise in this world."[37]

As Egeria pointed out, because it is grounded in shared human experience of time, the Christian year is the most inclusive of all spiritual practices. Rich, poor, young, old, city dweller or stranger—all are invited into the mystery of God as experienced physically in human time. The Christian year embodies the life of Jesus in readings, song, feasts, and prayers. As a French monk commented, Christian time is "the joy of the people, the source of light to the learned, and the book of the humblest of the faithful." As contemporary theologian Dorothy Bass writes, "In a single turning, the Christian year carries the content of Christian faith into present time, inviting us to experience the here-and-now in relation to a story that began before creation and continues into a future that is already dawning." She continues, "The Christian practice of living through the year cuts against the grain of despair, as the paschal mystery at its heart touches all our stories. . . . Time is for sharing the gifts of God's love and strength as we go about daily work."[38]

Spiritual Progress

A few years ago people began to use the term *spiritual progressive* as a replacement for *religious liberal*. The word *spiritual* seems more open and inviting than *religious;* and *progressive* avoided the dread *L* word.[39] The new phrase also signified new life for old-style liberalism, as the word *spiritual* indicates a more personal and more practice-oriented kind of faith life, in contrast to simply believing in a "religion." And *progressive* pointed past partisanship toward populist politics. One need not be a member of a particular party to be a progressive. Wherever *spiritual progressive* came from, it is quickly becoming the moniker of choice among some Christians.[40]

Although it is time to redefine religious liberalism, the term *spiritual progressive* seems vaguely secular and modernist, the sort of phrase tested in a focus group. The idea of social and historical progress formed the core of classical liberalism—that somehow, through effort, intellect, and technology, humankind would continue to better itself; civilization would advance to become more compassionate, peaceable, charitable, and tolerant until society reached some level of civic perfection. For progressives, moving toward this future was always superior to the traditions of the past. At the high tide of political liberalism in the late nineteenth century, several political movements, usually of the grassroots sort, deemed themselves "progressive" and won a good number of adherents and political victories.

By the mid-twentieth century, as was pointed out by Protestant theologians Karl Barth and Reinhold Niebuhr, the old liberal-progressive impulse had proved a political cul-de-sac; social failures like the Depression, two wars, and the nuclear bomb offered ample evidence that humanity was equally capable of going backward as well as forward. They undermined the optimism—perhaps fatally—that liberal politics and religion always advanced. Thus, the term *spiritual progressive* may well prove historically shortsighted. There is, however, an alternative way of understanding progressive spirituality, one rich in tradition, suggested by the fourth-century theologian, Gregory of Nyssa (ca. 331–395).

Gregory was part of a remarkable family—his brother Basil (330–379) a great theologian and bishop, and their sister Macrina the Younger (ca. 327–380) revered for her intellectual holiness and as the founder of an important monastic community. Along with their friend Gregory of Nazianzus (ca. 329–390), they were known as the Cappadocians, after the region of Turkey in which they lived and worked. The foursome, deeply influenced by Origen and Alexandrian Christianity as well as Trinitarian theology, produced a vast body of writings, including commentaries, sermons, and a monastic rule.

Gregory of Nyssa developed the doctrine of the eternal progress of the soul. All of the Cappadocians shared a cosmic vision of God's beauty, a Christ-restored universe: "The whole creation in the world and above the world, which once warred with itself, is bound together in the harmony of love."[41] Gregory essentially saw the whole of Christianity, in both its universal and personal dimensions, as the story of love—love lost, love regained, and surrender to love—a story, however, with a catch. However much one anticipates unity in the "harmony of love," it remains painfully obvious that such is elusive in our earthly lives. How can human beings participate in this vision? How can we touch such glory?

With these questions in mind, Gregory developed the idea of eternal progress in his book *The Life of Moses*. Using the allegorical method, he cast the ancient prophet's life as a metaphor for progressive spirituality, a never-ending process by which the individual moved toward God, a destination that can never be ultimately reached. "How then would he arrive at the sought-for boundary when he can find no boundary?" Because, in Gregory's mind, "the one limit of perfection (that is, God's goodness and love) is the fact that it has no limit."[42] Eternal progress, a never-ending pilgrimage. Spiritual progress is progress itself, always moving toward the vision of cosmic harmony, the true wisdom of Christ.

Gregory then related spiritual progress to Moses's journey of following God, a life that moved through humility to obedience and virtue to the mountain shrouded in the cloud; there Moses received the law, reestablished the priesthood, and "approached the divine nature." Yet not even Moses arrived; he simply walked off the stage of human history into the divine mystery of God, never reaching the Promised Land. Likewise, Gregory argued that once "you carve in your own heart the oracles which you receive from God; and when you destroy the golden idol . . . when you come through all these things . . . when you destroy everything which opposes your worth . . . then you will draw near to the goal." Only *near*, however; you will not arrive. And what is that goal? It is, very simply, to participate in bringing about God's harmony, "being called a servant of God."[43]

And that, for Gregory of Nyssa, is what it means to be a spiritual progressive: "tracing in outline like a pattern of beauty the life of the great Moses so that each one of us might copy the image of the beauty which has been shown to us by imitating his way of life." Or, distilled to its essence, to be a spiritual progressive is "to be known by God and to become his friend."[44]

This is a compelling vision for contemporary spiritual progressives. Progressive faith is not about winning. When progressivism becomes hubris, it always fails. Instead, ancient tradition, deeply formed in the ideal of spiritual progress, insisted that progressive faith was about humility—our lives and the world transformed through God's beauty. This, of course, does not fit on a bumper sticker or work very well in a party platform. But it should give progressive Christians pause, always remembering progress is a journey, not a destination.

THREE

Ethics: The Love of Neighbor

Trying to understand why and how Romans embraced Christianity, sociologist Rodney Stark states, "Conversion to a new religion involves being interested in *new culture*—indeed, in being capable of mastering a new culture." He argues that people converted initially, not because they found Christianity philosophically persuasive, but because Christianity was "efficacious."[1] In other words, it worked.

And it worked in some very particular ways. During the second century's great epidemic, known as the Plague of Galen (165–180), in which hundreds of thousands of people died in the streets, Christians proved their spiritual mettle by tending to the sick. As Bishop Cyprian of Carthage would later claim, that plague was a winnowing process, in which God's justice was shown by "whether the well care for the sick, whether relatives dutifully love their kinsfolk as they should, whether masters show compassion for their ailing slaves, whether physicians do not desert the afflicted."[2] Because they did not fear death, Christians stayed behind in plague-ravaged cities while others fled. Their acts of mercy extended to all the suffering regardless of class, tribe, or religion and created the conditions in which others accepted their faith. Christianity succeeded because it "prompted and sustained attractive, liberating, and effective social relations and organizations."[3] Translated from sociologist-speak, that means Christians did risky, compelling, and good things that helped people.

Christians did this on the basis of Jesus's Great Command to love God *and to love one's neighbor*, a quality that was, as Rodney Stark points out, often missing in Roman pagan religions. But for Christians, the principle was central. As John Chrysostom, one of the greatest early Christian preachers, proclaimed, "This is the rule of most perfect Christianity, its most exact definition, its highest point, namely, the seeking of the common good . . . for nothing can so make a person an imitator of Christ as caring for his neighbors."[4] Enacting love was a critical aspect of experiencing love. Devotion and ethics intertwined.

Hospitality

A television commercial caught my attention. Smiling people shaking hands, reaching out for one another, serving food to each other, offering gifts, with a voice overlay: "We're tracking hospitable acts across the globe. Tell us your stories of hospitality." I looked up, wondering who was soliciting testimonies about the practice of hospitality. A church or denomination? A nonprofit service organization? The words *Be*

Hospitable and the name of a major hotel chain flashed across the screen.

I wondered what would happen if I went to their Web site and posted this ancient story about hospitality:

> Come, you that are blessed by my Father, inherit the Kingdom prepared for you from the foundation of the world; for I was hungry and you gave me food, I was thirsty and you gave me something to drink, I was a stranger and you welcomed me, I was naked and you gave me clothing, I was sick and you took care of me, I was in prison and you visited me. (Matt. 25:34–36)

This testimony represents Jesus's notion of hospitality. Not a relaxing break at a fancy hotel with the disciples, hospitality is defined as the practice of welcoming those whom Jesus calls "the least of these" into the heart of community. Outsiders—unlovely, unwanted human beings—are brought inside the circle of protection and care as usual social relationships are disrupted or reversed. Jesus further overturns our typical idea of hospitality as a reciprocal relationship: "When you give a luncheon or a dinner, do not invite your friends or your brothers or your relatives or rich neighbors. . . . But when you give a banquet, invite the poor, the crippled, the lame, the blind, and you will be blessed, because they cannot repay you" (Luke 14:12–13).

We tend to equate hospitality with parties and social gatherings or gracious resorts and expensive restaurants. To us hospitality is an industry, not a practice, one that summons Martha Stewart to mind more quickly than Jesus Christ. But to ancient Christians hospitality was a virtue, part of the love of neighbor and fundamental to being a person of the way. While contemporary Christians tend to equate morality with sexual ethics, our ancestors defined morality as welcoming the stranger.

Unlike almost every other contested idea in early Christianity, including the nature of Christ and the doctrine of the Trinity, the unanimous witness of the ancient fathers and mothers was that hospitality was the primary Christian virtue. From the New Testament texts that unambiguously urge believers to "practice hospitality" (Romans 12:13) through St. Augustine's works in the fifth century, early Christian writings extol hospitality toward the sick, the poor, travelers, widows, orphans, slaves, prisoners, prostitutes, and the dying. As the preacher Ambrose (ca. 339–397) wrote, "Love hospitality, whereby holy Abraham found favor, and received Christ as his guest. . . . You too can receive Angels if you offer hospitality to strangers."[5] Or as Lucian (ca. 160), a pagan critic of Christianity, wrote of the lavish hospitality offered a local prisoner: "The efficiency the Christians show whenever matters of community interest like this happen is unbelievable; they literally spare nothing."[6] For all these people, from Paul to Ambrose to pagan reporters, hospitality equaled Christian morality.

Ordinary Christians practiced hospitality by opening their homes as house churches. Domestic hospitality included offering shelter for widows and orphans, providing rooms for itinerant missionaries and preachers, making meals for the poor, and hosting family funeral banquets and other ritual meals. Such arrangements were the purview largely of women, some of whom formed communities of domestic ascetics outside the control of the institutional church, including prayer, worship, and scripture study as a supplement to the practice of hospitality.[7] As early as the New Testament, the apostle Paul speaks of receiving hospitality from Priscilla, a missionary teacher in Corinth (Acts 18:1–3).[8] These practices extended throughout the empire and through the first centuries of Christianity. Shortly after the death of her husband, the wealthy Roman matron Marcella (325–410) organized a house church at her mansion on Aventine Hill, opening it as a center for Christian women seeking communal prayer, study, and service.

When Christianity became legal in the Roman Empire, pastors and bishops organized hospitality as an institutional function, and the "resources of the church were used for hospitality on a scale that cannot be exaggerated."[9] Gregory of Nyssa's brother, Bishop Basil, averted a disaster in Cappadocia during a famine in 368 when he used nearly all his family's fortune to feed the poor through the creation of a sort of ancient food bank, earning himself the popular title Basil the Great. He also built one of the first Christian hospitals and a hospice (*hospitality*, *hospital*, and *hospice* all come from the same Latin root) in his diocese.

Basil eventually wrote a rule for monastic community, and he structured hospitality as a cardinal virtue of the religious life. But monks had long practiced hospitality, even in the desert. In a report worthy of the *Be Hospitable* Web site, ancient traveler Rufinus testified,

> Then we came to Nitria, the best-known of all the monasteries of Egypt, about forty miles from Alexandria. . . .

> As we drew near to that place and they realized that foreign brethren were arriving, they poured out of their cells like a swarm of bees and ran to meet us with delight and alacrity, many of them carrying containers of water and of bread. . . . When they had welcomed us, first of all they led us with psalms into the church and washed our feet and one by one they dried them with the linen cloth they were girded with, as if to wash away the fatigue of the journey. . . . What can I say that would do justice to their humanity, their courtesy, and their love? Nowhere have I seen love flourish so greatly, nowhere with such quick compassion, such eager hospitality.[10]

Hospitality is the practice that keeps the church from becoming a club, a members-only society. Through hospitality, historian Rowan Greer claims, "an inclusive ideal of community life is affirmed, and we may suppose that implementing this ideal was no easier in the ancient world than in ours."[11] In greeting, meeting, eating, and caring, the church acted as a community with its arms open, attracting inquirers through a practical demonstration of God's love. "Observe, the hospitality here spoken of," preached John Chrysostom, "is not merely a friendly reception, but one given with zeal and alacrity, with readiness, as going about it as if one were receiving Christ himself."[12] From what historians can gather, hospitality—not martyrdom—served as the main motivator for conversions.[13] Early Christians found both spiritual and social power in such acts, for creating inclusive community, a community of radical welcome and love, can put one at odds with the authorities. "It is our care of the helpless, our practice of loving kindness that brands us in the eyes of our many opponents," claimed the African theologian Tertullian. "'Only look,' they say, 'look how they love one another!'"[14]

Communalism

In 1976 my high school youth group was studying the book of Acts. One night the passage was Acts 2:37–46. The first part of the reading recounted how Peter testified to the saving work of Jesus to the crowds and that every day more than three thousand people converted. As eager young believers, we liked the story. But the next part puzzled us. The new Christians in Acts hung around Jerusalem: "All who believed were together and had all things in common; they would sell their possessions and goods and distribute the proceeds to all, as any had need."

One skeptical teenager pounced on the youth pastor: "This is in the Bible? They sound like Communists, not Christians!"

The minister assured him that early Christians were not Communists. "The birth of the church was a very special time," he said, "different from the rest of history. God marked that occasion with strange signs that witness to God's power—like miracles and the sharing of property. After the book of Acts ends, these things cease and Christians form a more normal kind of church."

The look of relief on my friend's face said it all: Whew! Capitalism was safe from apostolic interference. After this Acts stuff, we could get back to normal.

Problem is, however, that is not what happened. Throughout the first five centuries of Christianity, people of the way struggled with their relationship to property and money—and in greater part concluded that wealth was, at the very least, somewhat unseemly. "While we try to amass wealth," noted Basil the Great in the fourth century, "make piles of money, get hold of the land as our real property, overtop one another in riches, we have palpably cast off justice, and lost the common good. I should like to know how any man can be just, who is deliberately aiming to get out of someone else what he wants for himself."[15]

Lucian, that pagan critic, attacked Christianity in 160, long after the book of Acts, on the basis of its practices of ownership: "They scorn all possession without distinction and treat them as common property." Their guilelessness, he wrote, made them easy prey for any sort of huckster, who because of Christian generosity could make "himself a millionaire overnight" with these "simpletons."[16] It seems that Lucian's targets took their baptism vows seriously, for early Christian instruction manuals, like the *Didache*, warned against the evils of loving money and failing to be generous, even condemning "advocates of the rich" to hell. Radical charity, such as selling all one's goods for the poor, was twinned with hospitality as part of the new Christian community's basic framework of morality and a mark of discipleship.

It was easy for the church to extol poverty and shun property as long as Christianity remained a persecuted sect. Although the church attracted wealthy people even at that time, almsgiving and hospitality were an expected path to holiness for the whole community insisting that the rich give generously. For people who knew the possibility of martyrdom, giving away possessions for the sake of Jesus was a small step.

However, after Constantine made Christianity the official religion of the empire in 313, Christians benefited from the state's largesse. The church, along with its pastors and bishops, became very wealthy—and Christians eagerly employed the principle of allegorical reading to texts such as "Go sell everything you have and give the money to the poor." Jesus did not mean it literally; rather, it is a sort of metaphor for giving up anything you love more than God.

The emperor Constantine, having evidently converted to the faith and happy to demonstrate the blessings of his new God upon the Christian political order, reconstructed the old city of Byzantium as his new capital of Constantinople. He poured money into the project, building gold-laden churches, a fine university, and new public spaces. He gave away land to middle-class farmers and free bread to the poor; people flocked to his city, quickly making it the wealthiest, most fashionable, and most cosmopolitan place in the empire. The still-standing Hagia Sophia, Church of Holy Wisdom, testifies to the imperial privilege Constantine and succeeding emperors lavished on Christianity. The emperors who followed Constantine continued to fill the city with treasure, a city sparkling with the riches of this world, an influential, endlessly powerful capital of a Christian Roman Empire.

Not surprisingly, the church changed in such an environment. While the benefits of imperial favor made for unimagined acts of charity through state coffers, morals and Christian practices grew lax. Indeed, in this period the crime of simony emerged in the church—priests and bishops stealing alms and offerings to benefit their own luxurious lifestyles.

In 397 the bishop of Constantinople died and a priest from the city of Antioch, John Chrysostom (ca. 347–407), was chosen to succeed him. John did not wish to become bishop. For many years he had preached and served happily as both a monk and a pastor, earning a reputation as one of the greatest orators in the empire; *Chrysostom* means "golden-mouthed" in Greek. Audiences and congregations frequently applauded and cheered his sermons. When word of his election to the office of bishop arrived, John evidently hid, having to be kidnapped and taken to Constantinople and installed as bishop by ecclesiastical captors. Antioch was an important city, to be sure, but it shrank in comparison to Constantinople's imperial glamour. Upon arrival, Chrysostom set out to reform both the city and the church through preaching the gospel.

One of his chief concerns was the corrupting power of wealth. "The desire to rule," he proclaimed, "is the mother of all heresies."[17] In one sermon, on the passage from Acts 2, he suggested that private property should be abolished, as it was in those first days of Christianity. "If this were done now," he insisted, "we should live more pleasant lives, both the rich and the poor." He conjectured that from his congregation alone he would gather "ten hundred thousand pounds weight of gold; nay, twice or thrice as much." The money should then be distributed to care for the poor. "What abundance there would be!" Knowing his flock would object, he asked, "What should we do after the money was spent?" John maintained that God would continue to pour out riches on the community. "Should we not make it heaven on earth?"

As the sermon ended John ruminated on what he considered the root of poverty: "It is the living separately that is expensive and causes poverty." Using the monastic ideal, he believed that even families with children should adopt communal arrangements for "division always makes diminution, concord and agreement make increase." But he knew that such remained a distant hope: "People are more afraid of this than of falling into a boundless and bottomless deep." Fear did not inhibit John's preaching: "I trust that we shall soon bring you over to this way of life."[18]

Chrysostom would continue to preach in this manner for several years, insisting that "it is not for lack of miracles that the church is stagnant; it is because we have forsaken the angelic life of Pentecost, and fallen back on private property."[19] He frequently argued for the social redistribution of wealth.[20] His views increasingly alienated the upper classes, especially the empress Eudoxia, whose fashionable excesses so appalled John that he called her "Jezebel" in a sermon, a comparison that did not amuse her imperial highness. To the elite, John Chrysostom bordered on being a traitor. After the attack on the empress, he deposed several of his brother bishops—from an entirely different city—who had been caught selling church property for personal gain. His enemies took the opportunity to charge him with heresy, and a kangaroo court convicted him on twenty-nine counts and banished him from his office and the city. Eventually city authorities recalled him, only to exile Chrysostom a second time; he lived the rest of his life in a remote village.

For all his tactlessness and political naïveté, Chrysostom championed the church's social responsibility toward the poor, the practice of hospitality, and the need for Christians to live in simplicity. His words still echo through time, ringing with Christian conviction regarding love for the neighbor. Speaking of the poor, John once reminded his comfortable parishioners, "They are the healers of your wounds, their hands are medicinal to you. You receive more than you give, you are benefited more than you benefit. You lend to God, not to people."[21] And his struggle to reinvigorate the early practice of shared goods points out how wealth and political power transformed—and perhaps deformed—apostolic faith.

Peacemaking

"That's a beautiful window," I said to Bob Tate as he took me on a tour of the church building where he serves as an Episcopal priest, St. Martin-in-the-Fields in Philadelphia.

High on the wall, well above the entry doors in the neomedieval building, a large round stained-glass window depicts a man, a soldier, sheltering another in his cloak. More than its execution, however, makes it beautiful. The picture communicates caring, the two figures appearing to glow in the practice of hospitality.

"You know the story, I suppose," Bob said. "That's St. Martin. He converted to Christ while a soldier. One day his regiment was guarding the city of Amiens, and he met a naked beggar on the road. Martin, though only a catechumen and not yet a baptized Christian, took off his cloak, tore it in half, and covered the beggar. He literally followed Jesus's teaching to give one's coat to the poor."

The night following the incident on the road, Jesus appeared to Martin in a dream, affirming the soldier's act of hospitality, saying, "Martin, a simple catechumen covered me with this garment." The episode became stuff of gossip in the regiment, and the cape was rumored to have miraculous power. After Martin's death, Frankish kings turned the cloak into a relic, claiming divine protection on their rule.

Martin of Tours (ca. 316–397) was born into a pagan family, but as a young man he expressed interest in Christianity. His father, however, was appalled by the religion and forced Martin to join the Roman army. While he served as a soldier, Martin's curiosity about Christianity grew, as did his strong sense of morality, until he became a catechumen. The cloak episode supposedly occurred when he was still an inquirer. The cloak is most likely the stuff of pious legend, a story told to make a point. But the point was clear: Martin was devout, even before baptism, and followed the way of hospitality and sharing.

When he was baptized, Martin demonstrated yet another early Christian practice by asking to be released from the army. "I am Christ's soldier," he maintained; "I am not allowed to fight."[22] Martin was not a conscientious objector in the modern sense; he was merely stating early Christian practice. Before theologians Ambrose and Augustine in later decades made a case for just war, Christians were not allowed to fight. No record exists that Christians served in the Roman army before the year 170.[23] The strong consensus of the early church teachers was that war meant killing, killing was murder, and murder was wrong. In the third century Cyprian of Carthage noted, "The world is going mad in mutual bloodshed. And murder, which is considered a crime when people commit it singly, is transformed into a virtue when they do it en masse."[24] Justin Martyr, Irenaeus, Hippolytus, Tertullian, and Origen all specifically condemned participation in war. "The Christian fathers of the first three centuries," states theologian Lisa

Sowle Cahill, "were generally adamant that discipleship requires close adherence to the nonviolent and countercultural example of Jesus's own life and his sayings about the nature of the kingdom."[25]

Related to their horror of killing was a second problem with warfare: soldiers were required to perform acts of worship to the state, the gods, and the emperor; thus, from a Christian perspective, soldiering demanded idolatry. Because the empire murdered Christians (among others), Tertullian pointed out that even a soldier's tokens of victory, especially the crown of laurel leaves, symbolized death; they were hollow triumphs made at the expense of other human beings: "Is the laurel of the triumph made of leaves, or of corpses? Is it adorned with ribbons, or with tombs? Is it bedewed with ointments, or with the tears of wives and mothers?"[26] Since the military practiced both violence and idolatry, Tertullian insisted that there was "no agreement" between serving God and the emperor. To even wear the uniform of a soldier symbolized killing; as a result, the church did not let Christians enlist or converts to continue to serve after baptism.[27]

While Tertullian emphasized the negative aspects of the military to Christian discipleship, Origen pointed out the positive vision of a life of Christian peacemaking. He criticized the army as a society of "professional violence," pointing out that Jesus forbids any kind of violence or vengeance against another. "We will not raise arms against any other nation, we will not practice the art of war," he wrote, "because through Jesus Christ we have become the children of peace."[28] To him the spiritual life means rejecting all forms of violence, an "absolute pacifism."[29]

In asking to leave the army, Martin was following the way of peacemaking as taught and expected in the early church. As soon as Martin was free from military obligation, he went to study theology with Hilary of Poitiers and eventually became a monk. In 372 the city of Tours chose him as their bishop. Like John Chrysostom, he turned down the honor—only to be forced into the office by popular acclaim. He succeeded as a bishop. He planted churches, converting many people throughout France, and founded the first Egyptian-style monastic community in the northern part of the empire. Many Christians believed that the former soldier, once a member of the feared Roman army, possessed the gift of healing; they came to him for relief from illness and disease. And he served the poor and outcasts, even on one occasion protesting the death penalty of a wrongly condemned man. Unlike so many of his peers, he died peacefully in bed of old age, having dedicated himself to a nonviolent way: a soldier for Christ.

Strangers and Aliens

"Have you ever noticed," Padre Jesus Reyes, an Episcopal priest, asked me one day, "that every time the media mentions Hispanic immigrants, they are called 'strangers' or 'aliens' who are 'invading' America?" He shook his head ruefully. "It can be just as bad in the church," he continued. "I think North American Christians have forgotten that we are all 'strangers and aliens' in this world."

On the night of his arrest, Jesus prayed for his followers: "I am not asking you to take them out of the world, but I ask you to protect them from the evil one." He went on, "They do not belong to the world, just as I do not belong to the world" (John 17:15–16). Jesus knew that those who walked his way would live out this prayerful paradox—being in the world yet not being of the world. Indeed, the writer of Hebrews would describe God's people as "strangers and foreigners on the earth" (Heb. 11:13).

The early Christian text (from the second or third century) known as the *Epistle to Diognetus* explains that Christianity is neither an ethnicity nor earthly citizenship but a way of life that is somehow at odds with the societies in which the faithful reside. Christians may look like everyone else, but their actions—including practices of hospitality, charity, and nonviolence—make them different:

> For the Christians are distinguished from other men neither by country, nor language, nor the customs which they observe. . . . They dwell in their own countries, but simply as sojourners. As citizens, they share in all things with others, and yet endure all things as if foreigners. Every foreign land is to them as their native country, and every land of their birth as a land of strangers. They marry, as do all [others]; they beget children; but they do not destroy their offspring. They have a common table, but not a common bed. They are in the flesh, but they do not live after the flesh. They pass their days on earth, but they are citizens of heaven. They obey the prescribed laws, and at the same time surpass the laws by their lives. They love all men, and are persecuted by all. They are unknown and condemned; they are put to death, and restored to life. They are poor, yet make many rich; they

> are in lack of all things, and yet abound in all; they are dishonored, and yet in their very dishonor are glorified. They are evil spoken of, and yet are justified; they are reviled, and bless; they are insulted, and repay the insult with honor; they do good, yet are punished as evil-doers. When punished, they rejoice as if quickened into life.[30]

Christians called themselves both "resident aliens" and "settled migrants." Yes, Christians were citizens of cities, regular people who seemed like all other people, but more importantly, they were citizens of another reality—one demonstrated by their actions. Thus Jesus's followers understood that they lived a paradoxical existence, part of an earthly city while at the same time finding a true home in the divine territory of practicing their faith.

The paradox of "in the world yet not of it" is sometimes expressed by modern people as the difficult relationship between church and state. But in the ancient world the tension ran deeper than political theology. For early Christians the state—the Roman Empire—was an all-encompassing world, not only a government or political arrangement but also a set of structures and a worldview that influenced every aspect of life, private and public. And the church was not yet an institution, a building, or a system of theology; believers were the church, the Jesus followers—a holy people enacting a Christian way of life that had transformed their beings. The paradox of being in the world yet not of it posed a crisis of identity and practice for ancient believers, and it served as the template upon which they built their lives and theologies: How to relate to the society in which they lived? Their former religions and beliefs? Their relatives who might not be Christians? Could their two worlds connect? As Tertullian put it, "What has Athens to do with Jerusalem?"

Early Christian thinkers developed two broad approaches to the question. Justin Martyr (100–165) developed the correlationist method by trying to relate pagan intellectual traditions to Christianity to prove the new faith's credibility in a skeptical and hostile environment. Justin knew that Christians were outsiders to the Roman world; he would eventually be martyred for his faith. He did not try to make Christians "of the world" in his theology. Rather, he hoped to show that Christianity was an intellectual system that, like the best of ancient philosophy, entailed growth in a life of virtue and deserved a fair hearing. Justin did not reject the philosophy and science of his day but rather tried to find elements of Christian wisdom in pagan thought and ideals. He appreciated ancient philosophy, arguing that "Socrates was a Christian before Christ." The best of the ancient world acted as a bridge to the fullness of Christian revelation. In essence, he hoped to convert the Roman world to Christianity by affirming the riches of ancient culture.

In northern Africa Tertullian (ca. 160–225) took the exact opposite approach by developing a separatist theological method. To him the world and church were completely distinct; indeed, worldly philosophy led to heresy. No one stated the conflict more sharply than he:

> It is philosophy which is the subject matter of this world's wisdom, that rash interpreter of the divine nature and order. In fact, heresies are themselves prompted by phi-

> losophy. . . . What is there in common between Athens and Jerusalem? What between the Academy and the Church? What between heretics and Christians?

Answering his own rhetorical question, Tertullian implied absolutely nothing. "The Lord should be sought in simplicity of heart. We desire no further belief."[31] To him scripture alone served as the guide for Christian reflection and practice. Dabbling in the world would lead away from truth. Theologies such as Justin Martyr's only accommodated the gospel to intellectual fashion, thus risking a corruption of the Christian message.[32]

For all their differences, Justin and Tertullian shared the presupposition that Christianity was distinctive, a community whose identity was grounded in the love of God and neighbor and a people who always resist the powers of this world. Anglican Archbishop Rowan Williams insists that "the foundational charter" of the Christian church was "in claiming a different sort of citizenship."[33]

In the end, however, Justin and Tertullian's argument may well have been moot, for the tension that inspired it disappeared in the mid-fourth century. In 313 the emperor Constantine opened the way for Christianity to become the religion of the empire, effectively replacing the old gods with Jesus Christ. Christians of his day hailed him as "the thirteenth apostle" because he, unlike Peter and Paul, had finally Christianized Rome. Constantine built churches, sponsored clergy from state funds and freed them from paying taxes, created Christian academies and universities, fostered the practice of pilgrimage to the Holy Land, and collected holy relics. Persecutions stopped, and the martyr faith became a faith only of memory. Christians were welcomed into the government and army; indeed, in the next century being a Christian became a requirement for serving in the army.

By the end of Constantine's reign, Christianity had been completely transformed. Christians no longer had to be "resident aliens" or "settled migrants." Instead they held dual citizenship in Rome and the heavenly city. Or, as seemed to many, with a Christian emperor and a court of bishops, Rome *was* God's heavenly city and the kingdom of God had taken up earthly residence. The paradoxical nature of Christian identity dissolved—the very paradox that had fueled the practices of devotion and ethics that made the faith both distinctive and compelling. The contemporary writer Verna Dozier referred to this as "the Third Fall," a fall as detrimental to faith as the original fall and Israel's insistence on a king.[34] The Christian paradox was lost, and the original vision of Christianity as a way of life yielded to faith as the prerequisite for worldly comfort and success.

The End of the Beginning

Augustine (354–430), an adult convert to Christianity and the reluctant bishop of the North African city of Hippo, emerged as the dominant theologian of Constantinian Christianity. His questions shaped Western Christianity for more than a millennium. Perhaps no one struggled more than he to understand doctrine, practice, and the institution of the church in the new cultural context, as shown by his thousands of pages of theological speculation on politics, the church, the nature of God, and Christian living.

In 421, toward the end of his career, Augustine summarized his own thought in a small tract, *The Enchiridion on Faith, Hope, and Love*, as a handbook on "true wisdom." The title echoes Paul's words to the Corinthians also summarizing the Christian way: "And now faith, hope and love abide, these three; and the greatest of these is love" (1 Cor. 13:13).

The Enchiridion is an odd and often overlooked book. Augustine devoted 113 chapters of it to faith, explaining, in pained detail, his understanding of sin and redemption—views that would form the basis of Western Christian orthodoxy.[35] He devoted three chapters to hope as described by Jesus in the Lord's Prayer. The final five chapters are dedicated to love, without which it is impossible to have either faith or hope. "All the commandments of God," claimed Augustine, "are embraced in love." The end of following Jesus's way is love; every practice "has love for its aim." Although he had written reams about original sin, predestination, the creeds, just war, and heresy, the mature Augustine returned to the central point of early Christianity: "This love embraces both the love of God and the love of our neighbor, and 'on these two commandments hang all the law and the prophets.'" So his handbook ended simply:

> We love God now by faith; then we shall love Him through sight. Now we love even our neighbor by faith. . . . But in the future life, every man shall love and praise in his neighbor the virtue that may not be hid.

For "God is love."[36] And all will be perfected in love.

Christians would need all the faith, hope, and love they could muster because the world in which they had grown so comfortable was about to collapse. In 410 the barbarian Alaric and his Goths sacked Rome, the symbol of immortal civilization and the cradle of the Christian church. "Eternal city," moaned Jerome, the translator of the Latin Bible; "if Rome can fall, what can be safe?" Christians had forgotten that they were citizens of two cities, the one Augustine called "the City of Man" and "the City of God." They conflated the two into one, fully identifying Roman interests with Jesus's way. The 410 attack proved the first of a devastating series of battles, culminating with a barbarian invader deposing the final Roman emperor in 476. Many centuries later, Thomas Merton would write in an introduction to one of Augustine's books, "The fall of the city that some had thought would stand forever demoralized what was left of the civilized world."[37]

Thousands of Romans fled across the Mediterranean to the North African city of Hippo, where Augustine was bishop. He sympathized with his fear-filled refugee congregation, those who had once lived at the center of power, the most important city in the world, and he began to preach. The problem, Augustine said, was that Christians had forgotten their true citizenship. Rome had been too alluring. "The heavenly city," he reminded them, "while it sojourns on earth, calls citizens out of all nations and gathers together a society of pilgrims of all languages. . . . In its pilgrim state the heavenly city possesses peace by faith; and by this faith it lives."[38]

Although Rome had accommodated the faith for a time, Augustine believed that Rome was the "City of Man," whose way of life ultimately was founded upon self-love, domination, possessions, and glory. Augustine contrasted that way to the Christian way expressed in the "City of God," the pilgrimage community that loves God, seeks wisdom, and practices charity and hospitality. "In truth," Augustine wrote, "these two cities are entangled together in this world." Sometimes the City of Man honors the City of God and its virtues, other times not. For those who follow Christ, their true home is God's city—always purer and more beautiful than any earthly one.[39]

As Rome—and the early church—passed into history, Augustine called Christians back to the way, the way of loving God and the neighbor. And as the old age closed and a new one opened, Christians could not imagine what would come next or how their faith would survive in a barbaric world.

PART II

THE CATHEDRAL

Medieval Christianity

500–1450

FOUR

Christianity as Spiritual Architecture

In August of 1980, while still a college student, I first visited Chartres Cathedral. From Paris the train takes about an hour, giving the adventure an air of pilgrimage. I arrived in the mid-morning and walked up to the famously beautiful building, the sight of which was difficult to comprehend spiritually. Thankfully, a sign at the entrance announced that an English tour would soon start. I signed up and waited.

A guide approached our small group, consisting mostly of Americans and Canadians, and introduced himself as Malcolm Miller, an Englishman who lived in Chartres and gave tours of the cathedral twice a day. He had been doing so since 1958; the cathedral, he said, was his life. More than a building, he explained, Chartres was in effect a library; in the Middle Ages, since most people could not read, architecture acted as story, as books. And among medieval buildings, Chartres was special. "It is alive," he claimed; "it changes, it breathes."[1]

As spiritual geography, Chartres has been special since ancient times. Long before Christians worshiped there, Druids revered a spring in Chartres and built a sacred well where the cathedral now stands. They believed that one day a virgin would bear a son who would heal the world, and the spring with its flowing water represented hope for this birth. Not surprisingly, when Christians first came to Chartres they built an altar to the Virgin Mary on the site. Roman authorities in Gaul did not take kindly to this development. They executed Christian worshipers on the spot and tossed their bodies into the sacred well. Eventually Christians built a church to remember these martyrs, dedicating it to Mary, the Mother of Jesus. By 800 the church claimed to hold the tunic that wrapped Mary during Jesus's birth—a relic of such stature that Chartres became an important pilgrimage site, complete with a new cathedral.

The building that now stands replaced an older one lost in a fire in 1194. As we walked around, a choir rehearsed medieval chant and rainbow-colored light fell across the floor. Miller retraced cathedral history, explaining Gothic architecture, pointing out an ancient labyrinth, and telling the Bible stories depicted in the windows. In the south aisle he stopped to teach us how to "read" a medieval stained-glass window. This one, given by the town's shoemakers, combined two scripture tales: the Old Testament story of Adam and Eve's exile from Eden and the New Testament parable of the Good Samaritan.

While such a combination might seem random, it was not. Other medieval cathedrals combined the same two stories. Although I certainly knew the stories, I did not know why they were paired. The guide explained that medieval people interpreted the Good Samaritan story as an allegory for humanity's spiritual condition. In their understanding, the wounded traveler was us—the children of Adam and Eve—exiled from paradise, dying in a ditch. Christ was the Good Samaritan, who poured oil and wine on humanity's wounds, rescuing us from death. Thus the stories intertwined, with the Good Samaritan fulfilling the longing sadness of Genesis to be restored to God's presence.

Sacred wells and living water. Martyrs and relics. Labyrinth and rose window. Music and allegory. Exile and return. Somehow, in Chartres time shifted. I had no idea how long I had been there, this world within a world; it was almost like being inside an icon of the cosmos. What kind of Christianity was this? Without words, medieval people left behind a record of faith in this building, a living witness to wonder.

"Come back," Malcolm Miller said to us; "I'll be here until Judgment Day." Caught up in the spirit of the place, I was pretty sure he spoke the truth.

Between Heaven and Hell?

If contemporary Christians draw analogies between our time and the world of the early church, they rarely do so with the Middle Ages. A society of monks and saints, kings and knights, clerics and peasants seems more a cast of characters from the local Renaissance fair than a place that actually existed. Indeed, it is fashionable in some circles to deride the medieval church as part of "Christendom," a political arrangement that joined church and state in a hierarchy of power that compromised vital faith.

At the same time, however, people appear to be rediscovering medieval spirituality. Books on medieval religious practices and monastic rules sell well. Prayer books based on the structure of medieval hours shape the lives of many of today's Christian faithful. Neo-Gothic churches seem to be attracting a new generation of the curious and seekers. Acting companies are reviving medieval mystery plays. Some Roman Catholic congregations are once again performing the Latin Mass. Formal liturgies based in ancient rituals have caught the imagination of younger churchgoers. Haunting medieval music accompanies many regular Sunday services, even in nondenominational congregations. And many seekers have found their way to Anglican, Roman Catholic, and Eastern Orthodox faiths, traditions that still bear strong resemblance to their medieval forebears.

I doubt that most North Americans are attracted to medieval spiritualities because they are hankering after Christendom; the social arrangements of the Middle Ages do not appeal to contemporary people. Rather, people seem to find some congruence between the sensibilities of medieval Christianity and their own. When viewed from the angle of sensibility, the medieval world does not seem quite so foreign.

Like us, medieval people lived in a culture with porous borders. Although the medieval church is often depicted as obsessed with orthodoxy and social control, the spiritual world of medieval Christians might be better described as messy. The boundary between sacred and secular was wide open, and the divine and mundane, Christian and pagan, theological and magical freely intermixed. The medieval world was indeed Christian. And when authorities felt threatened by this messiness, they cracked down. But for the most part medieval faith was a type of Christianity that blended traditions rather fluidly, a confluence of diversity and local custom. In contemporary parlance, medieval spirituality might be known—and criticized by purveyors of orderly religion—as "cafeteria Christianity."

And also like us, medieval people lived in a culture filled with stories told in pictures rather than only in texts. Their sculpture and stained glass were akin to our video and Internet. Their stories unfolded in image and light, much as ours do. They lived in a performance culture, where gestures communicated spiritual and moral lessons. They escaped the mundane by embarking on pilgrimages that took them to the far reaches of their geographical and spiritual worlds. Commenting on these similarities, French historian Regine Pernoud wrote, "We are actually closer to medieval times" than to those times of the more recent past.[2]

What makes us empathize with medieval spirituality? I think it may be our common sense of "in between-ness." Medieval people structured faith as in between heaven and hell, with the church mediating the mysterious territory of earthly existence, combining elements of both. The medieval church embraced both the mundane and the transcendent, making little distinction between spheres, acting as a thin place—a kind of permeable spiritual membrane—between the worlds.[3] Although many contemporary people lack the same certainty about heaven and hell, we nonetheless have the same sense that existence comprises the sacred and secular, as the old wall between the two thins once again. For us too the spiritual community mediates between work and play, surety and mystery, and the earthy and the divine; the church can be, as it was in the Middle Ages, the local geography of an unseen realm.

We also share with them the uneasy sense of being in the middle. The Middle Ages is named for the time between the ancient church and the modern one, with apparently little independent existence of its own. We too live in a historical middle. What was modern is quickly fading into the past; what will be is yet to come. Thus historians call our time postmodern, a discomforting and vague moniker if ever there was one. With no positive sense of identity, we, like them, stumble into the cathedral seeking some meaning for our spiritual lives.

Structured Spirituality

In 2007 I attended a meeting in which some clergy spent a good deal of time bashing the institutional church and organized religion, saying how outmoded, irrelevant, and wasteful they are. The conversation surprised me. After all, they were *clergy* and not a group of friends at Starbucks!

In an age when people claim to be "spiritual but not religious," it is fashionable to downplay institutions in favor of a direct experience of the divine. Yet as theologian Larry Rasmussen notes, structure answers an essential question, and one that was quite poignant for medieval Christians: "How do we order life together in a world with a nasty tendency to fall apart?"[4] Without some sort of architecture, spirituality cannot be sustained over time or taught to successive generations. At its best, structure carries life-giving wisdom beyond our immediate experience and limited individual memory.

Although contemporary people often think of architecture as static or perhaps stifling, buildings often "live," as Malcolm Miller proposed at Chartres Cathedral. Medieval Christians tried to translate their spiritual sensibilities into some sort of structure that would communicate life even long after the builders died. Chartres Cathedral would not exist if not for the two great institutions of the Middle Ages, the monastery and the parish church.

To medieval people, church buildings expressed their spirituality—their visions, virtues, and dreams of God. Church buildings were the geography of paradise, the actual location where God's reign of beauty and justice could be experienced here on earth. Buildings, and the arts and liturgies therein, demonstrated the mysterious interweaving of the worlds, the playful combination of this world and the one beyond. Holiness was translated into visible structures where people might see, touch, and feel the beauty of God. Medieval builders captured this sense, creating sacred spaces that were both spiritually unpredictable and theologically structured at the same time.

Because the church building was holy geography, communities spent enormous resources of time, money, and talent constructing church buildings; the church stood as both a location of paradise and an icon of communal identity. Medieval people associated the actual building with God's reign and were ferociously protective of their churches. In the 1130s Peter of Bruis, a French preacher, promoted the idea that God had no use for church buildings. To him they interfered with the purity and simplicity of faith. Peter urged Christians in the town of Saint-Gilles to give up their church and burn its ornaments, including its crosses, dramatically illustrating his point by lighting a pyre. The people of Saint-Gilles, whose church was a major pilgrimage site, responded by tossing poor Peter on his own bonfire.

Chartres Cathedral of the High Middle Ages—the church we know today—was unimaginable some five centuries earlier when the Roman Empire gave way to a "patchwork of rule and misrule"[5] that would eventually coalesce into medieval Europe. In 410 when the barbarians sacked Rome, Augustine bemoaned the city had been taken over by a "gang of robbers." For the next two centuries successive waves of northern invaders struck Rome, leaving in their wake an empire divided into East and West, with the political, social, economic, and cultural structures of the West collapsing more completely than those of the East. Pope Gregory the Great (ca. 540–604) observed:

> Everywhere we see mourning, from all sides we hear lamentation. Cities are destroyed, military camps are overturned, fields are laid waste. . . . We see some led captive, some mutilated, others murdered, and she herself [Rome] who once seemed to be mistress of the world, what has remained of her is abundantly afflicted with tremendous misfortunes.[6]

He thought that the end of the world was at hand.

In this difficult situation, however, Gregory helped shape Christian community in ways that would allow it to both survive and thrive for a thousand years—and he did so on principles drawn from his monastic predecessor, Benedict of Nursia (480–550). Between them, they ordered Christianity in a disordered world through both the actual architecture of the church and the spiritual architecture of Christian practices. Thus medieval Christianity emerged as a faith of the soul *in* the world yet not completely *of* the world.

Contemporary Christians are more familiar with Benedict than Gregory, thanks to a revival in interest in Benedict's rule as a spiritual path. Benedict, distraught by Rome's collapse, fled to the Italian countryside around the year 500. There, with his sister Scholastica, he gathered two communities of people "who were themselves looking for a more meaningful way of life" than what was offered by the remnants of Roman Christianity.[7]

Benedict developed a rule of life, a monastic handbook, that ordered community around the practice of humility. He envisioned the spiritual life as the "Twelve Steps of Humility," shaping the heart for "holy obedience," whereby external chaos would give way to an internally ordered soul. Although it emphasized authority and obedience, his rule was not severe. A wise abbot, the spiritual "father" of the community, would balance compassion with discipline, demanding "nothing too harsh, nothing too burdensome" of the monks. Such a communal life of prayer and good works, Benedict said, would be a "school for the Lord's service" where "our hearts overflow with the inexpressible delight of love."[8] In this modest hope lay the foundation of Western monasticism.

Not everyone, however, could escape to the countryside to monastic safety. Vast numbers of Christians remained in crumbling Roman cities, where their churches served as the locus of spiritual community. Amid the disorder, civil authorities abandoned their posts, and weakened churches often served as the only stable institution where people tended to the poor and sick, distributed food, provided education, and maintained law and order. Burdened by huge demands, the church found itself pressured by diminishing resources and declining clergy morale.

In 590 Gregory became Bishop of Rome, the position known as pope in the Western church. Concerned by political and spiritual challenges, Pope Gregory I set about reforming the church by strengthening its care for the social order, deepening the spiritual life of the clergy, and supporting mission work to the world. Gregory renewed the church on Benedictine principles, which he popularized through writing books. He reformed congregational worship by introducing choirs in order to lead liturgy, he emphasized preaching, and he raised standards of clergy education—all changes that had immediate impact on the lives of believers. By holding up Benedict's way of life as an example to regular Christians and their clergy, he tried to reshape their parish churches as monastic–like communities of humble service, regular prayer, and good works in the world.

During Gregory's time service to the world included not only charity and the administration of justice but also negotiating treaties with barbarian kings and taking political steps to protect the Christian community from being destroyed by war. Thus Gregory promoted missions as a pragmatic solution to a real problem; if the pagan warlords became Christians, they might refrain from attacking Christian churches and killing the Christian faithful. Pressed by the needs of the church in the world, Gregory expanded Benedict's vision to include mission as a practice for the parish church and its clergy. By the time of his death, Gregory had successfully established a practical spiritual framework for medieval congregations whereby the church, its buildings and its spiritual practices, served as the center point of village life.

Thus the ultimate model of medieval spirituality became the parish church infused with the devotion of the monastery—a lofty goal, no doubt, but one that influenced the practice of Christianity for a millennium. Benedict and Gregory intended to create a spiritual architecture that would shelter faith in difficult times. They lived when their world had collapsed; instead of abandoning religious communities in favor of some sort of personal spiritual quest, however, they attended to the need for and the patterning of Christian congregations. Arguably, Christianity would not have survived the fall of Rome without their innovative restructuring of church.

FIVE

Devotion: Paradise Restored

The story of Adam and Eve, as depicted in the windows at Chartres, acted as the foundational story for medieval spirituality. In the Old Testament book of Genesis, God created Adam and Eve and gave them a home in paradise, the Garden of Eden. God asked but one thing of them: not to eat the fruit from the tree of the knowledge of good and evil. But, tempted by the serpent, Adam and Eve ate. As punishment for their sin, God banished them from paradise. Absent God, the world devolved into a tragedy of pride, violence, and sin. Thus began the long human quest to regain paradise, to somehow find a way back to God's presence. Medieval spirituality was marked by its sense of exile and longing to return as Christians sought holy reunion with God in this life with hope for the next.[1]

Sacred Journey

My first course in medieval religious history was taught by Professor Eleanor McLaughlin, a noted scholar of both spirituality and women's history. One morning, with the day's topic posted as "Celtic Christianity," Professor McLaughlin walked into the classroom, paying scant attention to her students, and pretended to light a fire. As she knelt on the floor, she explained, "Celtic households began the day by blessing the fire." Her hands moved gracefully around the imaginary embers as she recited an ancient Irish prayer. "Celtic spirituality melded Irish folk ways and Christianity," she said. "It enfolded nature and grace, a kind of nature mysticism, in a pagan and Christian synthesis."

She recited the legend of Patrick coming to Ireland, the birthplace of Celtic Christianity. As it happened, Patrick landed on Easter eve, and he lit a Pascal fire that lighted up an entire hillside. The wizards who counseled the High King warned that if Patrick's fire were not put out by dawn, "it will not be quenched till doomsday" and that the one who kindled it "will vanquish the kings and lords of Ireland."[2] Wizards tried to extinguish Patrick's flame, but their powers failed and many converted to Christianity. From this mythical beginning a Celtic version of Christianity—one distinct from the traditions of the Roman Church—dominated Ireland. "Their learning, art, and song were placed in wholehearted service of God and the Church," one historian noted. "Nothing was done by halves."[3] Professor McLaughlin said it was a fire that could not be quenched.

This "wall of holy fire" swept across Europe.[4] The Celts, inveterate wanderers, could not sit still. Years before Gregory the

Great conceived of missions as politically advantageous, Celtic Christians set out on journeys as a practice of faith. They did not invent the practice of pilgrimage. Rather, the Celts defined the whole of the Christian life as a sacred journey. "God counseled Abraham," wrote Columba (ca. 521–597), "to leave his own country and go on pilgrimage to the land which God has shown him. . . . Now the good counsel which God enjoined here on the father of the faithful is incumbent on all the faithful; that is to leave their country and their land, their wealth and their worldly delight for the sake of the Lord of the Elements, and go in perfect pilgrimage in imitation of him."[5]

The Voyage of Brendan records the legend of a navigator, Brendan (484–577 or 583), who sets out to find "the island which is called the Promised Land of the Saints."[6] The *Voyage* recounts how Brendan and his companions sailed for seven years, encountering all manner of angels and demons in nature's beauty and fearful storms, in miraculous adventures that tested the pilgrims' faithfulness. It took so long, as Brendan learns at the end of the journey, because "God wished to show you his many wonders in the great ocean." When they arrived, they discovered "open land stretching out before them covered with trees laden with autumnal fruit," where night never fell and a wide river flowed through the center of the island. An angel greeted Brendan and his crew, instructing them to load their boats with fruits and gems before sending them home to their waiting friends. The *Voyage* was widely popular in written, oral, and pictorial forms through the Middle Ages, and it was translated into many European languages. It served as both an exciting tale and an extended metaphor for the Christian life.

Unlike early Christians, who made pilgrimage to specific locations associated with Christ or the saints, Celts tended toward no particular destination—except the "Island of Paradise." On this quest they wandered across the seas; they wandered on land. Occasionally they stopped to set up a cross, some huts, and a small monastic community. But then they started to wander again. Theirs was a vagrant life for Christ, a self-imposed exile from their beloved homeland to find a new way of being in God. As a chronicler from 891 wrote of three Irish strangers who arrived in Cornwall, "They wanted to go into exile for the love of God, they cared not whither."[7]

Celts took the story of Jesus with them to places like Scotland, the north of England, France, Switzerland, Denmark, and Germany. They wandered not for the sake of their own souls but for the sake of others as well, converting many pagan tribes to Christianity. As the missionary Columbanus (d. 615) wrote to a friend, "You know I love the salvation of many and seclusion for myself, the one for the progress of the Lord, that is, of His Church, the other for my own desire."[8] Celtic sacred journey strengthened both the inner spiritual life and the outer life of the church by forming Christian communities. As such, Celtic pilgrimage embodied Jesus's mission to be a faith community in the world.[9]

Eventually Celtic pilgrims encountered Roman monks and their genius for organization, a meeting that did not augur well for the less precise Celts. The Celtic church and the Roman one disagreed—among other things—over the date of Easter, the authority of the pope, and styles for monastic haircuts. Although the Celts lost on all these issues in a church council in 664, their spiritual fervor quietly strengthened the new Roman church in England. In this crucible of pilgrimage and institution, Western Christianity was reborn. Or, as Professor McLaughlin said, Celtic spirituality became "the life-giver of the structure, the fire in the hearth of faith." And throughout the Middle Ages, whenever the power of the institution threatened to overwhelm the heat of faith, pilgrimage continued to be a life-giving path for Christians who heeded the call to spiritual exile.

Icons

Protestant churches tend toward being plain. White or light blue walls, clear or inexpensive colored windows, red or gold carpet, and a simple cross or two constitute most spiritual decor of American congregations. In Sunday school classrooms hang discreet pictures of Jesus and some historical scenes of the Holy Land. Such simplicity comes from the fact that Protestants, unlike Roman Catholics and Orthodox Christians, believe that statues and paintings distract attention away from the Bible and sermon. Words of scripture and acts of goodness reveal God, not art.

Christians have been arguing for quite a long time about visual representation of God. In 600 Bishop Serenus of Marseilles destroyed all the pictures in every church in his city. Apparently the bishop felt that "images somehow cheapened the sacred words of Scripture."[10] When Pope Gregory the Great heard of Serenus's action, he chastised the bishop:

> It is one thing to worship a painting, and quite another to learn from a scene represented in a painting what ought

> to be worshiped. For what writing provides for people who read, paintings provide for the illiterate who look at them, since these unlearned people see what they must imitate; paintings are books for those who do not know their letters, so that they take the place of books especially specifically among pagans.[11]

Although Gregory stated the principle clearly enough, it did not stop icons from becoming one of the most controversial issues in the medieval church.

In 726 the Eastern emperor, Leo III, outlawed the use of icons and ordered their destruction. Up to that time, icons had not been the sole possession of saints, monks, and theologians. Ancient churches invited the laity to "enter an alternative world." There, in cool silence, worshipers were greeted by "the legions of saints—painted on the walls or captured on wooden panels. . . . Staring straight ahead, they waited the supplicant's entreaty, through which they would become animated. At that moment the martyrs of the past mingled with the faithful, blurring the line between the perceptible and that which is beyond human cognition."[12] Lay Christians were accustomed to using icons in public worship and private devotion, and it was assumed that the laity received benefit in healing and spiritual vision through praying with them. Holy images formed devotion throughout Eastern Christianity, opening the vision of paradise for all.[13] Upon Leo's decree to ban them, mass rioting broke out across the empire. The Christian poor revolted. Not even the emperor could close the window to heaven.

A series of edicts and counteredicts from successive popes and emperors further divided the church between *iconoclasts* (destroyers of images) and *iconodules* (worshipers of images). Elite Christians, whose piety was based on words and the Roman love of rhetoric, wanted to eliminate icons for fear that illiterate masses might take over the church. Complicating the class issue was the emergence of Islam in the East, with its strict prohibition against images of every sort. Leaders hoped to mute Islam's challenge to the faith by curbing the abuse of icons among lower classes. Eventually, in 780, the empress Irene ended the conflict and restored icons to the churches. But theological questions remained. She called an ecumenical council to resolve the problems.

The council drew largely from the work of John of Damascus (ca. 655–750). Ironically, John, the defender of icons, lived in the Muslim city of Damascus, where he served as chief councilor to the caliph. The caliph, despite his own distaste for representative art, protected John against several attempts by Christian partisans to have the theologian arrested or killed.

John addressed the issue rather simply. What is an image? "An image is a likeness and representation of some one," John argued, "containing in itself the person who is imaged. The image is not wont to be an exact reproduction of the original. The image is one thing, the person represented another." Thus, having made a distinction between the image and the thing, John explained the purpose of images. "Every image is a revelation and representation of something hidden," he stated. Human beings have limited knowledge; therefore images aid in our capacity to experience what is beyond time and space: "The image was devised for greater knowledge, and for the manifestation and popularizing of secret things." For

Christians this is "a pure benefit and help to salvation, so that by showing things and making them known, we may arrive at the hidden ones, desire and emulate what is good, shun and hate what is evil."[14]

John attacked the charge that iconodules committed idolatry by claiming, "Icons are not idols but symbols." When a Christian venerated an icon (used the icon in worship), John insisted that the act did not constitute worship of the image. "We do not make obeisance to the nature of wood, but we revere and do obeisance to Him who was crucified on the Cross."[15] Christ himself is an image, his human nature a reflection of the invisible divine nature. John believed that based on the nature of Jesus himself, representative art was necessary to Christian worship. The Second Council of Nicaea (787) affirmed John's view of icons and condemned iconoclasts.

Although the events of the iconoclast controversy seem trivial today, they shaped the practice of Christian art for the entirety of the Middle Ages in both the Eastern and Western churches. In the East icons continued to be the primary form of art to represent divine realities. In the West stained-glass windows and statuary replaced icons. Historian Peter Brown argues that medieval Christians understood art as a "bridge" to the spiritually invisible God in their quest to experience "Heaven-with-us." Images offered everyone the possibility of spiritual vision.[16]

In the 1500s Protestants rejected this medieval heritage and returned to the Roman emphasis on rhetoric alone. Most Protestant churches stand as a testament to iconoclasm, part of a long tradition of spiritual simplicity. Imagine my surprise, then, when in January 2008 I spoke at a youth ministry conference sponsored by Princeton Theological Seminary, a bastion of word-centered Protestant faith. When I walked into the meeting room, it was cluttered with icons—large and small—set on easels and surrounded by candles and flowering plants. The simple room had been transformed into a dazzling space of images, all representing Jesus and his ministry, beckoning worshipers to experience Heaven-with-us.

I laughed to myself. Princeton, huh? Sometimes it is good to admit when you got it wrong.

Praying the Hours

For a couple of years I was fortunate enough to live around the corner from the Santa Barbara Mission, a historic church complete with a monastic community. The mission, built in 1786, stands high on a hill overlooking the town and the ocean. From this holy perch, church bells ring out that can be heard throughout the neighborhood on a regular basis. Occasionally somebody complained—or mounted a petition—wanting to silence the loud, disruptive, and frequent ringing of the bells. The church, however, always won the argument. The bells are part of Santa Barbara's history. They have been ringing for a long time. To friendly neighbors, the bells mark time with old-fashioned charm; to the spiritually faithful, the bells call to daily prayer.

Of course, church bells mark both time and prayer. They act as a constant reminder of an ancient Christian tradition, the daily hours (or the daily office), whereby Jesus's followers practiced fixed-hour prayer. No historian knows who first developed this practice or where, but as early as the second and third centuries, writers like Origen and Tertullian assumed such prayers were a regular part of Christian life.[17] The hours included morning and evening prayers as well as devotions at 9:00 a.m., noon, and 3:00 p.m. In Christian Rome monks, clergy, and laypeople engaged in forms of hourly prayer.

When writing his *Rule*, Benedict ordered monastic life around fixed-hour prayer. By doing so, he enshrined a pattern of ancient prayer that became the primary form of Christian hourly prayer down to our own time. Benedict believed that prayer should be "short and pure" and should follow the cycles of days, seasons, and years. Joan Chittister, a contemporary Benedictine sister, says that it "is a spirituality that fills time with an awareness of the presence of God."[18] It is also, as any serious student of prayer knows, hard work. Benedict noted, "To pray is to work, to work is to pray." Hence the idea of fixed-hour prayer as *opus dei* (a term now popularly tainted by *The Da Vinci Code*), or "the work of God." To gather the community to prayer, Benedictine brothers eventually invented mechanisms that rang the *clocca*, the bells. "When the *clocca* rang," writes Dorothy Bass, "they drew attention to the eternity of God and brevity of human life."[19] Clocks and devotion; time and prayer interwoven.

For a few centuries following Benedict, *opus dei* flourished primarily in monasteries, making the daily office appear a clerical spiritual practice. Eventually, however, laypeople reclaimed fixed-hour prayer. As literacy increased in the High Middle Ages (1000–1300), a new "contemplative text-driven spirituality" moved out of monasteries into other Christian settings, driven by the establishment of cathedral schools and universities.[20] Although the invention of the printing press lay a few centuries in the future, medieval people had perfected and loved hand-produced books. In the early Middle Ages, the codex replaced scrolls, and by 1100 medieval Europeans were hand-creating vast numbers of texts, including prayer books. The daily office most often appeared in monastic breviaries, forms of prayer for use by brothers, sisters, and clergy. But most breviaries were anything but brief. They proved "dauntingly copious, complex and bewildering," needing "expert knowledge" to translate their rules into everyday life.[21] By the twelfth century shorter books of hours suitable for private use started to appear. Laypeople eventually picked up these books, referred to as prayer primers or a book of hours, a simplified version of the breviary, for use in their devotional lives.

Across social classes, people prized these short manuals. Personal prayer books could be carried around in a pocket, sleeve, or belt as a fashion accessory with pious purpose. Books of hourly prayer were given as gifts, in remembrance and thanks, honoring special occasions among families and friends. The books democratized fixed-hour prayer, making the daily office a fixture of piety—especially among women—in the Middle Ages. People jotted in them too, noting their hopes and petitions for health and happiness; they seemingly ascribed special spiritual powers to the pages of such prayer books. Lay practice of the daily office fostered an "essentially monastic form of piety," personalizing faith for regular people.[22]

Yet personal faith did not translate into mere individualism. Families, households, and groups of women recited the hours together, creating small lay communities of prayer. Around 1400 the Roberts family of Middlesex acquired an inexpensive book of hours, one aimed at the middle-class market for such devotionals. The well-worn volume, still extant in the Cambridge University Library, reveals both the formal devotion of regular prayer and the kinds of everyday prayers of informal lay piety. Over the years various members of the Roberts family scribbled over the daily office, marking their names and adding petitions to the traditional prayers. They enhanced the text with their own words, poems, and liturgies—including a Latin rhyme about the Virgin Mary, a prayer for conceiving children, petitions for protection against the plague, and a spiritual charm (saying the Hail Mary and giving alms) to ensure prosperity. Edmund Roberts included his own prayer—mixing both a traditional litany and his unique reading of scripture—to relieve fever "through the thousand names of Christ," commenting that he had "used the prayer well" over ten days. Historian Eamon Duffy describes the Roberts' prayers as "churchly, sacramental, attentive to the saints, concerned with meritorious acts of charity: they are highly supernatural, but in no sense otherworldly."[23] It was practical piety through hourly prayer.

Practicing the hours matched a new devotional seriousness among the laity, who appropriated the church's theology in their own voices. Regular prayer functioned in a surprisingly radical way: when conventional people engaged in such prayer they took on authority typically reserved for the ordained class, discovering their own spiritual power for service, healing, and prosperity. Through the Middle Ages the laity made what had become a clerical form of prayer their own once again, reclaiming for themselves an ancient practice of the church.

Hope

"I have a pop quiz," I announced to my church history class. "Read the quote on the handout and tell me who you think wrote it and when."

The students looked at the assigned quote:

> And so Jesus is our true Mother in nature by our first creation. And he is our true Mother in grace by taking our created nature. . . . He is our Mother, brother and savior.

I watched as they puzzled over the question; no one seemed confident about his or her answer. After a few minutes I asked for them to respond verbally, calling on them one at a time. The first replied, "I think this was written in the 1970s, but I can't say who wrote it." The second guessed, "Mary Daly? She's the only feminist theologian I know." A third suspected that I was the author. And so it went.

No one guessed that Julian of Norwich (ca. 1342–after 1416) penned these words around 1390, in the first English-language book written by a woman. Good thing the quiz was only for extra credit.

Julian of Norwich is a shadowy figure in church history. Her real name and the facts of her life remain unknown. For some reason this Englishwoman took up life as an anchoress—a solitary nun—walled into a cell at the parish church of St. Julian of Norwich, from which she took her name. On May 8, 1373, when she was around thirty years old, Julian was struck by a devastating illness from which she nearly died. During the sickness she received fifteen visions of God's love. For the next twenty years she reflected on these visions, writing down her reflections in a book called *Showings, or The Revelations of Divine Love.*

The fourteenth century was a particularly trying time in medieval England, complete with dynastic wars, the bubonic plague, and economic collapse. "Human life was cheap," one historian writes, "and fear of punishment by God ran high. A certain degree of pessimism, fear, and anxiety characterized the darker side of English life."[24] Despite this, and despite the fact that Julian received these visions during a life-threatening illness, the major theme of the revelations is hope in and through God's love.

According to Julian, this love has its most powerful expression in visions of God as Mother: "The deep Wisdom of the Trinity is our Mother, in whom we are enclosed." To her, fatherhood represented God's kingship, a kind of distant rule, whereas God's motherhood demonstrated the worldly, sensual, and active property of God. "In Mother Christ we profit and increase, and in mercy he reforms and restores us."[25] Only through the Mother God can human beings experience the comfort of the divine:

> The mother's service is nearest, readiest, and surest. It is nearest because it is more natural; readiest because it is most loving; and surest because it is truest. No one ever might or could perform this office fully, except only him. We know that all our mothers bear us for pain and for death. Oh, what is that? But our true Mother Jesus, he alone bears us for joy and for endless life. So he carries us within him in love and travail.

Julian explained that Jesus feeds us "with himself," drawing us to "his blessed breast." There the "tender Mother Jesus" revealed the "joys of heaven, with inner certainty of endless bliss."[26]

Thus "the fair, lovely word 'Mother'" belongs most truly to Jesus, "the kind, loving mother who knows and sees the need of her child guards it very tenderly." This is the essence of wisdom, that "precious and lovely are the children of grace in the sight of our heavenly Mother." And it is the genesis of holy assurance—that in the midst of suffering, illness, and pain, the Mother God says, "All will be well. You will see it yourself, that every kind of thing will be well."[27]

Julian goes on to say, "I marveled greatly at this vision." She was not, however, only marveling at the image of God as Mother. She marveled at the possibility of hope. For as singular as her own life was, she was not the only medieval person to delve into the divine feminine. Indeed, the imagery of Mother God appears two full centuries before Julian's *Showings* in the work of noted theologians such as Anselm of Canterbury and Bernard of Clairvaux. In this tradition maternity represented nurture, security, and comfort. The mother symbolism was most often expressed in relation to the Virgin Mary, but male theologians also employed it to describe Jesus, God the Father, and the Trinity.[28] "Mother" acted as a fleshy metaphor, a sensate comfort, whereby God's love became understandable, personal, and warm.

Therein lay hope, something that was in short supply in Julian's society. Against a backdrop of war and upheaval, Julian found assurance; a spiritual surety echoed through her written words, at the breast of the Mother God. No wonder that six centuries later, at the height of World War II,

T. S. Eliot would quote Julian of Norwich in his great poem, *Little Gidding*: "All shall be well / and all manner of things shall be well."

Passion

In my early twenties I attended Gordon-Conwell Theological Seminary, an evangelical school in the Boston area. One of my roommates, an outspoken Pentecostal pastor's daughter who could have passed for Anna Nicole Smith and who daringly coregistered for classes at Harvard, pinned a bumper sticker on her bulletin board offering a less-than-usual opinion in such a conservative place: Intelligence is the Ultimate Aphrodisiac. Not exactly a typical expression of evangelical devotion, it suggested some sort of heresy that caused me, with my own prim piety, to squirm.

Whatever my response to her bumper sticker creed, however, as a church history major, I knew the sentiment described a powerful aspect of medieval Christianity, whereby doubt and love merged into spiritual passion, a way of knowing God both prized and feared by the church. While the statement did not exactly fit in the dorm, it would in a church history text. And no one better exemplified it than the twelfth-century lovers Abelard and Heloise.

Young Peter Abelard (1079–1142) arrived in Paris in 1100 to study with a master teacher, whom he quickly bested in debate. Unlike many of his contemporaries, Abelard did not subscribe to realism, the cornerstone of medieval philosophy, which asserted that all things are grounded in some universal truth. Rather, Abelard emphasized particulars, the nuances that separate actual things from the words to describe them. Take humanity as an example. What is humanity other than a collection of very different individuals? Can one even speak of universal humanity? Abelard thought not; it was only a concept, not an actuality. As one biographer said of him, "The more you concentrate on these questions, the more they slip away."[29] Abelard challenged medieval theology by claiming that reason could and should be applied to faith. Abelard himself would assert, "By doubting we come to inquiry, by inquiry we come to truth."[30]

Doubting the reality behind words was one thing, but Abelard applied his method to Christian tradition. Abelard ruthlessly pointed out contradictions between particular traditions to show the folly of any universal principle of Tradition, thus opening the way for theological skepticism about everything from the lives of the saints to the doctrine of the Trinity. The result proved sensational. Students flocked to Abelard, forcing him to open a rival school, eventually exceeding other schools in enthusiasm and influence. He was more, however, than a celebrity or a pure skeptic. He employed doubt as a tool to find faith. If conflicts could be resolved and contradictions synthesized, humans might discover, not universal truth, but the truths of the universe.

At the height of Abelard's Paris career, a friend placed his niece, Heloise (ca. 1101–1162), a young woman of dubious parentage (her mother may have been a nun), with the philosopher to be tutored in Latin. The two began an affair, a liaison not permitted to philosophers whose intellectual purity was protected by celibacy. "So with our lessons as a pretext," wrote Abelard, "we abandoned ourselves entirely to love."[31]

The attraction was more than physical; Abelard and Heloise experienced intense spiritual and intellectual bonds. Abelard praised her "gift for letters," and their surviving correspondence attests to their mutual passion for theology, philosophy, science, and ethics. The interweaving of these things drove Abelard and Heloise to penetrating reflections on the meaning of life. "Surely I have discovered in you," wrote Heloise, "the greatest and most outstanding good of all." More than mere sentiment, their love, she claimed, embodied the Aristotelian highest good, the spiritual purpose of the universe. For both, skepticism dissolved in passion—as they found God through intimacy and in the heavens, a kind of erotic cosmic oneness, paradise here and now. They shared a "clandestine world where philosophy, love, and sex met and provided not just a shelter from the pain of the world but a key to its understanding."[32] A world beyond words, the ecstasy of God, the truths of the universe.

Medieval authorities praised passion when experienced by individual monks or nuns through the love of Christ, as with Francis of Assisi or Teresa of Ávila, as a foretaste of heaven. But they worried when men and women found it together, fearing that human sexuality would prove more powerful than divine love (something that Heloise herself would later admit was a temptation). If people could experience paradise on earth, religious authorities might lose the power of the keys to heaven.

Abelard and Heloise walked dangerously close to the theological edge. Their affair culminated in a secret marriage and became public knowledge with the birth of their son, an event that brought them unexpected misery.[33] In an act of revenge against their family's honor, Heloise's relatives castrated Abelard, robbing the lovers of their pleasure, thereby forcing the pair into holy orders and a life apart.

Heloise founded a convent, one noted for its tolerance and progressive rule; Abelard redirected passion toward his theological work. Perhaps not surprisingly, Abelard's work came to focus on the work of Christ on the cross. He related to the suffering Jesus. "In order to persevere bravely in the battle against our passions," Abelard preached, "we should always hold [Christ] before our eyes, and his passion should always serve as an example to us lest we fall away." For him, Jesus's words in John 15:13 held the meaning of Christ's sacrifice: "Greater love has no one than this, that to lay down one's life for one's friends." According to Abelard, we are united to Jesus in sacrificial love, through which the faithful "cling to him and to our neighbor in an indissoluble bond of love for his sake."[34]

External events did not end Abelard and Heloise's philosophical relationship. Instead, they continued to write steamy theological missives on love's pleasures. No doubt from his own experience of rough justice, Abelard rejected the idea that Christ died as a result of God's vengeance for human disobedience. Abelard was horrified by the novel teaching of his fellow theologian, Anselm (1033–1109), who proposed that Jesus died to satisfy the divine justice of his Father, as a payment of a legal debt required as recompense for sin and to restore God's honor. Abelard exclaimed:

> Indeed, how cruel and perverse it seems that [God] should require the blood of the innocent as the price of anything, or that it should in any way please Him that

> an innocent person should be slain—still less that God should hold the death of His Son in such acceptance that by it He should be reconciled with the whole world.[35]

Who, Abelard demanded, would forgive such a God for killing his own son?

Abelard proposed that Christ died for the sake of love, providing a model of self-sacrificial passion for humankind. Salvation entailed imitating Christ in his love for others, the love that God revealed in Jesus's death for his friends. As Christ had done, we also do. As contemporary theologians Rita Nakashima Brock and Rebecca Parker say of Abelard's view, "The atonement created a deeper love for God than would have been possible without it," creating the prospect that human hearts could be transformed "from fear to love."[36]

Later theologians refer to Abelard's idea as the moral influence theory of the cross, and it would eventually, in the nineteenth and twentieth centuries, shape liberal Christianity. The theory, however, was rejected by many of Abelard's contemporaries. Anselm's idea of blood sacrifice eventually won the day. Although some in the church attempted to have Abelard tried for heresy, the charges never stuck, and Abelard—as well as Heloise—died in communion with the medieval church.

Since the nineteenth century, romantics have interpreted Abelard and Heloise as a lovers' tragedy. But their story serves a more interesting purpose. Christians have often torn mind and heart asunder. Some have extolled doubt and embraced ambiguity while others acknowledged divine love and yet denied sexual passion. Abelard and Heloise, in a strangely contemporary way, put the two together in a compelling vision of paradise. For them the intellectual quest and the sensual quest formed a single path back to Eden. Passion, ignited not by chaste mysticism but rather by human sexuality and rigorous intellectual inquiry, opened the way to God. Through their own experience Abelard and Heloise grasped Christ's cross—the supreme Passion—as love.

Years after my seminary friend hung her bumper sticker, I read the work of Richard Holloway, an English theologian who claims that all that is left of Christianity in the contemporary world are "doubts and loves." Quoting the story of Abelard and Heloise to illustrate a "theology of life," Holloway says that faith "should prompt us to live passionately and intentionally and not waste the one life we have."[37] My friend may have understood this better than the rest of us.

Dying Well

One Sunday in 1989, when I was a graduate student, I went to Duke Chapel to hear the Reverend Will Willimon, then dean of the chapel, preach. Arriving at the chapel, I glanced at the bulletin. To my dismay, the sermon was on death. I grimaced—not a cheerful subject. But it was too late to go elsewhere. I sat down for worship.

Willimon addressed our fear of death—how we relegate the sick and dying to institutions where we cannot see them. "We beg God for a quick death," he said. "At night. In bed. Unexpected." He drew a contrast. "Not at all like our medieval forebears," he stated. "They prayed for long deaths, to die from cancer or other lengthy diseases. They wanted a protracted death so they might prepare for the end."

Unlike in our society, where we hide it, death surrounded medieval people. They had few hospitals, and so churches, poorhouses, and homes handled the dying and dead. Death was not a distant prospect at the end of a long, healthy life. It was integrated into ordinary experience. Medieval life was transitory, a journey through this world that often ended too soon and too abruptly. Death was often violent and unexpected. Extended death, through illness and in one's own bed, was actually a blessing. Death was part of everyday life; medieval people considered their deaths regularly. Indeed, as one medieval historian puts it, "One of the chief obsessions of medieval Christians was the need to make a 'good death.'"[38]

To this end Jean Gerson (1363–1429), a professor in Paris, wrote a mystical theology of dying that circulated among medieval clergy. One of his colleagues, an anonymous friar, excerpted and simplified the more formal book into a pamphlet, *The Art of Dying Well.* The booklet quickly became one of the most popular of its day, read widely in literate circles and appearing in several versions in Latin and in local languages across Europe. In its shortened form Gerson's book was a medieval best-seller.

Dying Well reminded readers that while "the death of the body is the most terrible, it is in no way comparable to the death of the soul." Souls die when tempted by the devil, and to die apart from Christ's grace would mean eternal separation from paradise. "It is thus of the utmost importance that a person take heed of his soul," said Gerson, "so that it not be destroyed at his death." Therefore Christians should "contemplate the art of dying" to prepare for the day that would surely come.[39]

Toward this end Gerson outlined six preparatory actions: (1) that a person should believe "what a good Christian is obliged to believe"; (2) he or she should acknowledge sin; (3) the dying person should swear to amend his ways if he recovered; (4) one must forgive those who have offended and seek forgiveness from those whom you have offended; (5) he or she must make restitution; and (6) the dying person must recognize that "Christ died for him." After these six conditions are met, the sick person could rest in good conscience and receive the church's sacraments. Although it seems rather mechanical, Gerson insists that this is a spiritual process. Throughout, the devil tempts the dying with doubts, despair, impatience, vainglory, and greed. All the while, however, angels assist the sufferer, thus placing the dying person in the center of a divine battle between evil and good, with the ending dependent upon the artful death of the believer.[40] Dying imitated the ancient practice of martyrdom, although here the heroic death happened not in a public arena but in one's own bed.

Despite its medieval notions of demons, angels, and the afterlife, *The Art of Dying Well* is surprisingly relevant today. As the Reverend Willimon pointed out, we do not often consider our own deaths and in many ways miss the opportunity for self-reflection and forgiveness that chronic illness offers. Contemporary theologian Amy Plantinga Pauw notes, "Dying well embraces both lament and hope, and both a sense of divine judgment and an awareness of divine mercy."[41] All of those elements—grief and expectation, repentance and forgiveness—formed the practical spirituality of the medieval vision of dying well.

Oddly enough, the six steps of *Dying Well* echo the twelve steps of contemporary recovery groups. In such settings addicts face their "deaths" and move through steps of remorse, repentance, and forgiveness, complete with temptations and spiritual victories along the path. By dying to their lives as they are, recovering people find hope for a new life beyond the life they have known. Perhaps the practice of dying well serves both the ultimate end and all the lesser ends we face along the way. Paradise found.

SIX

Ethics: Who Is My Neighbor?

The story of the Good Samaritan reminded medieval Christians that the way back to paradise could be found in caring for one's neighbor. In the Gospel of Luke a lawyer tests Jesus: "What must I do to inherit eternal life?" Jesus responds that he must love God and love his neighbor. "And who is my neighbor?" the lawyer challenges.

Jesus replies with the story of the Good Samaritan. A traveler is robbed, stripped and beaten, and left on the side of the road to die. A priest passes by, then a pious man. Eventually a Samaritan, a social outcast in Jewish society, sees the man and has pity on him. The Samaritan picks him up, cares for him, and gives him money. "Which of these three," Jesus asks the lawyer, "do you think, was a neighbor to the man who fell into the hands of the robbers?" The lawyer says, "The one who showed him mercy." Jesus ends the encounter with "Go and do likewise."

Although medieval people understood themselves as wounded travelers rescued by Christ, they also understood that Christ called the faithful to rescue the suffering. Such acts of charity contributed to salvation. No medieval person questioned Jesus's teaching that love for one's neighbor was a necessary part of a holy life. However, they were not always sure who counted as their neighbor. The lawyer's question, "Who is my neighbor?" was perhaps one of the most troubling ethical questions of the Middle Ages.

Medieval people believed that the universe consisted of a Great Chain of Being stretching from heaven through earth down to the lower ranks of hell, and on this chain everyone had a divinely appointed place and role. Baptism marked entrance to the faith and confirmed one's status in medieval society. But what of those not baptized—infants, pagans, Jews, and Muslims? And what of those who rejected their baptism? Heretics and witches? Did Christian charity extend to outsiders? And what constituted love toward others? Thus the question "Who is my neighbor?" dominated medieval ethics. Both within the Christian world and at its edges, the parable of the Good Samaritan loomed large as the faithful struggled with ethical practices toward their neighbors.

Jews and Muslims as Neighbors

At a gathering of rabbis, one attendee shared the story of his congregation. He was born in Jerusalem and now served a successful urban synagogue in the American heartland. The community had grown so large that it had recently bought a suburban piece of property to build a new synagogue. The congregation, known for its vital social justice work and prophetic witness, was not entirely happy with the prospect of moving to the suburbs. "So, we thought to ourselves," the rabbi said, "what is most needed in America today? How can we do something compelling for God in the suburbs?

"Over lunch one day," he continued, "I shared this dilemma with a friend, the imam from the local mosque. He confessed that his congregation needed to move as well and was equally displeased by the idea." Then the rabbi smiled. "Suddenly we realized that we could move together. We could build a synagogue and a mosque on the same piece of property!" Although the project had not been finalized, the rabbi and the imam had asked a local Christian group to join them. "The three great faiths of Abraham together," he sighed. "Where else could you do this? It is why I came to America: to be friends with Christians and Muslims."

Since the birth of Christianity and the subsequent emergence of Islam in the 600s, these two great faiths have contended for territory and adherents, with the Jews caught in the middle. All three traditions are monotheistic, and all three claim Abraham as their ancestor. And with the exception of Judaism, each claims to reform some corruption of the earlier faith. When the Qur'an denied the Christian doctrine of the Trinity on the basis that it violated faith in the One God, Christians responded by calling Islam a heresy. Thus even John of Damascus, himself defended by a Muslim ruler, attacked Islam as a false religion created by Muhammad so that the prophet might "indulge his personal sexual desires." From this inauspicious beginning, Christians and Muslims competed for both converts and territory on the battlefield.

Scholar David Chidester notes that "early medieval Christianity and Islam both embraced a military mission" as fundamental to their faith.[1]

Not many places exist where Christians, Jews, and Muslims have had the opportunity to live together without hating, persecuting, or killing one another. The rabbi's American city may well be one, but another long-ago place still serves as an example of such friendship: medieval Spain. Although the friendship was often strained and imperfect in its practice, in cities like Córdoba and Toledo, Christians, Muslims, and Jews formed a "society where the appetite for war gave way to the taste for intelligent coexistence between communities of faith."[2] The Spanish even have a name for it: *convivencia*, or "living together."

Muslim military forces gained control of Spain in 711, never managing further advance into Europe. There the new rulers set up a policy of toleration toward Jews and Christians, whereby they could practice their religions but not convert others. For the next seven hundred years Christians and Muslims would trade political control of cities and territories, yet the populations would remain multireligious, leaving rulers the necessary task of working out policies of accommodation and even tolerance. As part of their daily experience, regular Jews, Christians, and Muslims heard one another's bells and calls to prayer as they encountered three languages of worship and theology. On the basis of this interchange, the Spanish Jewish mystic Moses de León concluded that peace was ultimately God's way, "by praying earnestly and daily for that peace," and by respecting all one's neighbors—Muslim, Christian, and Jewish—as "beings fashioned in God's image and likeness."[3]

While the mystical traditions of Spain would provide experiential ways of relating to other faiths, philosophy actually created much of the intellectual energy of *convivencia.* Islamic Spain, unlike other parts of Europe, boasted libraries and genuine scholarly community, the best of all being in Toledo, a sophisticated multicultural city. There Muslim thinkers preserved the science, medicine, and mathematics of the ancient world as well as Aristotelian philosophy. Gerard of Cremona, an Italian priest who studied in Toledo, was overwhelmed, "seeing the abundance of books in Arabic on every subject, and regretting the poverty of the Latins in these things."[4] Gerard quickly learned Arabic and translated more than seventy major books into Latin, introducing them to the Christian West.

Thus learning became one of the primary ways that Muslims, Jews, and Christians related to each other in Spain's interreligious crucible. With Aristotle as their inspiration, Jewish and Muslim scholars launched an incisive critique of both scripture and the law on the basis of human reason. Moses Maimonides (1138–1204), born in Córdoba, both a doctor and a Jewish philosopher, appropriated Aristotle to interpret Hebrew scripture, arguing that the intellectual soul was "God's image and likeness," the part of the human being that would live forever.[5] Attempting to understand God through reason, Maimonides rejected literal interpretations of scripture. Instead he argued that scripture served as metaphor or allegory for deeper spiritual truths.

The same impulse to understand the relationship between faith and reason animated Ibn Rushd, known in the Latin West as Averroës (1126–1198). Averroës believed that philosophy provided "evidence of the Maker" and that the "door of rational speculation" opened to a knowledge of God.[6] Like Maimonides, Averroës advocated that both scripture and the law be subject to allegorical interpretation, not literal readings. One of his favorite tactics was to quote the Qur'an in defense of reason: "You who have eyes to see, reflect!" He wrote commentaries on both Aristotle and Plato; his work on Aristotle earned him the nickname "The Commentator." After his death his writing spread through Christian Europe. In his own day, however, Averroës pointed out the moral impact of philosophy. He irked Spanish authorities by questioning the role of women in Islamic society and by accusing Muslim political leaders of corruption. Cordoban rulers tried him for heresy and banished him from the city. They relented a year after the trial, but Averroës was never quite the same. He died two years later. As one historian sadly notes, "Adventurous study of philosophizing in the medieval Islamic world died with him."[7]

Maimonides and Averroës shared a common struggle for philosophical inquiry to shape religious faith. That struggle migrated north to Paris, where Christian theologians picked up Aristotelian method through the Jewish and Muslim philosophers. This new spirit of criticism inspired Christians to pursue religious reform on the basis of reason. In 1277 the church condemned much of their speculation as "Averroism," but their critical approach survived—often on the fringes of Christian theology—until the Renaissance.

In the pursuit of philosophy, Christians, Jews, and Muslims found common questions of faith and reason—and offered a common critique of corrupt religious authorities. Of the power of their work, historian Chris Lowney remarks:

> For most moderns, the term "medieval philosophy" conjures up sleepy images of musty tomes and academics pondering such irrelevancies as angels dancing on the heads of pins. In fact, rarely does a year pass without some small aftershock reverberating from this extraordinary moment in the history of human thought—in mosques and churches, on newspaper editorial pages, and among diplomats pursuing Mideast peace. Maimonides . . . and Averroës explored the relation of faith to reason, the proper interpretation of revealed texts, and the basis of religious law. The same concerns convulse modern societies far more violently than they shook Averroës' medieval one.[8]

If we share their problems today, might we too find friendship through *convivencia?* As our ancestors discovered in medieval Spain, studying philosophy seems preferable to conflict, terrorism, and war.

The Cosmos as Neighbor(hood)

In the 1970s one of the most popular Christian books was *The Late Great Planet Earth* by Hal Lindsey. The book, which claimed to unfold the mysteries of God's prophetic times, provided a guide to the hidden meaning of history. Lindsey popularized the theory of dispensationalism, the idea that God divided world history into special dispensations—or eras—of divine action. The final act of human history was quickly approaching, when the world would be consumed in a great tribulation culminating in a battle between good and evil. At the pitch of this conflict, Christ will return with all the saints to vanquish Satan and establish God's New Jerusalem. The end of the world, a cosmic vision.

And it is essentially a hopeless vision of a hostile universe. Lindsey's books borrowed the ideas of John Nelson Darby, a nineteenth-century English minister who invented this interpretation of prophetic texts.[9] Pessimistic about history, Darby interpreted the past as a series of inevitable human failures and corresponding divine punishments. To him the world was filled with despair from beginning to end—except for rare moments when God intervened. Because the universe was fractured by sin, dispensational theology undermined Christian motivation to change society. God provided believers with a convenient "out" called the Rapture, in which they would escape worldly suffering before Judgment Day. Widely popular in the United States, these views inspired Lindsey and led in the 1990s to the blockbuster Left Behind thrillers by Tim LaHaye and Jerry Jenkins. Considering the millions of books these authors have sold, dispensationalism may be the dominant way that contemporary North American Christians interpret history.

But critics, including many Christian theologians, reject apocalyptic thought as escapist. Dispensationalism is not the only version of Christian apocalyptic. Many Christians have interpreted apocalyptic stories as optimistic—as a vision of what the world can be, stories meant to motivate God's people toward a deeper engagement with justice. In its simplest form apocalyptic speculation is a cosmic reading of history, or a spiritual understanding of the universe, replete with promises of hope as well as warnings for the future. It places people in a larger story while helping them find meaning in their place in time.

Born in 1098 of noble German parents, Hildegard of Bingen (1098–1179) was known as the "Sibyl of the Rhine." A prophet and visionary her entire life, she received her first vision when she was only three years old: "I saw such a light that my soul trembled, but because I was an infant, I could say nothing of these things." She was not a mystic in the classical sense; her vision of God did not come as a result of divine union or a lifetime of special prayer. Rather, impressions of "fiery light of exceeding brilliance" would "permeate" her brain so that she "immediately knew the meaning of the exposition of the Scriptures."[10]

Her visions were, most surprisingly, recognized as valid by her male ecclesiastical and civil authorities. She became a Benedictine abbess and exerted great spiritual influence in her public preaching ministry throughout the Rhineland. In every sense she was a unique and unusual figure. Her contemporaries considered her a prophet and healer and came to her seeking her touch—renown for its ability to induce physical healing and spiritual insight. As in the case with Mother Teresa today, upon her death the faithful almost immediately called for her to be made a saint.

When she was forty-two Hildegard felt that God directed her to write down her visions, a process that continued in three major works and was not completed until her death almost forty years later. At the center of her work was an apocalyptic oracle—an interpretation of the cosmos that unveiled the hidden dimensions of human history—and that called for a prophetic reordering of church and society.

Oddly enough, Hildegard was a dispensationalist, but in a very different way than most Christians today use the term. She divided history into three ages represented, in order, by Eve, Mary, and a future female figure, the "bride of Christ," a seer named Ecclesia. Eve represented creation and the painful rejection of creation's promise; Mary symbolized the new birth of humanity in Christ; and Ecclesia embodied the struggle toward God's desire for justice. To Hildegard, God is the mother of history, who births redemption, justice, and virtue through an orderly process of human and divine activity. Hildegard referred to this cosmic unity as a "symphony."

Christians have most often depicted history as a line with a beginning and end—or the universe as a chain of being with a top and a bottom. Not Hildegard. She drew mandalas—complex circular patterns—to represent the universe.[11] To her, everything in the cosmos was related, circles of connection between God and humanity and humanity and nature. Hildegard's vision was not pessimistic. Instead of consigning humanity to perpetual defeat until rescued by God, Hildegard interpreted history as spiraling ages of "justice and injustice, each with its own deformations or reforms, [that] would alternate" until its consummation in love.[12] She described paradise as the time when "the whole world will exist in the full beauty of vitality and freshness":

> Then people will experience the justice that the world so sadly lacked. . . . All weapons manufactured for purposes of death and destruction will be forbidden and the only tools, devices, and machinery permitted will be those

> that serve cultivation of the land and are truly useful to humankind.[13]

This hope must shape the church as it moves through time; Christians are called continually to practice justice and reform the church as signs of God's unfolding future.

Sadly, in her own day Hildegard believed the church was deformed, having given itself over to vanities of "despair, greed, and worldly sadness" instead of justice.[14] To her, Ecclesia was not a religious elite; rather, it was the whole human community called to birth God's reign.[15] Justice had been despoiled because the religious authorities failed to enact this cosmic hope; they betrayed justice by greed, simony, fornication, oppression, insubordination, and negligence. She criticized monks as "enveloped in the blackness of acrid smoke because of their habitually foul behavior."[16] Their sins weakened the church by betraying God's people, marring Ecclesia's beauty. Hildegard called for renewal, warning that if the institutional church failed to do justice, civil rulers would strip it of its wealth and position and the faithful would desert and destroy it. Well into her seventies, Hildegard preached this message throughout the Rhineland, calling the church to account for its sins. She would eventually pay the price for her bold criticism of the establishment, however. In the year before her death her convent suffered the interdict: a local bishop withheld the Mass from her and her sisters.

Although few people today consider it, how we understand cosmic history has a direct impact on how we practice justice. For Hildegard, everything was really one, interwoven life that demanded justice for all. The whole universe was her neighborhood. A fractured vision of the cosmos leads to hopelessness and withdrawal from God's world; a connected vision empowers change.

Enemies as Neighbors

In October 2002, as the United States headed toward war in Iraq, Roman Catholic, Anglican, mainline Protestant, and progressive evangelical religious leaders urged President Bush to pull back, basing their argument on the just war theory, an ethical framework for warfare developed in medieval theology.[17] Sadly, conservative Protestant leaders—although they often appeal to tradition—neither agreed with their colleagues nor developed criteria for the war in Iraq. Instead, they supported the president's decision to go to war. For the most part they avoided obvious theological reflection or distorted tradition to suit the circumstances. As it now appears, George Bush listened only to them. He ignored Christian leaders who had urged caution and careful attention to the just war tradition.

Medieval Christians grappled with two cultures that venerated warfare. Although Christians were initially pacifists, they capitulated to the military norms of Roman society, and allegiance to the Christian God eventually replaced military oaths to pagan gods. In 312 the emperor Constantine (d. 337) secured his throne through military force. The night before the battle, God reportedly appeared to him in a dream with a cross saying, "In this sign, conquer." Constantine routed the enemy and attributed the victory to the Christian God and in 313 legalized the Christian faith. Augustine of Hippo (354–430), the greatest theologian of Constantinian Christianity, developed the rationale for just war on the basis of political realism. Because God's kingdom was not immediately at hand, earthly political authorities must use force to secure order and protect the church. Thus the medieval church inherited early Christian traditions that both explicitly forbade violence and permitted it under some circumstances.

When Rome fell, Christians found themselves face-to-face with Germanic peoples who lived in kinship societies based on blood warrior bonds. As these warrior tribes slowly converted to Christianity, their violent ethic blended with Christian practice. The combination of Roman military culture and pagan warrior customs proved literally explosive. Throughout Europe the fifth, sixth, and seventh centuries were times of terrible violence, murder, rape, and pillage, often committed in the name of Christ or as pagan backlash against Christianity. This was the true dark ages.

The church eventually quelled some of the worst excesses by instituting the "Peace of God" in 989, excommunicating anyone who attacked a bishop, priest, deacon, clerk, monk, pilgrim, woman, or child. Also subject to excommunication was anyone who robbed a church or stole from the poor. In 1017 the Peace of God was followed by the "Truce of God," whereby princes, nobles, and knights swore to desist from all warfare from Saturday to Monday and during the holy seasons of Lent and Advent. Any warrior who fought and died on these days would be denied last rites, Christian burial, forgiveness for his sins, and prayers for the dead. From the battles with Germanic warlords through the Crusades,[18] questions of war and violence were among the foremost ethical concerns in medieval Christianity.

Thomas Aquinas (ca. 1225–1274) was born more than a century after the Christian soldiers of the First Crusade burned Jews alive and slaughtered Muslims when conquering Jerusalem. As one Christian witness extolled in a letter home:

> If you had been there you would have seen our feet colored to our ankles with the blood of the slain. But what more shall I relate? None of them were left alive; neither women nor children were spared. Afterward, all clergy, laymen went to the Sepulcher of the Lord and his glorious temple singing. With fitting humility, they repeated prayers and made their offering at the holy places they had long desired to visit.

Medieval Christians assumed warfare. What we now understand as the hideous and inexcusable violence of the Crusades, along with the church's growing practice of conducting internal inquisitions against Christian heretics, acted as the backdrop to Thomas's reflections on war.

Thomas opens the subject by asking "whether it is always sinful to wage war." To answer, he drew from Augustine and Aristotelian theological methods. Thomas admitted that on the surface of it, war does seem to be a sin from a Christian perspective. However, three conditions made Christian warfare permissible: (1) sovereign authority (no private person may decide to wage war); (2) a just cause; and (3) an intention to promote good instead of evil. Even so, war must be carefully regulated toward the goal of peace, with a love toward one's enemies; attention to mercy, charity, and forgiveness during warfare; and limited violence. Certain classes of people—like parish clergy—are expressly forbidden to kill. He sanctioned the idea of military orders of monks to protect the church, but he equally resisted coercion to convert pagans and Jews. Thomas even suggested that "the common good may recommend toleration" toward Jews and others—although he insisted that killing for the common good might be, in some circumstances, an act of love toward an unwilling victim.[19]

Thomas's thought moved between the poles of war as sin and the common good as love in relation to "the needs of the present life."[20] Although one modern critic refers to his position as "dangerously naïve" and says that he "treats political matters with a certain optimistic abstraction," Thomas did construct a much more charitable idea of warfare than the Christian crusaders who sacked Jerusalem a century before his time.[21] Thomas's greatest failing may be that he seemingly ignored—or was perhaps blind to—the injustices committed by the Christian political system in which he lived. He tried to soften its excesses, but he never fully critiqued it.

Whatever Thomas's limits, his three principles for just war still serve as the template for the church to navigate the relationship between Christian faith and violence in a fallen world. Most ethicists insist that there are but two Christian theories of war as related to the common good: pacifism and just war—that is, peace by nonviolent means or peace by means of limited violence. All other moral positions are variants or modifications of these two. Any use of force that goes beyond them is expressly forbidden in Roman Catholic, Eastern Orthodox, and Protestant thought. From a theoretical and theological perspective at least, wars conducted by Christian societies—or those societies claiming to be Christian—must be submitted to these criteria or be deemed sinful.

No wonder that in the last years of his life Pope John Paul II objected so strenuously to the war in Iraq.

Animals as Neighbors

One of the most interesting people I know is my friend Paul Waldau, an ethicist working on questions of religion and animal rights. We first met in Oxford several years ago, and it was impossible to overlook Paul's concern for all creatures. He spoke of wild and domestic animals in personal terms, was a vegan who did not eat, wear, or use animal products, and would remove invading ants from his kitchen as if kindly ushering guests from his house.

Having grown up as a Roman Catholic, Paul is now mostly Buddhist in philosophy and practice. "Christianity doesn't have a very good track record about animals and creation," he says. It is hard to protest. In one of his books, *The Specter of Speciesism*, Paul unflinchingly analyzes Christian views on animals. According to him, Christian theology teaches that "it is members of the human species *alone* who matter among the earth's animals" and that "in general, the tradition has been locked into" a "negative evaluation" of "non-human animals." In other words, unless you are human, Christianity is a pretty bad deal.[22] Funny thing, though, about Paul: he always reminds me of St. Francis.

Francis (1181/2–1226) is probably one of the best known and best loved figures in Christian history. And he is also, perhaps, the most overly sentimentalized. Popular affection for Francis always strikes me as a little odd because his entire vision of the Christian life was predicated on the ideal of absolute poverty and service to the poor—something few people choose to emulate. The archetypal moment of Francis's life was when, as a young man, he rejected his father Pietro's success in business by using family money to rebuild a dilapidated church building. Pietro, intending to confront Francis and get back the cash, brought his son before the bishop in the town square. Instead of repenting and returning to his family's comfortable capitalism, Francis stripped nude and threw himself on the mercy of the church—thus forever rejecting material goods in favor of a fully spiritual life. Francis left Assisi naked, following the naked Christ.

Franciscan poverty took many forms, especially in service to lepers and the poor as well as in the mendicant lifestyle of the young men who followed Francis. One of its more unexpected aspects, however, emerged as Francis's connection with creation. Francis is often depicted surrounded by birds and other small animals or, in a famous image, shaking a wolf's paw. One of Francis's first biographers described how he exhorted birds, animals, and reptiles, preached to flowers, cornfields, vineyards, stones, and forests, and called all creatures brother or sister.[23] He never crushed worms or ants, and he fed bees wine and honey so they would not die in winter.

Although it is tempting to romanticize Francis as a supremely sensitive nature lover, his views seem to be drawn from a rather literal reading of Jesus's sermon on possessions:

> Therefore I tell you, do not worry about your life, what you will eat or what you will drink, or about your body,

> what you will wear. Is not life more than food, and the body more than clothing? Look at the birds of the air; they neither sow nor reap nor gather into barns, and yet your heavenly Father feeds them. Are you not of more value than they? (Matt. 6:25–26)

Jesus continued by extolling the "lilies of the field" and the "grass of the field" in the same manner. "So do not worry about tomorrow," Jesus said, "for tomorrow will bring worries of its own" (Matt. 6:34).

In a very real sense, creatures and creation exist as the ultimate teachers of holy poverty. Animals, birds, trees, flowers, and plants own nothing. Yet, as Jesus explained, they completely depend on God and at the same time are profoundly beautiful; "I tell you, even Solomon in all his glory was not clothed like one of these" (Matt. 6:29). Those beings that humans consider the least are actually the greatest because they exist in such close connection to God, a connection that illustrates a life of total dependence—and absolute poverty—in relationship to the Creator. Bonaventure, a later Franciscan theologian, wrote of Francis, "When he considered the primordial source of all things, he was filled with abundant piety, calling creatures, no matter how small, by the name of brother and sister, because he knew that they had the same source as himself."[24]

Beyond familial relation, however, animals possessed a more acute knowledge of God, which made them examples of holy wisdom. The brothers followed their example in not being dependent on property or utilitarian uses of land; to this day Franciscans do not "will to dominate or transform nature."[25] In fact, Francis appears to have submitted himself to the created order. He did not place either himself or human beings at the top of a Great Chain of Being; rather, he reversed the medieval hierarchy, an act with provocative political implications. In *The Canticle of the Sun*, Francis begins his song to creation not with humanity, but with "Brother Sun" and "Sister Moon," moving through the ranks of wind, water, creatures, fire, plants, and earth until ending with, in a seemingly ad hoc way, human beings and the humility of death. Indeed, scholars note that the song did not originally include human beings; humankind, they say, was a later addition.[26]

In linking poverty, politics, and nature, Francis articulated a completely orthodox Christian view. Indeed, a number of reform groups, including the Cathars, had arisen in the medieval church at approximately the same time as the Franciscans. The Cathars, like the Franciscans, upheld holy poverty and challenged medieval political authorities. But they eschewed the material world and ignored nature. The Cathars denigrated creation as evil, seeing it as the source of greed and opposed to a life of holy poverty. Francis's creation-based spirituality stood as a "direct rebuke" to the Cathars, and his love of creation was "an act of resistance to those who would totally 'spiritualize' faith."[27]

Although Paul Waldau is no doubt right about Christian tradition and creation, Francis represents the slender thread of an alternative vision.[28] English writer Sean McDonagh notes, "Francis shows a kinship with, and deep insight into, the heart of creation—animate and inanimate—which is probably unique in the whole European experience."[29] By drawing connections between economics, creation, peacemaking, and political organization, the medieval Francis anticipated much contemporary thinking on the web of relationships that make up a global ecology. One modern Franciscan claims that by "embracing both nature and neighbour in a healing and reconciling union," Francis provides a "pattern for both ecology and political relationship throughout the world."[30] Christianity as a whole may not have the best track record with nature, but Francis—and the Christians who have taken his vision seriously—certainly model a way to embrace the environment.

Outcasts as Neighbors

For several years John, an acquaintance of mine, was the minister of a large congregation in a gentrified neighborhood in Memphis, Tennessee. Under his leadership the church increased its membership, added almost $500,000 a year to its pledges, doubled its endowment, and successfully navigated a political argument over gay and lesbian ordination. John is a gracious minister who practices regular prayer, and no scandal or impropriety mars his character. Yet the congregation forced John's resignation. Why? Because he organized a ministry offering free hot meals once a week in the church building to the homeless and working poor. Neighbors—including some congregants—protested, insisting that the program attracted both criminals and unsavory characters. A task force studied options to move the program, but John stood resolute. The meal ministry would stay at the church. Opponents were furious; proponents kept feeding the poor. The congregation almost split in the squabble. His hand forced, the pastor resigned while remaining adamant that a Christian's primary moral duty is charity toward the poor.[31]

Charity, a word that comprises love and justice, may well be the most sublime of all Christian virtues. Of all of Jesus's teachings and works, his compassion toward the poor, suffering, and outcast claims the admiration of those even vaguely acquainted with the Christian religion. Oddly enough, however, ministry among the meek often provokes the ire of the established church. And those who serve the poor are often misunderstood and persecuted.

As the medieval church grew very rich, reformers like Francis of Assisi challenged the status quo with a renewed practice of both poverty and serving the poor. But the church did not embrace all such reformers as it did Francis. In the late 1100s a loosely connected movement of laywomen, called the Beguines, and a few laymen, the Beghards, emerged in the Low Countries and the Rhineland. These laypeople lived a semimonastic life outside of approved convents. Mostly single, the women were "neither cloistered nuns nor married homemakers," thus constituting an alternative female religious vocation.[32] They lived together (occasionally women and men occupied the same houses), wore simple habits, practiced the hours, and vowed simplicity and service. The women supported themselves in gender-appropriate professions such as weaving, spinning (hence, "spinsters"), sewing, nursing, and teaching. One contemporary historian refers to them as "the first urban 'base communities' in the new urban environment."[33] In 1215 Pope Honorarius III approved of "pious women" living in such arrangements.

Although no single theology linked all the Beguine houses in Europe, the same ethical practice did: charity. At this time most nuns were cloistered and under the authority of male superiors, their economic well-being and spiritual practices essentially out of their own control. With no obligation to stay in a convent—and with no male authority confining them—the Beguines were unrestrained and could do that to which they felt called, and many Beguine houses made good livings. Without families to support, they freely channeled their incomes toward whatever purpose they chose. Most of the Beguines chose to give their property away. They fed the hungry, clothed the poor, visited the sick, educated girls, offered hospitality, established homes for widows, nursed lepers, and cared for the dying. The Beguines both took alms and gave them away, thus creating a second economy, a monetary sphere outside the auspices of the institutional church.

Church legislation actually prohibited women from engaging in public religious work. Female spirituality was expected to be passive, not active. Writes one historian, "Neither charity nor voluntary poverty was prized above silence and obedience for women."[34] The Beguines, with all their conspicuous generosity, shocked other Christians by offering meals to hungry people or giving clothes to beggars in public. Jacques de Vitry, a sympathetic twelfth-century bishop, defended them, noting:

> In western lands, there are innumerable communities of men and women who renounce the world and regularly live in houses of lepers and hospitals for the poor, humbly and devoutly ministering to the poor and infirm. Men and women live separately and with all reverence eat and sleep in chastity. They do not omit to hear the canonical offices day and night as much as hospital work and the ministry to Christ's poor permit. . . . They take infirm

> people or healthy guests into their houses where they eat and sleep. . . . For them, the Lord changes the filthy shit which they are forced to clear into precious stones and the stench becomes a sweet aroma.[35]

Although Bishop de Vitry referred to the Beguines as the "new mothers of the church,"[36] their charitable acts won them few friends in the hierarchy, and established clerics attacked them.

Because of their work with the poor—and in response to the criticism—some of the more outspoken Beguines blamed the social order for medieval problems. They connected the increase in poverty and suffering to the growth of a moneyed class, new consumerism, and a tepid church. In her work the German Beguine Mechthild of Magdeburg (ca. 1212–1284) mixed mystical love poetry with apocalyptic insights and a call to reform the church, in much the same way as Hildegard of Bingen had done. For Mechthild, the church had failed in its vocation to love God and neighbor through the practice of virtue. Mechthild wrote of "corrupt Christianity," referring to the "poor church" as a "maiden whose skin is filthy." Not content to generalize, she called the local cathedral clergy "goats."[37] To perhaps no one's surprise but her own, the authorities tried to burn her books. Threatened by persecution, Mechthild fled to a convent in Helfta, where some sympathetic nuns protected her and her manuscripts.

Mechthild's words and the writings of another Beguine, Hadewijch of Antwerp (mid-thirteenth century), confirm the movement's central spiritual insight. Love is the Christian way of life, and Jesus's followers are called to enact his way of love.

"But nowadays," as Hadewijch stated, "Love is very often impeded, and her law violated by acts of injustice." To Hadewijch, "brotherly love" is justice, a virtue based on respect for all human beings that serves the common good. Therefore, she asserts, "Live according to justice, not according to your pleasure or satisfaction in any way whatever."[38] To the Beguines, love and justice met in the practice of charity.

In an age when the institutional church failed to act as Jesus had toward the poor, the Beguines turned their simple program of prayer and service into a popular platform for church reform, hoping that their devotion to poverty and the meek would renew apostolic fervor and holy faith. They saw the clergy and the church as rich, corrupt, and greedy; they identified the poor as the victims of avarice, those oppressed by wayward church leaders. In this climate "the ideal of imitating Christ came to rest on the concept of apostolic poverty."[39] And charity, acts like feeding the poor, amounted to a radical reversal of the social order in which those furthest from power and wealth would indeed inherit God's kingdom.

The authorities understood. By 1220 "religious poverty was being associated with heresy and Beguines were commonly accused of hypocrisy that amounted to heresy."[40] A number of church leaders condemned Beguines, ordering them to traditional convents or face the consequences. In 1311 the Council of Vienne denounced them as "an abominable sect." They lost their ministries and were sent packing.

And, John, I am sorry to say, but it appears you are in good company.

The End of the Middle

My friends Jonathan and Leah Wilson-Hartgrove are a twenty-something married couple with a small child. They live in Durham, North Carolina, in a modest house on the edges of Walltown, an impoverished community, and attend their local Baptist church. Jonathan and Leah chose to live in Walltown but not, however, to help gentrify the neighborhood. Nor do they live alone. Other young adults live with them in an intentional Christian community. They are neither clergy nor monks and nuns; they hold regular jobs in the real world. Yet the whole group is committed to keeping a way of life they call "the new monasticism," ordering their spirituality around twelve practices, including hospitality, communal prayer, peacemaking, and serving their neighbors.

On the community Web site they explain why they have chosen this path:

> Ours is a time of rapid social change. We are post-modern, post–Cold War, post–9/11, even post-Christian. All signs point to change, and we know things aren't what they used to be. But we hardly know who we are. Amidst wars and rumors of war, our global identity crisis threatens to consume us. . . . We're not sure just what will come of all this. But we're so grateful for the good news that God has not abandoned the world. Something new is stirring, drawing deeply from the old. People who've stumbled in darkness are glimpsing light. We pray for grace to remember who we are in Christ.[41]

In the 1400s European Christians may have felt much the same way. Although most could not name the changes beginning to affect them—shifts in the social order, economics, philosophy, and sciences—their world was moving in new directions that challenged the institutional church. These social changes were compounded by an extended religious crisis, when in 1309 Pope Clement V moved the papacy from Italy to France, thus resulting in three different popes, each claiming to be the vicar of Christ and head of the church. The schism lasted nearly a century and prompted a medieval identity crisis by undermining confidence in the church. It raised the question who could be counted among the faithful baptized, leaving Christians to doubt whether their priests or bishops held the authority of the sacraments or the keys to heaven. And it diverted Rome's attention away from the spiritual life of the laity, who felt increasingly distant from the traditional structures of the church. Reformers such as Peter Waldo, John Wycliffe, and Jan Hus all pressed for renewal that would include greater attention to the needs and ministry of the Christian laity.

Around 1375 a layman named Geert Groote (1340–1384) of Deventer in the Netherlands gave up a lucrative career as an intellectual and spiritual gadfly—he claimed to have "fornicated on every hilltop and under every spreading tree" in northern Europe—and adopted a simple way of life. He renounced his previous passions and began attending regular mass at a church run by the Franciscans near his home.[42] Instead of joining a monastery, however, he invited poor women to live in the family house as an act of penitential hospitality.

Groote's new sisters went beyond merely accepting his hospitality. They formed a religious community around their host's message of conversion and repentance, thereby creating a practical way of devotion to Christ. They held all things in common while continuing to make their livings in the world. They dedicated themselves to serious prayer, holy reading, meditation, and acts of kindness. And they understood themselves to be "restoring ancient spiritual traditions going back to the apostles, the Desert Fathers, and the Church's greatest teachers."[43] They did not, however, take monastic vows; they maintained relationships with family and friends outside the house. They worshiped both in their community household and at the local parish church.

Groote's experiment in practical Christian living soon expanded to include at least forty-seven additional houses of sisters and forty-one houses of brothers. Known as congregations or gatherings, these communities were nicknamed the *devotio moderna*, or "the new devotion," and their members were called "the New Devout."

The women of the New Devout were mostly poor, the kind of people whose memory is usually lost to history. But the sisters developed a practice of sharing the stories of the older members of their community as a way of encouraging faith. At first the stories were oral. Around 1456, however, one sister wrote them down: "It is most important to have their edifying lives present in our memory," creating a record of their faithfulness.[44] Gese Broekelants (d. 1407) was described as "kindly, patient, and never sharp." During her final illness she experienced an intense joy that manifested itself in laughter, "bearing witness that she was a child of God." Nyese Felix (d. 1411) was consumed with holy ardor, a sort of "burning" upon hearing the Word of God. Katherine Hughen (d. 1411) came from a prosperous family, and "she possessed all kinds of beautiful jewelry," a gift she gave to the other sisters. Lubbe Peters (d. 1413) was noted for keen business sense, a quality that sometimes interfered with practicing humility. Others were remembered for their frugality or their faithfulness at work. Heylewich van Grolle (d. 1454), for example, "sat and combed out wool for fourteen weeks straight." Her kindness extended to "nonrational animals," as she "would bring the little birds something to eat in the public square. . . . She knew each of the little birds as if they were people." Her sisters likened her to St. Francis.

These stories reveal lives of simple devotion, showing how seriously these people enacted their faith. One historian notes that the testimonies of the New Devout illustrate that "the higher ideals of the medieval Church" influenced the faith of "ordinary men and women." Far away from political popes and bloody crusades, Heylewich van Grolle fed her birds in Christ's name while praying, "Please, dear God, be kindly to them, for this is their heavenly kingdom."[45] Here, paradise is found by serving the least of God's creatures, and we witness an earthly and divine interplay of God's tender and transforming love. Thus this discreet tale, of a Dutch woman who dressed wool and worshiped in her parish church, summarizes the hope of a thousand years of faith—a spirituality that kept alive the ancient vision of Christianity as the way of Jesus. The *devotio moderna* reminds us how far medieval Christianity actually succeeded—even as the institutional church, the spiritual architecture that had for so long sheltered lively faith, was about to fail.

PART III

THE WORD

Reformation Christianity
1450–1650

SEVEN

Christianity as Living Words

On my twenty-second birthday I was sitting in a college course on Reformation theology. I would graduate in May, and this class was an intellectual gift to myself. For many years I had attended nondenominational churches marked by a disdain for history and a distinct attachment to contemporary worship. But their ahistorical faith was wearing thin. I wanted to understand the longer history and practice of being Christian. I had started to worship at an Episcopal congregation, which felt connected to a more ancient faith. A class in Reformation theology might help me understand the beginnings of my new church.

Professor Curt Whiteman was lecturing on late medieval theology and the birth of Christian humanism. "Europe," he claimed, "was set for the Reformation." He launched into the familiar story of Martin Luther—Luther's despair and anger with the Roman Catholic system of salvation, believing that the church taught salvation by works and not faith. He related how, in 1517, Luther initiated a debate about salvation with other scholars by nailing a list of propositions, called the Ninety-five Theses, to a church door in Wittenberg. As Luther questioned the basis of medieval Roman Catholicism, he summed up the opinion of many that the old church had somehow failed. Professor Whiteman laid out the main points of Luther's argument and said, "All the details point to the same conclusion: Luther's vision was 'Christocentric'; for Martin Luther, everything revolved around Jesus Christ, the Word."

Professor Whiteman became quite insistent, clearly wanting his students to grasp the significance of what had happened in the sixteenth century. "We bring our cultural theologies from the past, from previous generations. Yet theology must be redone, over and over. It is never static," he said. The Reformation serves as a historical example of theological dynamism, as "the word speaks again and again" in new social contexts. Christian theology is not about repeating formulas from the past. It cannot remain forever the same, because as Professor Whiteman said emphatically, "*Christianity is the living word.*"

By the sixteenth century the medieval church was failing, especially at the grass roots in northern Europe.[1] Local leaders complained bitterly about financial burdens of the church and moral laxity of the clergy. New interpretations of Christianity, offered to regular people in written and spoken words, opened hope for transformation. As literacy increased across Europe, words gave churchgoers the power to remake their world. During the Reformation people discovered Christian words afresh through the Bibles, books, and pamphlets being turned out by the newly invented printing press. But words were more than fancy speeches or symbols on a page. Words initiated and nurtured a religious revolution for both individuals and society. "Therefore God must speak to your heart," preached Luther. "This is God's Word. . . . A person can preach the Word to me, but no one is able to put it into my heart except God alone."[2] Words integrated one's inner life with outward actions; words led to both existential and moral commitments.[3] True Christianity, knowing God in faith, could—indeed, must—be articulated and acted upon by individuals. According to Luther, although the words of God could be read in scripture, the ultimate Word was the person of Christ. As the Gospel of John says, "In the beginning was the Word, and the Word was with God, and the Word was God" (John 1:1).

Of this experiential insight, contemporary theologian Richard Lischer says, "When you 'really have it,' as Luther said, there is no fundamental discrepancy between your identity and your interpretive acts. You are what you read."[4] Sixteenth-century people would have understood that. They loved words. Words changed things. Words were spiritual and political. And for them words opened radical new ways of loving God and loving one's neighbor.

A New Reformation?

In recent years many Christian leaders have called for a new reformation. About the same time that I was learning Reformation theology in college, theologian Frederick Herzog noted, "Reformation today is an issue raised every now and then among Protestants." He continued that such concern should be natural in Protestant spirituality: "Is not the church always in need of Reformation? Are we not heirs of an 'unfinished Reformation'?"[5] In the years since his observation, cries for a new reformation have become more insistent and widespread. Most people sense that modern religious authorities, institutions, churches, and organizations are eroding and in crisis. What once worked does not any longer. The reform of Christianity appears overdue.

More than a few spiritual leaders have noted historical congruity between the sixteenth century and our own time. In his book *A New Reformation*, Matthew Fox identifies four historical forces that combined to produce the first Reformation: the invention of the printing press, the rise of nation-states, corruption in religious institutions, and the emergence of an educated elite. He argues that now, almost five hundred years later, we are experiencing corresponding challenges in communications, politics, religion, and scholarship. Although these changes frighten some people, Fox argues, "We can start anew, that a New Reformation for a new millennium is upon us." To prove his point, Fox traveled to Wittenberg, where he posted his own Ninety-five Theses on Luther's door, arguing for a return "to the spirit of Jesus and his prophetic ancestors."[6]

Phyllis Tickle, who was for many years the religion editor at *Publishers Weekly*, also believes that Christianity has entered a new period of reform. She sees global renewal based on what she calls "the great emergence," an integration of religious traditions and spiritual insights across the Christian spectrum.[7] Other Christians, including Eric Elnes, Marcus Borg, John Shelby Spong, and Gretta Vosper, have likewise issued calls for a new reformation based on visions of justice and spirituality.[8] Most of these voices decry belief-based Christianity in favor of practice-oriented faith.

But liberal Christians are not the only ones calling for a new reformation. Across the conservative Protestant world, evangelical leaders have likewise articulated their hope for reform. Rick Warren, influential pastor of the Saddleback Church in southern California, has said, "I'm looking for a second reformation." In words that, perhaps surprisingly, echo those of his more liberal colleagues, Warren claims, "The first reformation of the church 500 years ago was about beliefs. This one is going to be about behavior. The first one was about creeds. This one is going to be about deeds."[9]

But the sixteenth-century reformers did not, as we do, divide words from works. For them, deeds without words were dead, and words without actions were moot. During the last five hundred years Western Christians increasingly equated words with the capacities of the mind, forgetting that words possess power to change human hearts and actions. One of the most important insights of the first Reformation was the idea that words did more than prove faith. Words enlivened faith. Indeed, words embodied the spirit. They spoke to the whole person, allowing those who really heard them to be changed, thus enabling hearers to transform both the church and the world. People experienced words.

Many contemporary people are searching for authenticity in spirituality and religion. They are looking for experiences and communities in which words and actions interweave, where Christianity is both proclaimed and embodied congruently and cogently. Indeed, the longing for authenticity is so strong that marketing gurus James Gilmore and Joseph Pine advise their corporate clients to be authentic—that a company should *"be what it says it is."*[10] Part of the problem of contemporary Christianity is that it has not been what it says it is. In the West it seems hypocritical and phony; its words and actions collide. A new reformation would find old wisdom in the sixteenth century's living-giving practices of the word.

The Word for All

At the end of the Middle Ages European Christians rediscovered the texts of ancient Greece and Rome. Universities started offering courses in the humane letters—that is, human literature—instead of teaching only theology. Nontheological subjects, like poetry, oratory, and rhetoric, captured a new generation's imagination. Students and scholars of humane texts became known as "humanists." Of them, historian Diarmaid MacCulloch says, "Humanists were obsessed with words and how to use them. . . . [They] were lovers and connoisseurs of words." To these late medieval people, words went beyond mere rhetoric. Words contained "power which could be used actively to change human society for the better."[11] A new optimism spread across Europe as people began to sense that the world could be transformed through a recovery of ancient words.

New technology aided their desire to change the world through words. In 1440 Johannes Gutenberg invented the first commercially viable printing press, making books faster, easier, and cheaper to produce. Once a devotional art of the monastery, bookmaking moved into the realm of industry. Printed books found an eager audience. In cities across Europe a new merchant class—formed by laypeople creating new businesses in a rapidly expanding economy—was learning to read. In most European cities around 1400, only a very small percentage of people, mostly clerics, professors, and rulers, could read. In rural villages the only literate person was often the priest. By 1650, however, literacy reached as high as 80 percent among urban males, and rural literacy hovered around 30 percent. Words spread quickly beyond the controlled structures of church, university, and state through an emerging class of businessmen and burghers, along with their wives and children. The more books were printed, the more the rising classes aspired to read, and printers produced more books to meet the demand. Medieval people had always loved words, but social class and technology had limited the power of books. Following the invention of printing, that was no longer the case. Not since the fall of Rome could so many Europeans read. And never before did words spread so quickly to so many readers and hearers.

In many ways the sixteenth century was an extended argument over words—the meaning of words, whose words had the greatest power, the role of words in faith, and the political impact of words. One of the first Europeans to grasp the power of words was Desiderius Erasmus (1466/9–1536), a Dutch humanist and illegitimate son of a priest, who became Europe's first literary celebrity. He carried on a massive correspondence with politicians and scholars across the continent, leading one contemporary historian to quip that Erasmus should be named the patron saint of networkers.[12] He wrote best-selling guides to the humane letters—sort of CliffsNotes on literary classics—and widely read satires on monasticism, the priesthood, and the papacy. "When I get a little money I buy books," he confessed to a friend. "If any is left, I buy food and clothes."[13]

Eventually Erasmus applied humanist methods of critical analysis to Christian texts. He learned Greek in order to read ancient theology and the New Testament in the original language. Up until this time most European scholars knew only Latin (the church's language) or Hebrew (which some learned from rabbis in their communities). Knowledge of Greek had passed from Western memory, leaving much of ancient Christianity known only to Eastern Orthodox scholars. Erasmus loved Greek. In 1515, some fifteen years into his study, he produced an edition of the New Testament in Greek, with critical notes and corrections of the errors he found in the Latin Bible, originally translated by Jerome in 384.

Errors? In Holy Scripture? Yes, Erasmus dared point out that for more than a thousand years the church had used a Bible that contained mistakes. The most notable of these errors was found in Matthew 3:2, where John the Baptist cried out to the crowd, "*Metanoeite!*" Jerome had translated this as "Do penance!" This text supported the medieval Catholic system of confession and penance, but Erasmus pointed out that the word actually meant "Repent!" As historian Diarmaid MacCulloch remarked, "Much turned on a word." Indeed, Erasmus overturned tradition with a phrase, questioning the entire Catholic structure of salvation. "To attack Jerome," states MacCulloch, was to attack the "understanding of the Bible which the western Church took for granted."[14]

But Erasmus was not content with a Greek Bible for scholars. He called for its translation into local languages. "Would that these were translated into each and every language so that they might be read and understood not only by Scots and Irishmen but by Turks and Saracens." His project was not intended for elites; rather he envisioned the words of the Word as the common property of all: "Would that the farmer might sing snatches of Scripture at his plough and that the weaver might hum phrases of Scripture to the tune of his shuttle, that the traveler might lighten with stories from Scripture the weariness of his journey."[15] He even hoped women would read the New Testament for themselves.

And that is pretty much what happened. Farmers, weavers, travelers, and women picked up the book and read. When people could not read the words for themselves, others made sure they heard.

EIGHT

Devotion: Speaking of Faith

Historians today generally agree that there was not a single Reformation; rather, sixteenth-century Europe comprised a host of reformations, all springing from and related to medieval Catholic culture. As the old ways broke down and new possibilities opened up, "the resources of word, song, and literature opened up endless options for the interior life and for communal experiments of all kinds."[1] The words that exploded across Europe ignited the Christian imagination and eventually cost people their traditions, property, reputations, and lives while opening an entirely new way of being.

Loving God meant hearing the word anew, in the spiritual and intellectual context of a radically changing world. Sixteenth-century Christians began to understand ancient Christian texts as worthy of both intellectual engagement and literary devotion, with an emotive power that revealed God. As Petrarch, the Italian humanist, observed, "Theology is actually poetry, poetry concerning God."[2] The English reformer John Colet, a friend of Erasmus's, referred to scripture as "nourishment for the soul."[3] Indeed, as one historian argued, the Reformation was a "stirring of the imagination" in which ordinary people found God for themselves. Sixteenth-century Christians were a bookish lot, with surprising biblical imagination, "a love of the languages, a sensitivity to syntax, [and] a historical empathy which flowed from humanism."[4] In their search to renew faith, they developed a host of spiritual practices—reading, speaking, singing, teaching, and praying—that enabled them to proclaim the word.

Reading

At the height of the Liberation theology movement in the 1980s, my friend Brad lived in Latin America, where he participated in a base community, a kind of radical Bible study group in an impoverished village.[5] Lay members rotated leadership, each week reading a text, offering an interpretation drawn from their own experience, and trying to relate scriptural stories to their own lives in order to inspire justice and social change.

One week the story was from Matthew 19, in which Jesus commands the rich young ruler to sell all his possessions and give the money to the poor in order to find eternal life—the same biblical text that in 270 had inspired Anthony to follow Jesus into the desert. Brad, an American evangelical, had grown up in a middle-class family and attended a good college. "It was fascinating to hear my new friends interpret this passage in such a different context," Brad said. "They were very poor and they understood it very literally. They were comfortable with Jesus's rejection of wealth."

Brad admitted that he felt uncomfortable, however, especially when one person turned to him and asked how "our brothers and sisters in America" interpreted the story. Brad explained that Americans do not read the story literally. Rather, evangelicals take the direction spiritually. "Jesus insists that we give up whatever means the most to us in order to follow him, not necessarily our possessions. The story isn't about money."

The group fell silent, and Brad was unsure of what he had said. Finally, one of the leaders asked how they could trust that Brad was really a Christian since it was obvious that he did not "take the Bible seriously."

Few in history have read the Bible as seriously, or with such powerful political consequences, as the German monk and theologian Martin Luther (1483–1546). Historians often quip that Erasmus laid the egg that Luther hatched. As Luther read Erasmus's Greek New Testament, the words of scripture discomforted the good monk. Luther was, like the sixteenth-century humanists, enamored of the new critical study. However, he interpreted the new learning through the lens of his own anxiety, born of his failure to find God's love in the monastic life. "I made a martyr of myself through prayer, fasting, vigils, cold," he reported. "What was I looking for in all that if not God? He knows how well I observed my rules and what a severe life I led." But no matter how much Luther did, it seemed he had to do more. This made him hate God; as he confessed, "I no longer believed in Christ, rather I took him for a severe and terrible judge."[6] In the midst of this spiritual crisis, Luther celebrated his first mass as a priest. At the moment he lifted the bread and wine toward God, Luther was so overcome by fear that he almost passed out.

Luther's mentor, Johannes Staupitz, sent his difficult charge back to the study by securing him a teaching post. Luther spent two years lecturing on the psalms and then an additional two studying the new Greek Bible and lecturing on Paul's letter to the Romans. One verse, the thematic key to the whole epistle, Romans 1:17, proved particularly vexing: "The one who is righteous will live by faith." Medieval interpreters, based on the Latin in the old Bible, believed that sentence to be active. Those who love God have faith. Luther did not love God; therefore he had no faith. No faith meant eternal damnation.

But the Greek opened up the words in a surprising new way. "Day and night I tried to meditate upon the significance of these words: 'The righteousness of God is revealed in it, as it is written: The righteous shall live by faith.'" These words stood at the heart of Luther's fear, since he knew that he was not righteous. "Then, finally, God had mercy on me, and I began to understand the righteousness of God is that gift of God by which a righteous man lives." The sentence, Luther realized was passive, not active. Faith does not consist in the right acts you do to earn God's favor; God bestows faith as God wills, thus making Christians right—the passive recipients of God's work. Faith is a gift. When Luther understood these words, his God transformed from dreadful judge to one of unconditional love. "The merciful God justifies us by faith. Now I felt as though I had been reborn altogether and had entered Paradise."[7]

Luther's conversion had everything to do with words:

> In the same moment the face of the whole Scripture became apparent to me. My mind ran through the Scrip-

> ture, as far as I was able to recollect them, seeking analogies in other phrases, such as the work of God, by which he makes us strong, the wisdom of God, by which he makes us wise, the strength of God, the salvation of God, the Glory of God.
>
> Just as intensely as I had before hated the expression "the righteousness of God," I now lovingly praised this most pleasant word. The passage from Paul became to me the very gate of Paradise.[8]

Eventually Luther's struggle with the word led him to question much of the medieval system of confession, penance, and salvation, especially as it related to selling indulgences (a kind of medieval "Get Out of Jail Free" card that could be purchased for time off purgatory). In 1517 he summarized his complaints in his Ninety-five Theses, a public invitation issued to his academic colleagues to debate the doctrine of indulgences. A local printer made copies of Luther's document and circulated them, thus provoking a pamphlet war across Germany. The anxious monk's words spread farther and had more influence than anyone could have imagined, and church authorities found they could not control the printers. Within a year it was clear that the Germans were questioning papal authority; within three years the Roman church, their hand forced by a popular uprising, condemned Luther for heresy.

Western Christianity split between the Catholics and the protesters because of a disagreement between an active and passive verb. Words had real consequences. And reading scripture for its transformative power emerged as the primary practice of Protestant piety.

Speaking

Several years ago a congregation was arguing about pews. In the midst of renovating their building, about half of the church members wanted to remove the pews and replace them with chairs. The other half, however, could not imagine the church without pews. "Churches have always had pews," argued one person. "They are supposed to be uncomfortable to make you pay attention to the sermon." This churchgoer was partially correct. Pews are intended to help congregants listen to sermons. But church buildings have not always had pews. Until the Reformation, churches had little furniture. They were instead large open spaces in which people stood, brought their own stools, or knelt on straw. Not until the sixteenth century did churches install pews—an innovation intended to aid in speaking the word.

"It is exactly like the interior of a school," noted a former monk of a Protestant church in 1550. "Benches are everywhere and a pulpit for the preacher in the middle. The women and children are seated on low benches in front of the pulpit, while around them the men are on higher ones." Indeed, this observer noted the primary change in sixteenth-century religious life—the shift toward "the pedagogical nature of the new piety."[9] Whereas worship once entailed wonder at the miracle of the Mass, reformed worship emphasized the word through preaching, proclamation, and prayer, all conducted in the local language of the people. In England reformers replaced traditional Catholic aids to worship, such as candles, statues, and altar cloths, with prayer books, Bibles, commentaries, and books of sermons. More than one parish, like the church at

Morebath in Devon, reported near bankruptcy in making the change to the new Protestant devotion of books and the spoken word.[10] Protestant ministers believed their primary tasks to be that of proclaiming the word and rightly administering baptism and the Lord's Supper. In some European towns secular rulers even determined the frequency, time, and place of preaching so that God's word was properly proclaimed.

It is not surprising that ministers took up the call to preach the new word of Reformation Christianity. During the sixteenth century, however, laypeople actively engaged in theological speech as well. Having read the Word of God in newly translated scriptures and listened to sermons from reformed pulpits, they added their voices to the devotional cacophony of the day. Speaking out for Christ became a measure of one's devotion. Historian Elsie McKee notes that as lay Christians discovered the word, they developed the ability for theological questioning and a "new confidence" in their own religious opinions.[11]

"Lay Christians" included, of course, women. In the early days of the Reformation, Protestant women likened themselves to biblical heroines such as Judith and Deborah, taking up both pen and spoken word to correct the corruptions of the church. One such person was Katharina Schütz (ca. 1498–1562). Upon reading the German New Testament, she was convinced that Luther was right and dedicated herself to the reform cause. On December 3, 1523, she broke with her Catholic faith by marrying Matthew Zell, a priest-turned-reformer in Strasbourg. Because clerical marriage was both unseemly and illegal, ugly rumors spread about the couple, leaving them open to personal threats and accusations of heresy.

Katharina was appalled when a resident of the nearby town of Kentzingen was executed for owning a German Bible. She wrote a pamphlet encouraging Protestant women there not to forsake their faith for fear of suffering but to more deeply embrace the devotion of the word. "Let [not] the invincible word of God go out of your heart," she exhorted, "but always meditate on that word that you have had with you for so long and heard with all earnestness and faithfulness."[12]

Later that year Katharina wrote a second pamphlet, this time defending both her husband and her marriage. In the preface, however, she needed to argue the case for a woman speaking out in public for God. She believed that speaking out is necessary for Christian devotion, that proclaiming truth demonstrates love of God and neighbor—especially if one's neighbor is spreading falsehoods. "To keep silence is not patience. To suffer is patience," she wrote. "By keeping silence I give him grounds to continue in his trumped up lies, and that, in my judgment, is against brotherly love." For Katharina, not to speak truth was to support error. And "honest people who in every way seek the truth" need to be instructed by learned teachers.[13] She declared that the Holy Spirit had given her authority to speak, as that same Spirit had animated Elizabeth and Mary, the mothers of John the Baptist and Jesus, for "in Christ there is neither man nor woman" (Gal. 3:28). Speaking out was her obedience to God. "I seek nothing other than that we may be saved together with each other." And for sixteenth-century people, salvation was the goal of the devout life.

Until the Reformation many European Christians had never heard theology in their own language, rarely said a prayer other than in Latin, and never celebrated a liturgy in their parental tongue. Once the word became embodied in the words of regular people, they not only heard the word but also felt called, like Katharina, to speak it. As was the case with Katharina Zell, speaking out often took the form of writing pamphlets, poems, and plays—short, cheaply produced editions of theology that attacked the Catholic church and encouraged Protestant beliefs and practices. The pamphleteers, like Katharina, were the bloggers of the sixteenth century, those whose words shaped religious rebellion by challenging traditional authorities and bypassing established channels of communication. Reformation historian Steven Ozment refers to the century as "the revolution of the pamphleteers," a largely lay-driven movement that "transformed the concept, practice, and institutions of late medieval religion in the most fundamental way."[14] In the words of the laity, words changed the Christian faith forever.

Singing

About a month after September 11, 2001, an adult education class at my church was discussing the ways in which Christian practices—things like hospitality, forgiveness, and Sabbath keeping—sustain our lives. One of the participants was intently studying the list of such practices posted in the room.

"You know," she observed, "two of these practices have carried us through the last month."

"Which ones?" asked another member of the class.

"Testimony. Everybody has a story. On the news, at the office, in church. We all keep telling our stories. We are compelled the testify to what we saw that day."

"And the other?"

"The other is singing. People are singing. Everywhere." She reminded us that when members of Congress returned to the city after the attacks, they gathered on the steps of the Capitol and sang. "And everyone is singing the same two songs: 'God Bless America' and 'Amazing Grace.' I'm not sure why," she laughed, "but maybe those are the only two songs every American knows!"[15]

Some experiences are beyond words; they call forth lyrics instead. Singing marks spiritual passages—both the formal ones of birth, marriage, and death, and the informal ones of commitment, doubt, and renewal. "Human beings have always sung," observes one musician, "at play and at work, on festive and solemn occasions, in joy and in grief. . . . The act of singing together is deeply and indelibly human."[16] In many ways Christians sing faith. Musicians Don and Emily Saliers think of music as "soul practice," because music awakens "our souls to matters beyond the ordinary." At moments of change in Christian history, music often opens the path that cannot be articulated, for poetry and song take us to places that prose cannot. "Music is not simply an ornament of something already understood in words," write the Salierses. "Rather, ordered sound mediates the world to our senses and animates—literally, ensouls—those who enter it deeply."[17]

As the hunger for change overtook Europe during the Reformation, music carried the longings of the people. Martin Luther wrote hymns for congregations to sing in their own languages—a daring innovation. Although medieval people participated in the Mass, vernacular singing enabled people to experience the church's liturgies in powerful new ways. Luther loved music. He played several instruments and once commented, "Next to the word of God, music deserves the highest praise." He desired that church music be clear and not overly complex, harmonious and not monotonous, popular and not arcane. Luther thought music aided people in memorizing scripture, thus deepening their understanding of the written word. Luther advised clergy to sing Bible readings during Sunday worship and encouraged congregants to sing during Holy Communion. He personally wrote many hymns as well as settings for the Lord's Prayer, the creed, and for baptism and the Lord's Supper. Beyond Germany, followers of the French reformer John Calvin (1509–1564) busily translated the psalms into metrical verse to be sung in unison during services. Calvin himself extolled music's power to "delight," recognizing its "almost incredible power to sway hearts in one sense or another."[18] And English reformers created entire sung services of biblical texts, psalms, and prayers in their native tongue.

But not only the leaders of the Reformation sang the new faith into being. With the Bible translated into their own languages, Europeans discovered a myriad of biblical songs—from the psalms to the protest verses of Miriam, Deborah, and Mary. Much Protestant hymnody was based in the stories of biblical prophets, songs of freedom and liberty. Gerard Roussel, writing from Strasbourg, reported that the singing of psalms in the local church "ravish(ed) the soul."[19] Katharina Zell published a biblical songbook to be sung by "the artisan at his work, the maidservant at her dishwashing, the farmer and the vine dresser on the farm, and the mother with the wailing child in the cradle."[20] In short, Reformation music was intended as music of liberation for regular people. In Nürnberg alone in the fifty years following the Reformation, printers produced more than three hundred songbooks and song sheets for an eager audience.

Lazarus Spengler (1479–1534) served as city clerk of Nürnberg, an important political post in medieval Europe. A lawyer and humanist, Spengler met with a small gathering of civic reformers who welcomed Luther to their town in 1518. Evidently Spengler found Dr. Luther's views convincing. In 1519 he published the first lay defense of Martin Luther's teaching and began to enact civil reforms based on Protestant principles of freedom of conscience. For his trouble Spengler along with Luther was excommunicated by the Roman Catholic Church in June 1520.

Besides his work in law and theology, Spengler wrote hymns, including his best known, "Durch Adams Fall" (Through Adam's Fall), which extols the power of the word:

For my feet your holy word
is a blazing lantern,
a light that shows me the way forward;
as this morning Star
rises upon us we understand
the great gifts
that God's spirit has certainly promised to us,
and in these we have our hope.[21]

Spengler's verse captures the breathless sense of the Reformation as a new way of being, a transformation of words. Spengler sings that the word is the light, at the dawning of a new age, with the imminent fulfillment of God's most ancient promises. Luther's famous hymn, "A Mighty Fortress Is Our God," reaches toward the same as it describes the word as a castle that can never be breached—implying that the old fortress, or the old church, had indeed been stormed by a new Protestant people. Thus Reformation hymns were not *about* doctrine. These songs communicated an experience of God that Reformation people encountered through the word. The Reformation was not only carried in song, it was, in and of itself, "a new song."[22]

Teaching

When I was a girl in the 1960s, my Methodist church stood directly across the street from a Catholic parish. In those last days before Vatican II, Protestants and Catholics still viewed one another with suspicion if not occasional hostility, vying for the spiritual affections of the neighborhood. No matter that we attended the same public school and shopped at the same market. We lived in different religious worlds, worlds that seldom understood the other's traditions and practices—and that competed for the neighborhood's soul.

Catechism was one such competitive practice. Protestant children had no idea why Catholics had to attend classes after school or on Saturday when it seemed children should be roller-skating or playing baseball. The Roman Catholic children had to go to catechism, a mysterious-sounding program that, Protestants were convinced, brainwashed youngsters into a lifetime of spiritual darkness. Other than the fact that catechism had something to do with First Holy Communion, the Methodists had no idea what it was. We only knew it was

Roman Catholic and therefore "bad." It was not something enlightened Protestants would do.

Words like *catechism* and *didactic* have fallen on hard times, and contemporary Protestants generally eschewed these as moralistic forms of teaching. *Catechesis* simply refers to oral instruction in question-and-answer form; *didactic* means only moral teaching. Early Christians employed both to spread the new faith—as in the Catechetical School of Alexandria or the early text of the *Didache*—and written catechisms were popular ways of sharing Christian theology. Ancient statements of faith like the Apostles' Creed, now much maligned and misunderstood, were originally question-and-answer catechisms to prepare new believers for baptism, oral teachings that at some point were written down. In a pluralistic society like that of the ancient Roman Empire, teaching one's faith was a matter of survival and success.

Throughout the Middle Ages the Catholic Church used catechisms to teach the faithful. Since most people were baptized as infants, or since the church assumed that most Europeans shared a Catholic theological outlook, catechism appeared rote—as it seemed in my childhood. It would have surprised Methodists greatly, however, to discover that their Protestant ancestors were the very Christians who renewed and expanded the practice of catechism. Sixteenth-century reformers understood the importance of teaching regular people the word through catechisms and creeds. They believed that the spiritual energy of the reform could not be sustained without being shaped in God's word through teaching.

In many ways the French reformer John Calvin (1509–1564) was the great teacher of the Reformation. Calvin believed that everything—nature, scriptures, and the church—was a school for Christ. While Calvin was a humanist scholar and emphasized the importance of academic learning, he also was skeptical about the ability of the human intellect to grasp spiritual things. "There are many poor dunces today," Calvin stated in a backhanded but vaguely democratic way, "who, through ignorant and unskilled use of the language, make Christ known more faithfully than all the theologians of the pope with their lofty speculation."[23] To him faith resided in the heart, not in speculative philosophy.

Because of these views Calvin and his followers believed that every Christian—male and female, adult and child, literate or illiterate—should and could learn the faith. Most Calvinist churches included a catechism service (in addition to a regular service) on Sundays. Although this may smack of rote memorization to us, Charles Perrot, a pastor in Geneva, describes catechism's echo process as a dialogue where he would "come down from the pulpit . . . and sit on a bench" with the children, having each converse with him in turn.[24]

MASTER.—What is the chief end of human life?
SCHOLAR.—To know God by whom men were created.
MASTER.—What reason have you for saying so?
SCHOLAR.—Because he created us and placed us in this world to be glorified in us. And it is indeed right that our life, of which himself is the beginning, should be devoted to his glory.
MASTER.—What is the highest good of man?
SCHOLAR.—The very same thing.
MASTER.—Why do you hold that to be the highest good?

SCHOLAR.—Because without it our condition is worse than that of the brutes.

MASTER.—Hence, then, we clearly see that nothing worse can happen to a man than not to live to God.

SCHOLAR.—It is so.

MASTER.—What is the true and right knowledge of God?

SCHOLAR.—When he is so known that due honor is paid to him.

MASTER.—What is the method of honoring him duly?

SCHOLAR.—To place our whole confidence in him; to study to serve him during our whole life by obeying his will; to call upon him in all our necessities, seeking salvation and every good thing that can be desired in him; lastly, to acknowledge him both with heart and lips, as the sole Author of all blessings.[25]

To dismiss this as formulaic misses the point. Here, in a parish church in Geneva, a pastor leaves his pulpit and sits with a boy or girl, a radical egalitarian act in itself, to recite faith together. To small children, memorization was a way of reading. The reformers specifically rejected theological formulas and rote religion. They used catechism to personalize faith through teaching in community.

This style can be interpreted as a nudge to learners to adopt reformed theology for their own, thus enabling the young to "interiorize the faith" and "acquire a framework for their lives."[26] In addition, catechism acted as a springboard to literacy. All of this empowered regular people—especially women, servants, and children—in faith and learning to read Scripture for themselves. Teaching both transformed the individual and made him or her part of a larger learning-and-teaching community, or as the reformers put it, "a priesthood of all believers." The reformers' insistence on learning the word was well summed up by Ekhardt zum Drübel, a Dutch layman: "I can and may, I and every Christian, write, sing, talk, advise, speak, teach, instruct in a Christian way."[27] Pastors were not the only teachers. Laypeople instructed one another as well. Early Protestants understood that catechism was not brainwashing; it was an oral practice of teaching that amounted to social protest and reorganized the very structure of church.

Or as Johannes Schwöbel, a German reformer from the town of Pforzheim, stated: "The game has been turned completely upside down. Formerly one learned the laws of God from the priests. Now it is necessary to go to school of the laity and learn to read the Bible from them."[28]

Praying

Tony Jones, national coordinator of a network of emerging Christian leaders, tells the story of sitting in first class on a flight to New York next to a chic and clearly successful editor. "About halfway through the flight, she closed her Mac and tilted her seat back," he recalls. "What happened next has stuck with me ever since. She took a rosary out of her pocket and spent the next hour surreptitiously praying with her eyes closed." Thunderstruck by this apparent incongruity, Tony confesses that he had pegged her as an "enlightened, liberal member of the East Coast elite," but there she was—praying to the Virgin Mary.[29]

During the time of reform, Roman Catholics did not sit back and allow Protestants to simply destroy the old faith. Many faithful Catholics were painfully aware of their church's shortcomings and challenges but chose to remain part of the ancient institution and to try to reform it from within. They, too, emphasized a renewal based on the word—arguing that better teaching, preaching, and theology would stop the spread of Protestantism. They believed that Roman Catholicism had within it everything needed to revitalize the Christian faith: the problem was that the laity had not experienced the beauty and fullness of Catholic life.

To that end, many Catholics emphasized the importance of personal prayer as a way of spiritual renewal. Catholic reformers like the Spanish nun Teresa of Avila (1515–1582) wrote extensively on prayer, trying to open the way toward a practical mysticism that could be experienced by all the Christian faithful. After struggling mightily with the practice of prayer, Teresa came to believe that all Christians could cultivate a rich life of prayer, and "a beginner must look on himself as one setting out to make a garden for his Lord's pleasure." Although she laid out four stages of watering the garden—each involving greater spiritual difficulty—Teresa insisted that anyone may develop a soulful prayer practice, find him- or herself in the companionship of Christ, or even achieve a state of ecstasy with the God and the saints.[30]

But prayer was more than a monastic practice adapted for lay use. During the Reformation, Catholic women and men enthusiastically promoted prayer through use of the rosary, a practice of praying to the Virgin Mary with prayer beads. Although no one knows the exact history of the rosary, repetitive prayer to Jesus or Mary by counting beads was ancient, maintained in Eastern churches through many centuries. Around the year 1200, the practice seems to have been reinvigorated for Western Christians by the Spanish monk Dominic de Guzmán (1174–1221). During the sixteenth century, as the Protestant message spread in northern Europe, Roman Catholics in Spain, Italy, southern France, and southern Germany found new meaning around personal prayer through the rosary. They joined together in communities of prayer, called confraternities, supporting and teaching the practice. Often, villagers introduced their neighbors to the rosary, not waiting for clerical approval to share the practice with their friends. They developed additional spiritual practices, such as special masses and festive processions, as communal celebrations of praying the rosary. Many rural villages boasted rosary confraternities long before Roman officials introduced ecclesiastical mechanisms of the Catholic Reformation, leading one historian to refer to the use of the rosary as a "flowering of communal piety."[31] Confraternities advertised the rosary as a way of inner peace that "produces fruitfulness of virtue and curbs cursing tongues." Additionally, they promised practitioners "the achievements of virtues and of all spirituality."[32]

Praying the rosary emerged as one of the most popular devotional practices of the reform era. In one French village alone, two-thirds of all the adults joined the local rosary prayer group. The rosary made the mystical path of the saints readily available to regular parishioners through a "disciplined, meditative recitation of prayers [that] fostered an interiorized and individualized spirituality."[33] The rosary offered a personal and practical way to cultivate the garden of the soul that the church had long neglected. Faithful Catholics thus promoted renewal through the transformative power of words in prayer. If people only prayed, then the church would find new life, and would have no reason to embrace Protestant theology.

Across France, prayer did slow the Protestant advance. Rosary communities attracted large numbers of people, especially women who shared in the spiritual leadership of such groups, and who endowed masses and built churches as testimony to a new experiential faith. Personal prayer led to communal reformation, and opened laypeople to surprisingly innovative—and grassroots—expressions of a renewed Catholic devotion. In the sixteenth century, words uttered to God appeared as important as a way of devotion as the words said about God.

NINE

Ethics: Walking the Talk

Robert grew up in a staunchly Roman Catholic family. As a teenager, he began to attend a Protestant church with his friends. Eventually, he decided to join. "But I was shocked," he said, "when I figured out that Protestants honestly believed in 'justification by faith alone,' that God alone saves us." He rightly understood that Protestants insist that human beings contribute nothing to their own salvation. Faith, not good works, makes men and women right with God. He went on, "We do nothing? How can that be? If our works don't add to salvation, then what keeps us from doing whatever we please?"

Although he did not know it, his question was not original. After Luther and other reformers argued that faith alone—and not works—saved human beings, sixteenth-century critics raised the same concern about the new faith. If faith alone saves, then what is the role of works in the Christian life? What is the basis for ethics?

Luther tackled the question in his 1520 tract, *The Freedom of a Christian.* His argument opened with the proposition "Many people have considered Christian faith an easy thing."[1] But that is a misunderstanding of faith, Luther insisted. Christianity is never easy. It is difficult and calls forth great courage to act on faith in the world. To help readers grasp what a Christian way of life entails, Luther laid out two principles upon which ethics must be based:

1. A Christian is a perfectly free lord of all, subject to none, and,

2. A Christian is a perfectly dutiful servant of all, subject to all.[2]

Luther admitted that the two ideas seem contradictory. But in his love of spiritual paradox, he insisted that the tension could be resolved through love.

Works without love, he explained, produced hypocrisy. Therefore a person must be free from the church or any authority telling him or her how to behave. Good works must flow from a loving heart. Faith in Christ was a gift freely given and freely embraced; therefore, as free agents, Christians were indeed subject to no one. "One thing, and only one thing," Luther claimed, "is necessary for Christian life, righteousness and freedom." Thus even the simplest peasant, delighting in redemption, was the "freest of kings."[3]

That brought Luther to the second part of the paradox. Although works did not save—only love of Christ freely bestowed can do that—those who experience God's love would freely choose to do good for their neighbors. "Insofar as he is free he does not works," Luther stated, "but insofar as he is a servant he does all kinds of works." True Christians demonstrate love through doing good, when "faith is truly active through love." People should not care for the neighbor to save their own souls; rather, they do good because faith "finds expression in works of freest service." Therefore, as Luther concluded, "Although the Christian is thus free from all works, he ought in this liberty to empty himself, take upon himself the form of a servant."[4] Accordingly, "Genuine Christians were those who both believed in Christ and acted as Christs to one another."[5] Works validated the truth of one's words.

In the sixteenth century the motivation for ethics shifted from obligation to intention. This process had begun several centuries before—Abelard had argued for much the same thing—but a widespread social impulse toward choosing love did not emerge until Luther's time. People across Europe longed for spiritual freedom. "There is repeated reference to the living Word of God," notes historian Peter Matheson, "in itself an extraordinary image when one thinks about it, and among the biblical images those of deliverance are perhaps the most prominent: Moses and Egypt, Deborah, Daniel and the lion's den, the ever-present resurrection of the lamb."[6] Freedom—liberation—was the mood of the day.

But people not only yearned for personal freedom, they also wanted freedom to make the world according to God's word. Sixteenth-century Christians took it upon themselves—as an act of love to their neighbors—to work for justice, reform marriage, testify to the power of change, and practice reconciliation. It was a heady time, the dawn of a new age.

Justice

New Testament scholar Marcus Borg says, "Almost anywhere in the Bible where the word *righteousness* appears, you can replace it with the word *justice*. Modern people tend to interpret *righteousness* as a private and devotional word—a little smug, perhaps—but *justice* is a robust political term." It is perhaps no coincidence that Borg grew up Lutheran. For Martin Luther loved the interplay between the words *righteousness* and *justice*. In his theology God bestowed justice on human beings, therefore saving us; the world, however, was still plagued with injustice and cried out for the justice of God, that is, social justice. In 1560 the English poet Anne Locke perfectly expressed this in her *Meditation of a Penitent Sinner:*

> Perform mercy: so as in the sight
> Of them that judge the justice of thy cause
> Thou only just be deemed, and no more,
> The world's unjustice wholly to confound:
> That damning me to depth of enduring woe
> Just in thy judgment should thou be found.[7]

Personal salvation and the conundrums of political justice were inexorably linked, playing off each other in unexpected and unanticipated ways throughout the sixteenth century.

One of the most powerful words of the sixteenth century was the word *justice*. From its spiritual meaning, to make a person "just" or "right" with God, to its political meaning of making society right, reformers argued about the nature of justice and its relation to the civic order. As European

Christians tended to the state of their own souls, they equally noticed that their society remained spiritually untended. For a supposedly Christian world, many aspects of communal life were not in line with God's justice. "But alas in our day [Christian] life is unknown throughout the world," bemoaned Luther; "it is neither preached about nor sought after; we are altogether ignorant of our own name and do not know why we are Christians or bear the name of Christians."[8] God's justice seemed elusive, and people longed for social transformation.

Although Christians have always longed for justice, medieval people tended to view justice as obedience. They attended to their rightful place in a divine order, punished those who defied their status, and offered charity to those below them in the Great Chain of Being. It did not, in general, occur to medieval Christians that the structure of society could be altered or that justice might include a different social arrangement than that which was. As the Reformation dawned, however, Europe was changing and people speculated that they could foster social change through the work of human hands in order to right society's wrongs.

"All agreed on the need for change," writes historian Miriam Chrisman, but "how change was defined, what it should include, laid bare fundamental divisions in society."[9] Although reformers sought justice in different ways, they shared an underlying assumption: that somehow their political order had to be made more "Christian"; it needed to be brought into line with Jesus's Great Command. Justice meant to behave toward one's neighbors as Jesus intended. And in the context of the sixteenth century, this entailed a profound restructuring of society. "For reformers both Catholic and

Protestant," claims historian Scott Hendrix, "religious transformation and social change were more important than intellectual renewal."[10]

In 1501, sixteen years before Luther published his Ninety-five Theses, a serf named Joss Fritz entered a church and placed a banner over an image of Christ crucified. The banner featured a *Bundschuh*, the laced boot of a peasant, and bore the slogan Nothing but Divine Justice. According to his contemporaries, nearly twenty thousand people followed him in an uprising to rid the bishopric of all taxes and tithes and to make common property of all water, woods, and meadows. For the next few decades rural and urban protests increased, leading historian Heiko Oberman to suggest that Luther's call for justice dovetailed with a "gospel of social unrest" already present in Germany, where peasants had connected "justice before God" with "justice before human beings."[11]

Luther and Calvin, along with other leaders in Germany, France, and England, tried to Christianize Christendom through the already existing civil authorities, and they emphasized obedience more than revolutionary change. Reformed princes and magistrates carried out God's justice in newly Protestant provinces and cities. Despite their overall conservative approach to social change, even mainstream reformers hoped for civic reordering. John Calvin's followers, in particular, seemed given to utopian schemes, such as the establishment of the Calvinist city of Geneva, where they enacted their own vision of heavenly society in sometimes restrictive ways.

A more radical reforming impulse, however, accompanied the new theology in southern Germany, Switzerland, and the Netherlands, where some people wanted to both purify the church and separate it from a corrupt state, thus instituting a kind of New Jerusalem that would embody millenarian dreams. "Lay people wanted their village, their town, to ring to the Psalms of Zion," writes historian Peter Matheson, "but also to incarnate the righteousness of the prophets so they could follow their Captain Christ right into the interstices of day-to-day life."[12] To that end, entire families left their villages and walked across Europe to join bands of like-minded believers to form God's new commonwealth together. Some of these groups were peaceful; others were more forceful in the quest for justice. As the energetic reformer Argula von Grumbach, referred to by one opponent as a "female desperado," reminded her magistrate cousin of God's justice, "My words are like a fire, like a hammer which smashes rock."[13]

In 1525 shopkeeper Sebastian Lotzer (1490–?) wrote a small pamphlet summing up the grievances of the people of Memmingen against both the church and civil authorities; it was titled *The Fundamental and Chief Articles of All the Peasants and Subjects of Spiritual Authorities by What They Believe Themselves to Be Oppressed.* Reading the Bible, Lotzer had become radicalized, attacking the church for its lack of concern for the poor and arguing for a common holding of wealth. His pamphlet became known as *The Twelve Articles*, and it pressed for the right of communities to choose their own pastors, an end to tithes, freedom from slavery (called "serfdom" in medieval Europe), free access to fish, game, and firewood, new rent assessments, a return to common fields, and abolition of the death tax. The Word of God, he argued, and "divine law" justified these demands.

On March 6, 1525, the Memmingen shopkeepers drew up a constitution based on the twelve articles and created a political entity, "A Christian Union," based on the practice of social justice. The experiment lasted about six weeks, when Austrian authorities clamped down in a series of violent attacks and demanded Lotzer's arrest. The shopkeeper escaped to St. Gall, where he then disappeared from history.[14] Although many of the sixteenth century's millenial communities failed, the impulse for social justice remained a theological cornerstone of Protestant practice.

Family

As a lifelong churchgoer, I have heard innumerable sermons on marriage and the Christian family. The preacher typically appeals to Adam and Eve as the perfect example of marriage as well as the divine pattern for marriage established in the Garden of Eden. "Marriage is," as often proclaimed, "the one unchanging institution upon which the rest of society is based. God ordained it in the book of Genesis." It is a little odd to hold Adam and Eve up as examples of Christian marriage. Besides the obvious fact that they were not Christians, they ran around naked, could not have actually married since no marital laws existed, lied to and deceived one another, and demonstrated such fine parenting skills that one of their sons murdered the other.

Bad biblical interpretation aside, however, preachers often overlook the fact that marriage has changed over time. What counted as a good Christian marriage in ancient Rome differed from that of a successful medieval one, where marriage was considered a sacrament but seemed a lesser spiritual state than celibacy. Medieval marriage existed for the procreation of children. During the sixteenth century the reformers expanded the sphere of marriage, its spiritual dimensions, and its practices. Their social agenda included a new understanding of marriage, the family, and the home.[15]

Reformers began rethinking marriage when they married. Most of the early Protestant leaders had been clergy or monks, and while some of them kept concubines, others were celibate. Thus any sort of clerical sexual activity was secret—and not something that pastors could theologically reflect upon in public. For early Protestant preachers marriage was both a pleasure and a way of defying Catholic authorities. But more than anything, clerical marriage embodied Christian freedom—its right to choose to be celibate (if God had so gifted one) or to choose to be married. Martin Luther argued that priestly celibacy violated the "pact of freedom" God entered into with believers upon their baptism. According to him, vows of celibacy went against common sense; he argued that only men over seventy could honestly make them.[16]

The reformers spoke boldly of sex and sexual pleasure, believing that marriage was the only appropriate vessel for sexual expression. As Luther once remarked, marriage was a hospital for lust. To make the theological point, Luther himself married in 1525. Katherine von Bora had been a nun whom Luther arranged to be kidnapped from the convent along with several other sisters in the back of a fishmonger's wagon among barrels of herring. The two made quite a pair, as was testified to by Luther's own writings and that of his students and boarders. Together they raised ten children—six of their own and four orphans. Luther clearly adored Katherine, jokingly referring to her as "my Lord Katie" and "my chain." Of sex, Luther wrote, "This plighted troth permits even more occasion than is necessary for the begetting of children." Marriage vows, unlike clerical celibacy ones, freed men and women to experience romantic love and sexual pleasure as the foundation for Christian union. Historian Lyndal Roper remarks, "This is certainly a positive attitude toward sex within marriage, and Luther can with justice be said to have made a genuine break with pre-Reformation views of sexuality."[17]

Protestants not only shifted European views of marriage, but they also changed the understanding of Christian households. Katherine Luther managed a large estate—a former monastery that had been given to them as a wedding present—that included a herd of cattle and a brewery. Female Christian leadership moved from the convent to the family and home, thus hallowing the sphere of activity that most European women already occupied. Although the ideal Protestant household was still headed by a pious father, husband and wife were to be spiritual partners. "The clergy wife," writes historian Diarmaid MacCulloch, "came to provide a new model for all the wives of Protestant Europe." Of her qualities, "she was, of course, obedient to her husband, but she was also a calm and experienced companion, ready to give advice and help to parishioners."[18]

As was modeled by the Luthers and other clerical couples, the home became the Protestant equivalent of the monastery, where all members of the household strove for greater piety and a pure knowledge of Christ. Protestants demonstrated the new prominence of families by changing the seating in church. Before the Reformation, men and women sat or stood in different sides of the church. After the introduction of fixed pews, families sat together in groups. Some conservatives attacked this innovation as distracting and clannish, but Protestants continued to insist that their families were the primary spiritual community forming the church. This "new image of the family" amounted to, as one historian put it, a "radical redefinition" of the sacred.[19]

Although the most profound rethinking of the family came in the early part of the sixteenth century, Protestants continued to experiment with family arrangements. In 1625 Nicholas Ferrar, an English businessman turned Anglican deacon, settled at a ramshackle estate called Little Gidding with the intention of establishing a household where his family "might live and serve God together."[20] Ferrar was not married, but Little Gidding became home to him, his married brother and sister, their spouses and families, his mother, and some single friends—around forty people in all. Together they created a family monastery, gathering daily for morning and evening prayer, keeping the hours, and maintaining a prayer vigil in the community chapel.

The ideal of a "godly household" was deeply ingrained in English Protestantism, but the Little Gidding community took the ideal much further than most families could or did. The primary purpose of Little Gidding "was the steady, rhythmic routine of prayer and worship and consecrated effort provided in the daily rule of the household."[21] Together the extended Ferrar family managed the estate, cared for each other, raised children, and tended to the farm and gardens, interlacing fixed prayer and worship with everyday life through a new monastic-style rule. Like monks and nuns before them, the Little Gidding residents educated local children, offered charity to the poor, and practiced hospitality. More radical Protestants, the Puritans, discerned a dangerous social aspect to their prayers and good works—that the community might be secret Roman Catholics and therefore traitors to the Protestant cause and democratic government. Their radical reordering of family went too far. In 1646 Oliver Cromwell's soldiers raided the manor house, attacked the chapel, and dispersed the community.

Their routine of prayer and worship may have seemed Catholic to some of their neighbors, but their willingness to experiment with marriage, family, and community marks the Ferrars of Little Gidding as the heirs of the Reformation. When it comes to sexuality and family, Protestants are always willing to change the rules.

Testimony

Several years ago the Reverend Lillian Daniel became the pastor of a struggling New England church. In the early years of her ministry, she tried to figure out what might revive the flagging community. During Sunday worship she felt frustrated as the announcements from the membership went on too long, cutting down on the time for her sermon and singing. "I felt angry at the announcements," she said. "Then suddenly it dawned on me: people wanted to talk in church."

Lillian's insight led the congregation to a regular practice of testimony. Given the context—that of a reserved and socially liberal Connecticut congregation—having people stand up in worship to share their faith stories was unusual. Practicing testimony changed their faith community, renewing the old congregation and empowering them to practice social justice. "Our church's practice is giving testimony, having people talk about their experience of God," Lillian explains. "We didn't invent it; it was in the early church." She says, "Words are like an earthquake." Learning to give testimony transformed her congregation; they learned "releasing control and risking," and they heard each other's voices. The church grew more confident, more sure that God was still with them, and the congregation found new energy. Lillian, herself an excellent preacher, having a way with words, confesses, "The Holy Spirit uses all of us."[22]

Although testimony featured prominently in early Christianity, the practice waned through the Middle Ages. But as Europe changed during the Reformation, more democratic impulses emerged, and the need to share one's story took on renewed importance. People testified to their embrace of the new Protestant religion in church, in town squares, in print, and—when called to do so—before the local magistrate. For some Protestants testimony acted as the portal to the new community, as acceptance into reformed congregations often depended on one's ability to witness to God's power in one's life. Testimony shifted spiritual authority away from the learned clergy to the people.

In the United States testimony is often viewed as a devotional practice, even referred to as "personal testimony." Yet, as the good folks at Lillian's church discovered, testimony is more than personal; it is a public practice with public consequences. "I know that it will be considered shameful or worthless for a woman to dare to answer such big guys," proclaimed Ursula Weyda, a German tax collector's wife asked to defend her Protestant views in 1524. "[But] I know that Christ said to me as much as to all bishops: 'Whoever confesses Me before men, that one I will confess before My Father who is in heaven. . . .' I will not cease doing what I am obligated to do; God will require an accounting from all of us." During the sixteenth century regular people claimed the authority of their own voices, thus challenging both the church and the social order. Testimony was not personal. As a public practice, it enabled people to create new political realities for themselves. Testimony was, as historian Elsie McKee argues, "historically unprecedented" in its scale and effects.[23]

In 1524 English authorities arrested gentlewoman Anne Askew (1521–1546) for her Protestant beliefs. Anne came from a mixed religious family—her grandparents were Roman Catholics, her brother served the household of the Protestant reformer Thomas Cranmer. As a young woman, she was forced to marry Thomas Kyme, a conservative Roman Catholic. But she had converted to the Protestant faith. It was an unhappy union. She bore two children, but she left Kyme, hoping to secure a divorce, after he shut her out of the family house for abandoning the Catholic faith.

Anne went to London to join other Protestants—including those in Queen Katherine Parr's circle—to push for greater religious change in England, especially with regard to the practice of the Lord's Supper. She did not believe that the bread and wine actually became the body and blood of Christ during the Eucharist and that such "superstitions" contradicted the teachings of scripture. For speaking too freely on this account, and for her political connections to the queen, Anne was imprisoned for heresy, tortured, and burned at the stake.

Before her captors did their worst, however, Anne Askew wrote down her story, a testimony of Protestant beliefs, in a document called the *Examinations*.[24] Her book recounts her court testimonies to Catholic authorities regarding her understanding of the Eucharist and other doctrines. Throughout, she appealed to the source of her authority: "I believe as the scripture doth teach me."

While Askew testified to the power of the new theology, other laypeople witnessed to faith's more emotive side. A Dutch mother, Janneken Munstdorp, wrote her testimony to her infant daughter, also named Janneken, from prison in 1573. Munstdorp, an Anabaptist, had been arrested and was waiting execution for her faith. Like Askew, Munstdorp's faith challenged tradition: Anabaptists rejected infant baptism in favor of adult believers' baptism. But more politically provocative was their pacifism; for this European rulers viewed Anabaptists as traitors. Like many others, Munstdorp was condemned to die for these beliefs.

"My dear little child," she wrote to the newborn taken from her,

> I commend you to the almighty, great and terrible God, who only is wise, that He will keep you, and let you grow up in His fear. . . . Hence, my dear lamb, I who am imprisoned and bound here for the Lord's sake, can help you in no other way; I had to leave your father for the Lord's sake and could keep him only a short time. We

were permitted to live together only half a year, after which we were apprehended, because we sought salvation of our souls. They took him from me, not knowing my condition, and I had to remain in imprisonment, and see him go before me; and it was a great grief to him, that I had to remain in prison. . . .

And now, Janneken, my dear lamb, who are yet very little and young, I leave you this letter . . . and this I leave you for a perpetual adieu, and for a testament; that you may remember me by [this letter]. Read it, when you have understanding, and keep it as long as you live in remembrance of me and your father. . . . Be not ashamed to confess us before the world, for we were not ashamed to confess our faith before the world.

Let it be your glory, that we did not die for any evil doing, and strive to do likewise, though they should also seek to kill you. And on no account cease to love God above all. . . . Seek peace, and pursue it, you shall receive the crown of eternal life.[25]

Each woman had a story, a story she shared with the larger community of which she was a part. Anne Askew testified to the power of scripture and her experience of the Lord's Supper. Janneken Munstdorp witnessed to the Anabaptist commitment to peace. These testimonies do more, however, than tug at the heartstrings. Both tales became part of the martyr literature of the sixteenth century, inspiring countless others to embrace and persevere in the new faith. Such stories, especially when they came from women, undermined the credibility of the old authorities. In their testimonies both

Askew and Munstdorp stand as innocent victims of a corrupt system—a system that needed to be reformed. Testimonies functioned as political tracts, intended to stir discontent and move others to action. John Bale, an early editor of Askew's *Examinations*, said it plainly enough: in the burning of "this godly woman Anne Askew . . . behold the tyrannous violence there showed." The authorities were worse than Pilate because they treated a woman with the "most terrible tyranny." Their fate is their "damnation," and true Christians must rise up and reject their hypocrisy.[26]

Discipline

Not long ago, NPR broadcast a story on Internet gambling and government attempts to control it for the sake of the "public good." More than a dozen people called in decrying the "nanny state" and what they viewed as an intrusion on their freedom to gamble. Some civic leaders, including some religious leaders, tried to make the point that young people and the poor were the most adversely affected by gaming debts, thus adding to the social problems of American cities. The exchange went nowhere, each side regarding its opponents as hopelessly immoral or boneheaded. The show's host cut off some callers—as well as his guests—in a desperate attempt to restore order.

On August 24, 1542, the Geneva Consistory, a Reformation church court, called Jaques Bornant, a cobbler, to appear. He was charged with skipping Sunday worship in favor of "wasting time in gambling games." Bornant protested, saying that he always attended church. To prove it, he recited the Lord's

Prayer and the Apostles' Creed. He could not, however, remember the Ten Commandments. For his infraction, the consistory "admonished" him "to cease to gamble and to give an example to others" and to remember to "frequent the sermons."[27] No other punishment was meted out.

For all the radical energy of the Reformation, critics often point out that some killjoys like John Calvin quickly quashed the impulse of Christian freedom by instituting tight social controls over Protestant communities; one calls it "some pettifogging interference by humorless self-appointed tyrants."[28] Indeed, from Erasmus onward, and for Protestants and Roman Catholics alike, the sixteenth-century longing for freedom was accompanied by an equal desire for social discipline. Viewed from only a contemporary perspective, the sixteenth-century reformations may well be seen as midwife to the oft-criticized "nanny state."

Social discipline, however, needs to be placed in its context in order to understand its relation to Christian ethics. In the sixteenth century *discipline* was a positive word, almost a sales slogan for an orderly community in the midst of a chaotic world.[29] Discipline was both internal and external, a kind of spiritual control intended to curb human sin and to further virtue in society. Martin Luther's *Shorter Catechism* placed social order alongside right doctrine in its teaching of faith, and all the reformers emphasized the Ten Commandments as the basis of communal discipline. For the Reformers, a disciplined community was a just community.

Why discipline? Because, quite simply, in the sixteenth century other forms of justice eluded regular people. In the late Middle Ages justice was arbitrary and expensive, well beyond the means of common folk. Ecclesiastical or secular courts meted out punishments, but lawyers rarely pled cases, nor did juries judge evidence. There existed no justice system as we know it, and disputes between neighbors were most often settled on the basis of who had the most power, status, or money. A poor man could be tossed in jail for looking cross-eyed at a duke or be executed for stealing a rich farmer's pig while a feudal lord could evoke legal privileges to rape the daughter of a peasant. Women could be burned as witches for inheriting their father's property or healing a sick child with herbs. It was nearly impossible for most Europeans to hope for anything like restitution for wrongs committed against them, their relatives, and their property. Justice was an elusive dream.

Thus when the new ethics taught freedom, regular people quickly used that freedom to institute forms of control to ensure wider justice in church and society. Discipline was intended to create the possibility for reconciliation between arguing parties, thus establishing a just society. Much of the early Protestant vision of justice was based in the words of Jesus in Matthew 18:15–17:

> If another member of the church sins against you, go and point out the fault when the two of you are alone. If the member listens to you, you have regained that one. But if you are not listened to, take one or two others along with you, so that every word may be confirmed by the evidence of two or three witnesses. If the member refuses to listen to them, tell it to the church, and if the offender refuses to listen even to the church, let such a one be to you as a Gentile and a tax collector.

Jesus's teaching was, of course, directed toward the Jews who followed him—Jews under the authority of a Roman legal system stacked against them. Thus Jesus commanded them to make their own community, rather than depending on civil courts as the locus of justice.

Early Protestants took this literally, reforming existing church courts and creating new ones to carry out social discipline—geared toward the practice of reconciliation. For followers of John Calvin, that meant setting up consistories, or boards of church elders and pastors, to hear disputes and hold church members—such as Jaques Bornant—accountable for their behavior. Such courts delivered justice "free of charge" and, unlike civil courts of the time, were "reactive and local," thus ensuring quicker results for the parties involved and administering discipline from below, not imposed by a prelate or prince.[30] Discipline tended toward correcting behavior, not enforcing doctrinal conformity. Judges handled all manner of infractions, but "peacemaking in an admittedly disputatious world was perhaps the largest task to which they applied themselves."[31]

The first step toward reconciliation was penitence, often involving some public act such as wearing sackcloth, sitting on a repentance stool during Sunday worship, or being shunned from a congregation. One historian refers to this as "a theater of forgiveness," intended to "bring an offender back into the fold of the community." During the Reformation, not unlike the contemporary practice of victims addressing perpetrators of a crime before sentencing, both the sinned against and the sinners had to make public speeches decrying their misdeeds. Through their speeches the congregation determined the sincerity of their penitence. Then members offered tokens of peace to each other—handshakes, kisses, or other embraces—to mark reconciliation and forgiveness. Whether through the consistory or the whole congregation, justice became the work of the people, and even the upper classes and clergy were subject to it.[32]

John Calvin's followers favored consistories (church courts), but other Protestants worked for discipline through other means. Always looking for the "visible fruit of faith," Anabaptist reformers attempted to create congregations that held out Christian perfection as an ideal, with all believers held accountable for their spiritual lives, much as monks and nuns were held accountable in Roman Catholic monasteries. In the city of Augsburg Anabaptists regularly complained that Lutheran preachers had never "enlightened or improved anyone" and that the city fostered no more Christian virtue than it had under the rule of Roman Catholics.[33] Led by Jacob Dachser (1486–1567), the Augsburg Anabaptists called for a "Christianity of obedience" and separated themselves from other reformed churches to lead a more disciplined life. The new community shared its goods and earned a reputation as particularly generous to the poor. To ensure justice, it instituted shunning (refusing to associate with sinful church members) and the ban (exiling unrepentant sinners from the community) as forms of discipline, intended to reconcile believers. In a short time over 1,100 people joined Dachser's congregation, making it a sort of sixteenth-century radical megachurch.

Not surprisingly, the group proved controversial, and one of its Lutheran opponents railed at it for peddling a "new monasticism," a derisive term to accuse someone of being Catholic.[34]

The real threat, however, centered on the group's practice of communalism and its insistence that people could achieve a truly Christian way of life, a state of disciplined perfection, on this earth without being subject to civic authorities. Because of its views, the group was eventually forced to hold secret meetings and worship services. Not an easy feat for a congregation of more than a thousand people.

The Augsburg Lutherans had little patience for the Anabaptists' vision of a just society and questioned their practice of discipline. The authorities arrested their leaders, including Jacob Dachser, who remained imprisoned for three years. Eventually city leaders were sufficiently convinced of his orthodoxy, freed him, and made him assistant pastor at St. Ulrich Lutheran Church. For the next two decades he served in the regular ministry and became known as a hymn writer. It must have been difficult, however, for Pastor Dachser to hold his tongue. Some sources imply that he and his wife, Ottilie, well into their sixties, may have held clandestine Anabaptist meetings in their house. In 1552 Emperor Charles V ordered him and two other pastors to leave Augsburg "because they spoke, acted, and practiced all sorts of things that might lead to sedition, revolt, and all mischief."[35] To the authorities, the exercise of spiritual discipline was suspect.

Although it is very difficult for contemporary people to grasp sixteenth-century practices of discipline as Christian justice, we have an example of this reformation vision closer at hand: South Africa's Truth and Reconciliation Commission. After gaining political freedom, the citizens of South Africa created a public tribunal of repentance and forgiveness in 1995, declaring by their actions that liberation must, of necessity, lead to reconciliation. Without the public practice of reconciliation, based on disciplined forgiveness, a truly just society would be impossible. Those who had oppressed others were called to account for their sins and asked to publicly repent, and those who had been oppressed were asked to offer public tokens of forgiveness to their enemies.

This, I think, was similar to the practice of the early Protestant reformers. Some of the "sins" they thought serious look petty to us today, but they surely believed that to continue in such sins would impede good relationships and social justice. Thus discipline, the right ordering of the soul in society, formed the basis of God's new world and transformed politics.

The Unfinished Reformation

One of my favorite professors in seminary was Richard Lovelace, a church historian with a gracious spirit. Although he served on the faculty of an evangelical theological school, he was a deeply committed mainline Presbyterian and one of the most thoroughly ecumenical people I have known. He believed that Christianity was a generous way of life, a process of ongoing personal and communal reformation centered in the love of God. "Reforming doctrines and institutions in the church was futile," he wrote, "unless people's lives were reformed and revitalized."[36] The reformed church, he insisted, must always be reforming. As a scholar, he studied Christian renewal movements and taught several classes in the history of spirituality and post-Reformation church history.

In his most popular class, The Dynamics of Spiritual Life, Professor Lovelace explained that shortly after Martin Luther's death in 1546, Protestants began to fight over the particulars of their revolutionary movement. Second-generation leaders demanded theological clarity and ecclesiastical order. In response, Lutherans and Calvinists developed precise systems of theology and clear boundaries as to what constituted the church. They fought among themselves while continuing to argue with Roman Catholics and Anabaptist Protestants. Instead of experiencing the word as fluid, Protestant leaders made their faith rigid, concretizing the passions of their ancestors into dogmatic intellectual systems. They fought real wars—like the English Civil War and the Thirty Years' War—over words.

The post-Reformation theological turn is known as "Protestant Scholasticism," a method "that insisted legalistically on the acceptance of precisely worded doctrinal confessions" as the basis of faith.[37] People lost the sense that words resided in human wholeness, that they enlivened the heart. Theologians pitted devotion and morality against belief, defining faith no longer as a way of life but rather as intellectual assent to certain creeds or confessions; their books were filled with "quarrelling, disputing, scolding, and reviling."[38] Words became weapons.

"By the end of the sixteenth century," Professor Lovelace told us, "Protestants in both Lutheran and Reformed spheres were referring to the 'half-reformation,' which had reformed their doctrines but not their lives."[39] The historical stage was set: modern Christianity would struggle between the head and the heart; orthodoxy and piety had been severed.

While he lectured about this tension in the classroom, we witnessed it at the seminary. In the mid–1980s the school was racked with controversy between those faculty members who insisted upon creedal purity and those committed to spiritual liveliness. The seminary "scholastics" launched a crusade against colleagues who in their view were guilty of sloppy thinking or questionable orthodoxy—a charge that led to a heresy trial, some firings, and a good many faculty retirements. For those of us who were students, it was a fearsome object lesson in church history. Inquisitions are ugly things. In the battle of orthodoxy versus piety, at that particular seminary, orthodoxy won. And in the pitch of battle, the love of God vanished from the place.

In 1675 Philipp Jakob Spener (1635–1705), a Lutheran minister, lamented the state of the church and hoped for better days in a small book titled *Pia Desideria.* Disillusioned and divided by the violence of religious wars, people found little in the church to inspire them. "There are probably few places in our church in which there is such want that not enough sermons are preached," wrote Spener. "But many godly persons find that not a little is wanting in many sermons." The clergy were largely trying to impress their congregations with their learning, their "suitably embellished" orthodoxy, and dry presentations of Christian teaching. Such sermons failed "to awaken the love of God and neighbor." Spener believed that Lutheran Christians had lost their capacity to experience the transforming Word. "It is not enough that we hear the Word with our outward ear, but we must let it penetrate to our heart."[40]

Spener diagnosed the problem in simple terms: an ecclesiastical elite cared more about theological purity than the "universal priesthood" of God's people, who constituted the real church. Leaders had directed their attention to church "disputations" and were more concerned with "human erudition" and "artificial posturing" than the pursuit of Christian wisdom. Spener warned that this turn of affairs harmed the church. Quoting one of his colleagues, Spener stated, "The consequence is that the *theologia practica* (that is, the teaching of faith, love, and hope) is relegated to a secondary place, and the way is again paved for a *theologia spinosa* (that is, a prickly, thorny teaching) which scratches and irritates hearts and souls."[41] Why would anyone even want to be a Christian in such circumstances?

So Spener reminded his readers that "it is no means enough to have knowledge of the Christian faith, for Christianity consists rather of practice" and that "love is the real mark" of Jesus's followers. The church could never be reformed on right belief alone. Rather, "love is the whole life of the man who has faith and who through his faith is saved, and his fulfillment of the laws of God consists in love." Christianity does not mean assenting to a creed, for "conviction of truth is far from being faith"; true Christianity is the "practice of love."[42]

Not surprisingly, his "orthodox opponents" attacked him, saying that Spener's theology was questionable because it was too subjective. It weakened ecclesiastical authority, they warned, if the laity truly embraced his radical ideas. They accused Spener of taking the Reformation too far.

Will words prick and irritate? Will they inspire hope? Is faith a way of dogma or a path of love? At the end of the course, Professor Lovelace asked his students, "If you had to pick, what kind of Christianity would you rather have: a

Christianity with the right answers that was dead or a Christianity, loose around the intellectual edges, that compelled people to act in love?" We sat and stared at him. No one wanted to answer. We really wanted both, but we also knew how seldom that has happened in Christian history.

I hoped that Professor Lovelace's question was relegated to the generations immediately following the Reformation—or to a cranky evangelical seminary north of Boston, Massachusetts. But the questions of the "half-reformed" Reformation still resonate. As I write, in the summer of 2008, Anglican bishops from all over the world are meeting in Canterbury and having an argument over homosexuality, biblical interpretation, and the nature of the church. It is a nasty dispute, as scratchy an ecclesiastical quarrel as has ever been, made worse by instant communications and the Internet. The whole thing brings to my mind some words uttered by Martin Luther to the people of Erfurt in 1522:

> Beware! Satan has the intention of detaining you with unnecessary things and thus keeping you from those which are necessary. Once he has gained an opening in you of hand-breath, he will force in his whole body together with sacks full of useless questions."[43]

I don't suppose I can do anything to quiet the din from Canterbury. But I do have an overwhelming desire to board an airplane bound for London with a suitcase full of copies of the *Pia Desideria*.

PART IV

THE QUEST

Modern Christianity 1650–1945

TEN

Christianity as a Quest for Truth

During my senior year in college I was walking down a path near the main academic building on campus. I heard an exceedingly loud voice from a second-floor classroom and looked up. At that moment a book flew out the window and landed about two feet in front of me. I leaned over and picked it up. It was Albert Schweitzer's *The Quest of the Historical Jesus.*

Several friends who were in the classroom from which the book was thrown—a course on Jesus—reported to me what had happened. The professor had been lecturing on developments in liberal theology, on Schweitzer's 1906 book and how it tracked the scholarly search for the Jesus of history—and that nineteenth-century people were seeking the Jesus as he existed, not the Jesus of pious legend. They were looking for the true Jesus or, at the very least, the historical truth of Jesus. To do this European scholars employed new critical tools to scripture, trying to read the Bible as they would any ancient document instead of as the inerrant Word of God.

The professor read them passages from Schweitzer's survey of these developments, explaining it as he went. Committed to a conservative view of scripture, he ridiculed Schweitzer's task and methods, dismissing him out of hand. Even though Schweitzer criticized many aspects of the nineteenth-century quest, the professor was not impressed. Using Schweitzer's own image, he argued, "His quest ended not with Jesus, but with Schweitzer. It was as if Schweitzer—like all the other liberal Protestants—looked down the deep well of history and saw his own face. And so it was with modern theology. An inadequate vision of Christian faith." He pondered the book in his hand. "Schweitzer said the historical Jesus remains a 'stranger and enigma' to us. Well, this is what I think of Schweitzer's *Quest*," and he tossed the book out the window.

Thus it could be said that *The Quest of the Historical Jesus* hit me over the head one day. Well, almost, anyway.

When Schweitzer's book appeared in 1906, it did seem to hit many Christians over the head. In it Schweitzer argued that Jesus proclaimed the imminent kingdom of God and that he had been sent to initiate God's messianic end-times reign. Jesus's message was intrinsically knit into this context, a context of Jewish thought and culture that we can no longer understand. Thus Jesus was a real person in history, but one whose contextual meaning cannot be recovered. Schweitzer separated the historical Jesus from the "Christ of faith." He argued that the truth of Jesus cannot be found in history but is found rather in "the present experience of Christ as a living spiritual reality."[1] Schweitzer's conclusions surprised many

Christians, and *Quest* sparked controversy among theologians and churchgoers.

Perhaps, however, Schweitzer's book should not have been such a surprise. It both summarized and capped two centuries of theological speculation regarding God, scripture, and the nature of theology—a quest for the real Jesus. Since the Reformation Protestants and Catholics had been reassessing Christian thought and practice in the modern world, trying to make sense of ancient ideas in the challenging new social, economic, and intellectual environments in Europe and the Americas.

Even though Protestants view the Reformation as a success, the events of the sixteenth century unleashed a host of problems with which Christians had to grapple. To say, for example, that the Word of God acted as spiritual and theological authority for life created a problem: Whose interpretation of the word was correct? How could a believer adjudicate between conflicting views of scripture? What happened when those in authority contradicted each other? And even worse, when those authorities—all claiming to be Christian—persecuted or went to war with each other, what then? The Reformation eroded traditional sources of authority and unity in Europe, opening Christian communities to questions and concerns unimagined by the medieval church. As the questions provoked many different answers, they also provoked warfare. Catholic kings challenged Protestant princes over territorial claims, and those in authority—whether Catholic or Protestant—crushed heresy and heterodoxy within their own borders.

This, combined with the European encounter with new worlds, cultures, peoples, and religions in the first age of global exploration and conquest, changed both the context and content of the Christian faith. Philosopher Charles Taylor refers to the transformation of Western society following the Reformation as a "shift in background" or "the disruption of an earlier background," a change in which the "whole context in which we experience and search for fullness" becomes something it has not been before. "To put the point in different terms," he states, "belief in God isn't quite the same thing in 1500 and 2000." In those five hundred years belief has become an "option," and the new "background" is the slow "coming of a secular age."[2]

This shift in background—all the new questions it entailed, along with its quest to understand—challenged believers. Faith was no longer what it had been for their ancestors. Over several generations Christian faith would increasingly become one option among many. As the modern age dawned, Christians set off searching for a new kind of Christianity.

A Modern World

As we move closer to our own time, the lines of past and present blur. Where are we in history? Modern Christianity is problematic because we still experience it; we live in its wake of unresolved questions and open-ended quest.

In recent decades, however, philosophers and scientists have argued that modernity is grinding to an end, or has ended. Accordingly, Western society—and the societies influenced by Western culture—have entered a "postmodern" age. As a historical epoch, modernity is slipping into the past, as did the Middle Ages. Theologians talk about the "end of Christendom," "postmodern Christianity," and "post-traditional religion."[3] These concepts are reshaping popular Christianity, and in some Christian circles it has become fashionable to dismiss—or belittle—modern conceptions of Christianity.

In 1989, several years after Albert Schweitzer fell at my feet, I was sitting in a class at Duke Divinity School called the English Church in the Eighteenth Century and taught by Professor Ted Campbell, noted historian of British Methodism. It was a small group; only six of us braved the complex theological territory of early modern Europe. Ted had stretched the definition of "eighteenth" century a bit; we were studying Christianity from 1688 to 1820. The course included everything in England and North America from the Glorious Revolution (1688) under William and Mary through both the American (1776) and French (1789) Revolutions and ending with the Battle of Waterloo (1815). Not only did the period include three political revolutions that reshaped world history, but it also included the publication of some of the most influential works in the English language, like the American Declaration of Independence and Adam Smith's *The Wealth of Nations.*

The early modern period was a time of intellectual, political, and social upheaval. It was a time of optimistic possibilities, revolutionary change, and economic prosperity when scientific and social visionaries believed they could solve all the world's problems. These modern impulses shaped the centuries that followed in ways that continue to influence the globe. In this environment Christians reworked theology. They de-emphasized the supernatural aspects of faith, rebased faith on morality rather than doctrine, celebrated tolerance, and elevated the role of the natural world and humankind in relation to the divine. The new spirit was captured in the titles of books such as John Toland's *Christianity Not Mysterious* (1696), John Locke's *An Essay Concerning Human Understanding* (1690), and Joseph Butler's *The Analogy of Religion to the Constitution and the Course of Nation* (1736). Although these Enlightenment theologians wrote in the polite cadences of their day, their books revolutionized Christianity by making it more rational, irenic, scientific, and liberal.

One discussion day, as the students in my class struggled with Butler's *Analogy,* Professor Stanley Hauerwas was lecturing on postmodern Christian ethics across the hallway. That class was much larger; more than sixty students crammed into the room to hear Hauerwas hold forth in his distinctively forceful style. "Nothing good came out of the Enlightenment for Christians," he argued. Although his classroom door was shut, we could still hear him loudly insisting, "Modernity was a theological mistake" while critiquing a host of twentieth-century theologians. Modernism had failed in its optimistic assessment of reason, human morality, and progress. We closed our door. Over the harmonious logic of Butler, however, we could still hear Stanley Hauerwas railing against modernism. We were trying to grapple with the Enlightenment while the class across the hall was busy dismissing it as an irrelevant failure. Two classes, studying at the bookends of modernity, trying to come to grips with its beginning and its end.

British sociologist Anthony Giddens takes issue with the idea that we are somehow postmodern, arguing instead that Western culture exists in a "high modern" context, and he cites continuities between our time and that of early modernity. The Enlightenment created the conditions with which we now struggle, "the institutions and modes of behavior established first of all in post-feudal Europe, but which in the twentieth century increasingly have become world-historical in their impact." However, Giddens finds this condition ironic. Instead of answering questions and providing security, modernity opened the way for less certainty and more social and political risk.[4]

Whatever the debate between modern and postmodern, Giddens makes an interesting point. Modernity began with questions about human community, the existence of God, certainty and doubt, and the anxieties of nature. For a few hundred years modernity reduced social stress by breaking with the medieval European past—especially with traditional ways of conceiving religion—and providing new answers to these concerns. In the process, however, modernity would come to question the very assumptions on which it was founded: reason, logic, and objective inquiry. As Giddens states, "Modernity turns out to confound the expectations of Enlightenment thought—although it is a production of that thought," thus creating a kind of circular process of anxiety, questions, solutions with unanticipated consequences, doubt, further risk, and stress.[5]

Oddly enough, Western culture now experiences as much—or perhaps more—anxiety as when post-Reformation turmoil roiled Europe. No matter how postmodern we might imagine ourselves to be, most people still live with the continuing questions and conundrums of modernity while many take for granted—and still grapple with—modern ideas, especially about how philosophy, science, social science, history, and politics relate to the Christian faith.

Christianity as a Quest

Modernity rested on new questions about God, human beings, and society. It presupposed that answers could be found as singular truth or, as modernists commonly remark, "Truth with a capital *T*." Modern people assumed there existed *one* truth about the universe and its various components. Modern life, therefore, developed as a quest to find the universal truth about God, the self, science, philosophy, society, and nature. If human beings understood truth, then we could fix—or, at the very least, correctly anticipate—the problems that plagued humankind. In its unflagging quest for truth, modernity promised intellectual certitude, social order, universal harmony, and political security.

Quests were, of course, nothing new for Christians. Early Christians practiced pilgrimage and understood faith as a quest for God; medieval believers did likewise and further developed spiritual quests into literary forms and poetry; and Reformation people imagined faith as a journey back to the primitive church, a quest to recapture the purity of New Testament belief. Before 1650 the idea of spiritual quest had a certain open-ended quality, of going but never quite arriving. Premodern Christians tended to emphasize the adventure encountered on the quest rather than the object of the journey.

Modern Christians, however, defined quest as a finite intellectual search in which their questions would be answered; exploration took a backseat to a journey's completion. In the modern mode Christians were less interested in pursuing God than they were in pursuing knowledge *about* God. For in their world knowing *about* God equaled *knowing* God. Modern quests were also sensory quests; metaphoric, poetic, and mystical quests largely fell from spiritual fashion. Modern Christians embarked on quests to see, touch, hear, or feel God—and they developed specific practices to do just that. They needed assurance through their senses, a kind of divine data that enabled believers to know God. And they were optimistic that such sensory evidence existed and would enable them to discover truth.

Modern quests for God unfolded in two directions: an internal grasp of divine things and an external experience of faith through good works. By exploring both the inner territory of faith and its public consequences, Christian truth was demonstrated through both piety and morality. Thus the quest for spiritual truth entailed a dual journey—inward to understand the soul and outward to make the world a better place. Of course, Christians differed on what constituted piety and morality, but most boldly asserted that the spiritual quest was a closed system—marked by certain predictable patterns of action and consequences—whereby one moved from questions to answers. The spiritual life was a puzzle to be solved.

This confident quest marked modern Christianity, acting as the template through which Jesus's followers interpreted the command to love God and love their neighbors. In his *Quest of the Historical Jesus* Albert Schweitzer still framed the Christian life as a journey of assurance that entailed both spiritual enlightenment and practicing morality:

[Jesus] comes to us as one unknown, without a name, as of old, by the lakeside, he came to those men who did not know who he was. He says the same words, "Follow me!", and sets us to those tasks which he must fulfill in our time. He commands. And to those who hearken to him, whether wise or unwise, he will reveal himself in the peace, the labors, the conflicts, and the suffering that they may experience in his fellowship, and as an ineffable mystery they will learn in who he is. . . .[6]

ELEVEN

Devotion: The Quest for Light

Medieval people knew where God was—the Father sat on the high throne of heaven, was mysteriously present in the bread and wine of the Eucharist, and was manifested through the authority of the church. They took literally the words of Jesus's prayer, "Our Father, who art in heaven." As the Reformation fractured this traditional arrangement, God appeared to move away from familiar spiritual geography, leaving modern people to relocate the divine. Modernity opened the terrifying possibility that God was not reliably present—and that God may even be absent. Was God really in heaven, as generations of Christians had recited in their prayers? Although modern Christians struggled with many questions, an overarching one was achingly simple: "Where is God?"[1]

Since God could no longer be assumed, modern devotional quests sought to answer this question and find God. In order to find God people had to determine what the divine might look like. Despite the fact that early modern people gloried in human capacities and experience, they somehow found God to be more ineffable and less physical than had medieval Christians. As evident in art, medieval painters often depicted God in graphically mundane ways; modern artists rendered the divine as more elusive, often as diffused light.

Although from Hebrew scripture onward God had often been described as light, light became a primary descriptor for divine things in the early modern period. Historian George Marsden points out that light was a dominant theme in "the preaching and philosophizing" of the seventeenth and eighteenth centuries.[2] To modern people light acted as more than a metaphor. Light was an actual property that mimicked divinity. It could be scientifically studied, thus providing the possibility of rational data to assure them of God's existence and presence.

Perhaps no modern Christian handled the theme of light more deftly than Jonathan Edwards (1703–1754), the New England theologian. In his sermon *A Divine and Supernatural Light* (1734), Edwards explored the question "Where is God?" According to Edwards, God constantly emanated love as a kind of "divine light" shed over the universe.[3] The light of God's beauty is everywhere, at every moment, throughout nature. However, human beings lack the capacity to see the light until God instills in them the Holy Spirit, who gives believers "a new spiritual sense" to "apprehend the things of God." Thus the "spiritually enlightened" person does not "merely rationally believe that God is glorious, but he has a sense of the gloriousness of God in his heart."[4] When a Christian sees the light (as it were), he or she experiences this "sweet and joyful" knowledge of God that transforms one's life and provides evidence of God's being in all things.

In a rigorously democratic way, Edwards did not believe that the apprehending light was limited to the learned, mystics, or saints. Indeed, God's light was accessible to all—or at least to those who had eyes to see. And across Western Christianity, in the midst of change and turmoil, people strained to glimpse the light wherever it could be seen.

Inner Light

For several decades now the question "Where is God?" has been felt acutely. Since the 1960s North American and European Christianity has been in a seeking mode, as vast numbers of people have become spiritually unmoored, moving from one religious option to another. I have one friend who has embraced nine or ten different spiritual options, only to conclude that what mattered was "experiencing the light within." Thinking her search unique, she did not know that her realization resembled that of the seventeenth-century English Quakers, who after breaking with tradition discovered the same.

George Fox (1624–1691) was a cobbler, a man of humble devotion. In 1643, when England was in social and religious upheaval during their Civil War, a youthful Fox abandoned family and job and embarked on a spiritual quest to find a more meaningful life. God appeared to him in a dream (perhaps the result of a drunken revel) and said, "You see how young people associate in vanity, and old people into the things of the world; but you must forsake all, young and old, keep out of all, and be as a stranger to all."[5]

Fox wandered from one religion to another, seeking answers to his questions about theology and church order. In his day, there were two primary religious options: Anglicanism and Calvinism. To him, both faiths seemed to distance God in outward rituals. No one could assuage his doubts. "And when all my hopes in them [that is, preachers] and in men were gone, so that I had nothing outwardly to help me, nor could I tell what to do; then, oh then, I heard a voice which said, 'There is one, even Jesus Christ, that can speak to thy condition,' and when I heard it my heart did leap for joy."[6]

Fox testified to having a direct experience of Christ separate from the institutions of the church, claiming, "This I knew experientially." Fox saw that others needed to be likewise enlightened: "Christ, the great heavenly prophet, the true Light coming into the world that illumines every person; that they might believe in it and become the children of light, and so have the light of life, and not come into condemnation."[7]

As Fox shared his experience, he gathered followers who became known as the Society of Friends, also called Quakers. The doctrine of the Inner Light formed the heart of their community:

> That there is an evangelical and saving light and grace in all, the universality of the love and mercy of God towards mankind—both in the death of his beloved Son, the Lord Jesus Christ, and in the manifestation of the light in the heart—is established and confirmed against the objections of those who deny it.[8]

Fox's aimless wandering ceased as he called his friends away from established churches and, as he described it, "I directed the people to their Inward Teacher, Christ Jesus, who would turn them from darkness to the light."[9]

The doctrine of the Inner Light may not seem terribly radical today, but in the seventeenth century it was a revolutionary idea that upended the traditional order of society. Most Christians—Protestants and Catholics alike—believed that God's presence was mediated through hierarchical institutions, theology, and the written word. But Quakers argued that everyone had access to God within by virtue of the Inner Light, thus leveling the ancient structure of the church. The implications of this belief manifested themselves most dramatically in the lives of Quaker women, who quickly moved into leadership in the new movement.

Elizabeth Hooton (1600–1672) was one of Fox's first acquaintances to embrace the Inner Light (although some speculate that theirs may have been a mutual conversion). Like Fox, Hooton felt called to preach the new doctrine of the Friends. Traditionally the Christian ministry was reserved for men, and women preachers were not common.[10] But the Friends believed that the Inner Light came to all people regardless of gender. To them, women and men were equally enlightened by Christ—that the "Spirit is poured upon all Flesh, both Sons and Daughters."[11] Thus Elizabeth Hooton, well into middle age, left her family and "became the first person in England to preach the doctrines of George Fox the Quaker."[12]

Hooton claimed the authority of God on her ministry, railing against both the traditional clergy and civil magistrates. Having found the light, Hooton, like other early Friends, embarked on a spiritual quest to bring others to the truth. In three different English cities in only four years she was arrested as a disturber of the peace. Not content to preach only in England, in 1662 she journeyed to the New World. There she preached on the Inner Light, only to have authorities in Massachusetts and Rhode Island arrest, whip, and abandon her in the wilderness. She made her way back to England but returned to the New World on two successive trips, with similar results. Undeterred, Hooton joined a group of Quaker missionaries and sailed for Jamaica, where she died at age seventy-two. Of her Fox wrote, "Elizabeth Hooton, a woman of great age, who had traveled much in Truth's service, and suffered much for it, departed this life. She was well the day before she died, and departed in peace, like a lamb."

An oddly modern twist in the Quakers' quest: they were willing to travel to the ends of the earth to help people discover the Inner Light, yet that light resided within.

Where is God? The Quakers responded, look within.

Light of Learning

It is striking how many college seals are designed with pictures of lamps, candles, stars, and the rays of the sun. Such depictions, of course, equate light with knowledge. An educated person is an enlightened person. From a Christian perspective, the symbolism is rich. For light is more than factual knowledge. Indeed, Christ is understood to be the Light of the World, the source of both spiritual and intellectual enlightenment. Learning and faith were intertwined, the two paths seen as one.

But the double journey of knowledge generally had been reserved for male clerics, philosophers, and lawyers. Through much of history, few women could read. During the Reformation that began to change as a powerful reorientation toward the written word swept through Europe. God's light, it appeared, could be found in books. Laymen, and eventually laywomen, learned to read. The new learning was not only a Protestant phenomenon; Roman Catholics too embarked on the modern quest to find God through learning—something that had often been resisted by the church in the Middle Ages. In modernity Protestants and Catholics approached learning differently. Protestants tended to read the Bible so that they might understand the world; Catholics reversed this, seeking to learn about the world in order to understand the Bible.

Inés Ramirez de Asbaje y Santillana (1651–1695) was born on a ranch southeast of Mexico City. She was most likely illegitimate and was raised by her grandparents. As a young girl, she displayed a precocious intellect and learned to read before she was six. Her grandfather owned a substantial library—and Inés had to be physically restrained to keep her away from his books. Because of her obvious talent, she was sent to Mexico City to live at the viceroy's court. Her family wished her to marry well, but Inés embraced celibacy and scholarship instead. "Given the total antipathy I felt toward marriage," she wrote, "I deemed convent life the least unsuitable and most honorable I could elect. . . . Such as wanting to live alone, and wishing to have no obligatory occupation to inhibit the freedom of my studies."[13] She entered a convent and took the name Juana Inés de la Cruz.

The convent was not particularly rigorous. There Juana could pursue her interests. She wrote poetry, carols, and plays, studied science and philosophy, and read and collected thousands of books in Latin, Spanish, and Portuguese. Juana gained fame for her intellect, was christened the "Tenth Muse" of New Spain, and held court at the convent with nobles, political leaders, and intellectuals, many of whom corresponded with her on a regular basis. The new viceroy and his wife (to whom Juana would write erotic love poetry) befriended her and acted as her patrons.

Sometime in the 1680s Juana wrote *El Sueño* (The Dream), a poem extolling the soul's desire for knowledge. Composed for her own pleasure, the poem described learning as a fearsome quest wherein "reason ignobly flees from confrontation" and "comprehension turns away, dismayed whole, dreading failure, acumen evades the daunting challenge." Despite such intimidation, Juana went on to say that "it seemed fainthearted meekly to yield the laurel wreath before the battle started." So she persevered to find the light that infused the world:

> . . . while our Hemisphere was inundated
> by a flood of gold that radiated
> from a solar aureole that impartially restored
> color to all things visible, and
> gradually,
> reactivated the external
> senses, an affirmation that left
> the World illuminated, and me awake.[14]

The poem is compelling, the testimony of a nun, a Mexican woman finding intellectual enlightenment. In a very real sense, throughout her work the light has passed from the institutions of the Old World to the peoples and geography of the

New. And, interestingly enough, the light was not particularly supernatural or mystical. Rather, it was found in her immediate experience of nature through human senses. In making this move, Juana shifted the Catholic emphasis on learning from the illuminating word to "the world illuminated."

All of this worried church authorities, who feared both her political influence and her powerful intellect. Her first confessor determined that her poetry was too secular and ordered her to stop writing. She dismissed him. Trying to control her, the bishop published one of her private letters—it criticized a priest's sermon—and called upon her to cease her studies and embrace the more feminine vocation of silent prayer.

Juana responded vigorously, claiming that her studies were her attempt to understand "the eminence of sacred theology," the discipline that Catholics considered to be the "queen" of the sciences.[15] Defending her scholarly pursuits, she asked, "How can one who has not mastered the style of the ancillary branches of learning hope to understand that of the queen of them all?" To Juana rhetoric, physics, music, mathematics, architecture, law, history, and astronomy all figured in Holy Scripture, and without knowledge of each of these fields, the Bible could not be properly understood. "In sum," she argued back to the bishop, "how to understand the book which takes in all books, and the knowledge which embraces all types of knowledge, to the understanding of which they all contribute?"[16] Studying was a religious vocation. The church did not protest that point. They disliked both her method and the fact that a woman employed it. Juana's approach was from the bottom up: secular learning led to holy understanding, not the other way around. "Continuing prayer and purity of life" must complement mastery of the natural world, but only a combination of the two led to the "illumination of the mind" that amounted to wisdom.

In a bold move Juana accused the bishop of persecuting her for her "love of learning and letters." The quarrel lasted five years. The church opened an investigation into her conduct. In 1694 she appears to have been forced to sign documents of contrition, give away her library, and abandon scholarship. She died a year later. Although the church treated her unjustly, the modernist impulse to find God through studying human sciences would expand in Catholic thought and piety. Modern Catholic education would in many cases be more open to new knowledge in the arts and sciences than some forms of Protestantism.

Where is God? Pick up a book—any book—and read.

New Light

When my preschool daughter asked me, "Mama, where is God?" I answered, "Honey, God lives in your heart." Inwardly I chuckled at my own answer. Although I have been an Episcopalian for many years, I responded straight from my childhood Methodism, an answer based on John Wesley's insight that Christ resides in the hearts of those who have been renewed through the waters of baptism and an experience of one's heart being "strangely warmed."

The Quakers and the Methodists did not arrive at the exact same answer to the question of "Where is God?" George Fox insisted that everyone possessed an innate Inner Light, God dwelling within, and salvation was a matter of seeing that light. The Methodists, in contrast, believed that people were innately sinful and needed God to imbue them with light through an experiential encounter with Christ.

John Wesley (1703–1791) was a Church of England minister who founded the spiritual movement that eventually became the Methodist Church. As a university student, he practiced a spiritually disciplined way of life, and he eventually chose to become a missionary priest to Georgia. The mission was not successful; indeed, disgruntled parishioners sent him packing after he tried to seduce a young woman whose family filed legal charges against him. He returned to London and, doubting both his faith and his future, confessedly suffered from "indifference, dullness, and coldness and unusually frequent relapses into sin," Wesley began to search for a renewed sense of God.[17] Some Moravian Christians, part of a spiritual community that emphasized heartfelt religious experience, befriended Wesley. On May 24, 1738, he had a particularly powerful experience of God's presence during one of their meetings:

> In the evening I went very unwillingly to a society in Aldersgate Street, where one was reading Luther's preface to the Epistle to the Romans. About a quarter before nine, while he was describing the change which God works in the heart through faith in Christ, I felt my heart strangely warmed. I felt I did trust in Christ, Christ alone, for salvation; and an assurance was given me that He had taken away my sins, even mine, and saved me from the law of sin and death.[18]

Unlike the Quakers, who found light within, John Wesley encountered light as external to everyday experience. That light changed his sinful nature by renewing his heart.

Wesley's spiritual insight was not singular. In both England and the American colonies, preachers like Howell Harris,

Jonathan Edwards, and George Whitefield reported similar movements of God's spirit. In the 1730s and 1740s, many thousands of people on both sides of the Atlantic were caught up in a movement known as the Evangelical Revival or the Great Awakening, whereby they, like Wesley, newly experienced the light shed upon their hearts. These eighteenth-century people encountered light that went beyond reason; it was an intuitive apprehension of divine things, an experience of the light of biblical revelation in the heart. Struggling to explain it, they called their encounter the "new birth" and referred to their congregations as "New Light" churches.

The Methodists quickly discovered, however, that this evangelical light could be ephemeral. Since spiritual light was not intrinsic to human beings, it had to be sought as a series of unfolding experiences. Thus the new birth saved a believer from sin, and God's light also led to a life of deeper holiness. American Methodist preacher Jerena Lee (1783–1850), an African American woman from Philadelphia, recorded her experience after conversion: "Now there seemed to be a new struggle commencing in my soul, not accompanied with fear, guilt, and bitter distress, as while under my first conviction for sin; but a laboring of the mind to know more of the right way of the Lord. I began to feel that my heart was not clean in his sight."

Methodists refer to this spiritual process as sanctification, or growing in a life of holiness. For them, encountering the light accomplished two things: first, it renewed the heart; and second, it created awareness of needing to live in continual light. Lee explained, "By the increasing light of the Spirit, I found there yet remained the root of pride, anger, self-will, and many evils." She asked Christ to sanctify her—make her holy—and "that very instant, as if lightning had darted through me . . . a new rush of the same ecstasy came upon me, and caused me to feel as if I were in an ocean of light and bliss."[19]

Like Wesley and a host of early evangelicals, a spiritually enlightened Jerena Lee felt called to preach. She approached her pastor to share this desire, and he told her that the order of the church "did not call for women preachers." But the impulse remained—even through an unhappy marriage—until "it was as a fire shut up in my bones."[20] Eventually church leaders confirmed her calling and Lee became a Methodist preacher with her own congregation and led a successful ministry of healing, forgiveness, and evangelism, mostly in her hometown of Cape May, New Jersey.

Although it is very difficult for contemporary Christians to grasp it, Lee's story is not atypical of eighteenth-century evangelical religion. Early evangelicalism, with its insistence on a life transformed by the blinding light of God, undermined "the perpetuation of a hierarchical social system" maintained in most Protestant churches. The original experience of new birth resulted in "dissatisfaction with authority," which created an alternative community of equality between men and women, black and white, slave and free.[21] In the American context evangelicals equated spiritual light with the light of liberty—an idea that would have dazzling political consequences in both the Revolutionary War and the subsequent struggle over slavery.[22]

Where is God? The evangelicals answered, in the transformed heart of those born again.

Enlightenment

About a dozen years ago the local Unitarian society asked me to preach for their congregation, which met in a beautiful and historic building. Never having visited a Unitarian church before, I arrived early that Sunday morning to check out the arrangements. As I looked about, one stained-glass window—clearly the most extravagant and prominent in the building—surprised me. It depicted Thomas Jefferson.

America's third president, a figure more often associated with politics and philosophy than faith, is not a common subject of religious windows. Preaching was a little intimidating with Mr. Jefferson's stained-glass gaze so firmly fixed behind me. People do not usually consider Jefferson a figure of much importance in church history. But the Unitarian Society's window invites us to understand President Jefferson's role in Christian spirituality. Depicting Jefferson in stained glass is oddly, and perhaps ironically, appropriate. For he, like other early modern people, engaged in the search for light, a desire to be enlightened. For Jefferson, however, light would be divine and yet not—in any way—supernatural. Light is the light of reason, like the natural light of the sun streaming through a window.

Although in his own day Jefferson's opponents called him an infidel, he ranks with two other American presidents—Abraham Lincoln and Jimmy Carter—as our most thoughtful presidential theologians. Historian Martin Marty cites him as a "reverent" and "respectful" thinker who represents the religious impulse of the Anglo-American Enlightenment and who believed that "religion was a major grounding for, or instrument of, virtue and morality."[23]

Unlike Jonathan Edwards, whose vision depended on a powerful sense of a supernatural God, Jefferson's vision of God derived from nature and was revealed through reason and ethics. Jefferson's own faith changed through his life. As a young man he shared the growing European opinion that Christianity was both absurd and corrupt, having seen the conflict and violence wrought by religious wars in the Middle Ages and following the Reformation. Indeed, Jefferson displayed a collection of gory religious artwork at his home—paintings intended to remind his guests of the unsavory consequences of religious excess. Jefferson believed religious extremism had led "millions of innocent men, women, and children to be burnt, tortured, fined, [and] imprisoned," thus making "one half the world fools, and the other half hypocrites."[24]

To Jefferson, the evidence of history proved that Christianity was not rational and that religions needed to be judged by reason. "Fix reason firmly in her seat," he wrote to a young friend, "and call to her tribunal every fact, every opinion."[25] On the basis of this test Jefferson believed Roman Catholicism to be superstition and harshly criticized Calvinism, a religion that he considered a form of "Daemonism."[26] Instead of trusting faith alone—"blindfolded fear"—Jefferson advised, "Your own reason is the only oracle given you by heaven."[27]

Despite this unflinching criticism, Jefferson did not reject Christianity outright. Instead, he embarked on a journey to discover the primitive purity of Christianity, hoping to reform the faith. "The Christian religion," he wrote, "when divested of the rags in which the clergy have enveloped it, is a religion of all others most friendly to liberty, science and the freest expansion of the human mind." Thus Jefferson tried to strip away all the irrational bits of faith—the doctrine of the Trinity, Jesus's divinity, and the miracles—and retained only those parts that withstood the light of reason. "To the corruptions of Christianity, I am indeed opposed," he confided to a friend, "but not to the genuine precepts of Jesus himself." Those "precepts" were, according to Jefferson, enlightened, as they instilled "universal philanthropy, not only to kindred and friend, to neighbors and countrymen, but to all mankind, gathering all into one family, under bonds of love, charity, peace, common wants, and common aids."[28]

Jefferson considered Jesus a great moral teacher, a "benevolent and sublime reformer," whose life exemplified the principles whereby humanity would be improved through the spread of Christian charity. By enlarging the sphere of benevolence, Jefferson argued that republican government would flourish and social harmony—a kind of reasonable Christian utopia—would result. Jefferson crafted a vision of Christianity that was rational, natural, and orderly. He believed the goals of true religion and politics were the same: human prosperity and happiness through Jesus's universal law of love.[29]

Contemporary philosopher Charles Taylor describes the theological vision of eighteenth-century men and women like Jefferson as "providential deism." They understood Christianity through four important and interrelated ideas: (1) that human happiness is religion's primary purpose; (2) that God's will is clearly visible through reason; (3) that mystery should be replaced by the design of nature, and (4) that human beings have no need of a spiritual transformation beyond the bounds of our natural condition; indeed, everything needed to aid human happiness exists within the laws of nature. In this view

God created the order of the universe so we may discover morality and goodness through the light of Reason.[30]

There were, of course, more radical renderings of reason—writers like Tom Paine and David Hume who, unlike Jefferson, completely rejected both Christianity and theism. Taylor makes a convincing case that eventually Jefferson's softer form of providential deism became widespread—closely tied to enlightenment ideals of freedom, liberty, and benevolence. Without reason, faith devolved into mere superstition, something feared by many eighteenth-century people. The light of reason, a divine but natural capacity, acted as the engine that drove vast cultural change, spreading this vision of religion to people well beyond Jefferson's elite intellectual circles. Writing of his student days at Yale around 1800, Presbyterian minister Lyman Beecher lamented that only five students belonged to the college church in New Haven: "That was the day of the infidelity of the Tom Paine school. Boys that dressed flax in the barn, as I used to, read him and believed him."[31] In the early Republic, deism was a populist faith.

Where is God? The deists answered, in a life of reason and good works.

Nature's Light

Like many baby boomers, Richard left church in college. He had grown up as a Presbyterian in the 1950s and '60s, and his familial faith was a rationalist sort, not entirely different from the reasonable religion suggested by Thomas Jefferson. He found church uninspiring, spiritually cold, and not in any way transcendent. Presbyterian minister Graham Standish describes that kind of Protestantism as "rational functionalism," which he calls a "disease" whereby church leaders "subscribe to a view of faith and church rooted in a restrictive, logic-bound theology that ignores the possibility of spiritual experiences." It is, according to Standish, "an excessively rational, empirical, quasi-scientific approach."[32]

Richard returned to church some twenty years after he left. In the meanwhile, however, he spiritually migrated toward the American Transcendentalists, a group of early nineteenth-century writers, philosophers, and social activists who emphasized sentiment, intuition, and mysticism in religious knowledge over pure reason. They believed that God, or the Spirit, resided in a dynamic encounter between the self and nature.

It is not entirely surprising that Richard could relate to the transcendentalists. They too grew up with rational religion and found their ancestral faith "corpse cold."[33] In 1836 a small group of Unitarian ministers from Boston met to discuss the moribund state of their church and what they sensed to be "a promise of a new era in intellectual life."[34] They formed the Transcendental Club, comprised of both men and women who sought to reform American religious life on the basis of a new Romantic philosophy from Europe. No single doctrine bound them; rather, they represented an open-ended spirit of the day, completely tolerant seekers, all looking for new ways of understanding the self and God. "The novel ideas then beginning to circulate," comments historian Philip Gura, "began to move American liberal religion in wholly new directions."[35] That new direction was away from "the frigid utilitarianism of the last century," wrote transcendentalist Orestes Brownson, toward a future church "more fervent, living, and soul-kindling," a vision of faith that would unify "Spirit and Matter."[36]

In 1836 Ralph Waldo Emerson (1803–1882) published an essay titled "Nature," positing the idea that human beings could discover God in unity with nature. Since the eighteenth century Christians thought God could be found by observing nature, its orderliness and harmonies. To Christians like Jefferson, Nature (with a capital *N*) revealed a rational Creator. But Emerson rejected this idea, suggesting instead that nature was beyond rational comprehension. Nature is the "Not-Me," the mystery that lies beyond ordinary human experience.

For Emerson, God could only be experienced when a person, "Me," merged with the "Not-Me." Writing of a walk in the woods, Emerson said,

> Standing on the bare ground,—my head bathed by the blithe air, and uplifted into infinite space,—all mean egotism vanishes. I become a transparent eye-ball; I am nothing; I see all; the currents of the Universal Being circulate through me; I am part or particle of God. The name of the nearest friend sounds then foreign and accidental: to be brothers, to be acquaintances,—master or servant, is then a trifle and a disturbance. I am the lover of uncontained and immortal beauty.

Only through nature does this fundamental unity—the wholeness of divinity and humanity—emerge. "I am not alone and unacknowledged," wrote Emerson. "They nod to me, and I to them. The waving of the boughs in the storm, is new to me and old. It takes me by surprise, and yet is not unknown." He insists that nature alone cannot inculcate this experience, nor can human beings accomplish it without nature: "Yet it is certain that the power to produce this delight, does not reside in nature, but in man, or in a harmony of both."[37] The Me and Not-Me are united. God is everywhere.

For their part, the transcendentalists thought that the Enlightenment had overplayed science and reason, leaving no room for the "poetic use of nature." Drawing from European scholarship, they believed that the early church had based faith on "an imaginative understanding of the natural world," and they sought to restore the sensibilities of early Christianity. The first Christians, wrote one transcendentalist, "had not learned to write their poetry," but they "had lived it." They argued, therefore, for a return to "the influence of feeling" in vital Christianity.[38] As a result, they did not reject reason as unimportant, but they tried to relocate it in relationship to the spiritual or intuitive faculties, what they called the "understanding," of individual human beings.

Most of the transcendentalists were not pastors or professors; they were anything but ivory-tower intellectuals. Instead, they were poets, novelists, social activists, and popular writers who used the media of the day to spread their ideas. They published short pieces in newspapers, novels, poetry, book reviews, lectures, and intellectual articles. And they spoke in one of the most important public venues of the day: the lyceum. In early America most towns established lyceums, buildings where public events and entertainments were held to benefit adult education. In many ways lyceums constituted a nineteenth-century version of the Internet, a connected, grassroots community of free-flowing opinion. Transcendentalists (especially Emerson) regularly spoke on the "lyceum circuit" across the country, with newspaper reporters in every town duly covering their lectures, thereby creating a large following that "shaped the popular mentality" of nineteenth-century American religion.[39]

Where is God? The transcendentalists answered, in the subjective unity of the self and nature.

Light Everywhere

A popular contemporary answer to the question "Where is God?" is that God is found in all denominations and all religions, a kind of universal light shining through the varieties of faith. Critics often treat this answer with contempt, depicting it as "cafeteria Christianity," with uneducated masses simply picking and choosing what they like from a variety of faiths to construct a truth that fits their own longings. To me, this answer is less a matter of sloppy thinking and more often a response to the problem of religious diversity. How can it be that so many different religions claim to be true? And how can human beings, limited as we are, commit to any one form of faith?

As was the case for so many modern Christians, "religious oppositions" that resulted in "repugnant" division repulsed Congregationalist minister Horace Bushnell (1802–1876). To him, Christian disagreement and sectarianism obscured the light of God's love. In 1848 he addressed the problem of religious pluralism in an essay titled "Christian Comprehensiveness." While many of his colleagues were busy trying to prove that only their denomination was true, Bushnell argued the opposite point: that religious diversity does not undermine truth; rather, diversity can be seen as the pathway toward "a more complete and perfect whole."[40]

Throughout the essay Bushnell contends that all forms of Christian faith contain partial truths that need to be seen as equally true. He does not argue for a kind of mushy middle, whereby people develop some mediating ground between extremes. Rather, Bushnell calls for true universalism, or *catholicism* with a small *c*. "There rises up now a man, or a few men," Bushnell writes, "who looking again at the two extreme schools, begin to ask whether it is not possible to comprehend them—that is to receive, hold, practice all which made the extreme opinions true to their disciples?" This kind of truth "ascends, as it were, to a higher position," since it "is in fact a disciple of the extremes, taking lessons of both" and thus creates a new sort of "radical agreement." Bushnell believed that "embracing the opposite" would reveal wisdom and holiness through faith-filled unity.[41]

At a time when most American Protestants were vigorously anti–Roman Catholic, Bushnell extended his comprehensive vision to the argument between Protestants and Catholics. Protestantism had suffered, Bushnell suggested, by being cut off from history; Catholicism had suffered, he believed, because it lacked a positive view of the future. By connecting "the Christian future with the Christian past," Bushnell speculated that a new, broader, more organic catholic Christianity, the church of the future, would emerge.[42]

In this process Bushnell believed the light of truth would be revealed. "We simply require it of all Christians to look for the truth," he wrote, "and the truth only."

> And if we require them to look beyond themselves and across their own boundaries, we see not that there is any thing specifically frightful in this, if they look for nothing but the truth. Or if we prepare a previous conviction, in their minds, that there is somewhat of truth in all Christian bodies, does any one doubt that there is? . . . We recognize, the great principle that truth is a whole and is to be sought only as a whole—anywhere, everywhere, and by all means.[43]

As a nineteenth-century theologian, Bushnell wrote specifically about Christian division, trying to comprehend the variety of Christian sects and theologies. However, it is not difficult to extend his vision to contemporary tensions between different religions. He depicted universal truth as harmony—whereby all forms of Christianity are "strung together" as bells in concert, "every bell must have a tongue and a voice of its own" for "there is yet some element of truth, something which makes it true to its disciples." In "embracing and comprehending all . . . Christian souls will ring in peals of harmony, as a chime that is voiced by the truth."[44] To Bushnell, right harmony—not right opinion—sounded God's truth.

Where is God? The light, answered early Protestant liberals, can be found in comprehending the harmonies of the whole.

Light, Maybe

In late summer 2007 *Time* magazine reported on Mother Teresa's "crisis of faith." Commenting on a then-new book, journalist David Van Biema wrote that contrary to the spirituality portrayed in public, Mother Teresa's private spiritual life was "an arid landscape from which the deity had disappeared." For nearly fifty years the great contemporary religious leader felt nothing but God's absence. "As for me," she wrote to a friend, "the silence and the emptiness is so great that I look and do not see, listen and do not hear."[45] It turns out that one of the world's most revered spiritual figures lived a life of doubt.

While doubt has a long history in Western society, modernity has proved especially amenable to the erosion of religious certainty. Persecution and wars of religion branded Christians guilty of "cruelty and intolerance," and new developments in philosophy and science opened the genuine possibility that God did not exist.[46] Although these changes enabled many people to opt out of Christianity, others tried to in some way interweave faith and doubt.

Emily Dickinson (1830–1886), the American poet, grew up in revivalist New England, where she several times flirted with her peers' evangelical religion. Ultimately, however, she refused to confess the evangelical faith, ceased attending church, and accepted the language of doubt as the primary language for God. She expressed her experience as "A loss of something ever felt I— / The first that I could recollect / Bereft I was—of what I knew not." Dickinson's biographer, Roger Lundin, writes of this as her encounter with modernity, the experience of "disenchantment" that would "become an intellectual commonplace and a widespread cultural phenomenon in the twentieth century."[47] Thus, a full century before many people experienced the same, Emily Dickinson had already anticipated that doubt and faith exist in a paradoxical relationship.

In her book *Doubt: A History* Jennifer Hecht calls Dickinson "the Cheshire Cat" of doubt, who welcomed ambiguity "playfully" and depicted an unsettled version of Christianity that "doubts as fervently as it believes" (poem #1144).[48] Dickinson certainly rejected traditional religion, favoring instead humility in relation to an ultimately unknowable and discomforting mystery—and maelstrom—of God. In many ways Dickinson's poetry was her religion, the artistic realm wherein she explored the range of spirituality from an absent God's "amputated" hand (poem #1551) toward the "rendezvous of light" (#1564).

Throughout the moods of her poetry, however, she remained "eccentrically Trinitarian to the core."[49] She emphasized human and divine suffering in and through Jesus Christ:

Life—is what we make it—
Death—We do not know—
Christ's acquaintance with Him
Justify Him—though—

He—would trust no stranger—
Other—could betray—
Just His own endorsement—
That—sufficeth Me—

All the other Distance
He hath traversed first—

No New Mile remaineth—
Far as Paradise—

His sure foot preceding—
Tender Pioneer—
Base must be the Coward
Dare not venture—now—
(#698)

A vision of Jesus as "tender pioneer" provided Dickinson some access to the absent Father and the comforting Spirit. In her reverence for Jesus's humanity, she showed doubt as a way of spirituality. Even to the doubter, Jesus remained a compelling figure worthy of both imitation and love. For a thoroughly modern thinker, like Dickinson, doubt served as a necessary aspect of the Christian faith and the Christian God. "On subjects of which we know nothing, or should I say *Beings*," she wrote, "we both believe, and disbelieve a hundred times an Hour, which keeps Believing nimble."[50]

Where is God? The doubters answered: Who knows? But that is what makes belief an art.

TWELVE

Ethics: Kingdom Quest

One of the major differences between modern Christianity and earlier forms of faith emerged in ethics. Through much of Christian history ethics amounted to charity, spiritual practices of aiding the distressed or alleviating the suffering of the poor. Only rarely did it occur to Christians that they might be able to change the actual conditions that created poverty, violence, and oppression. Christians typically accepted social structures as part of the divine order. Thus Christian ethics tended to acquiesce to the circumstances in which human beings found themselves, preferring instead to bandage those most harmed by poverty, illness, and war. Ethics was doing good works toward one's neighbors.

During modernity, however, this changed. As Walter Rauschenbusch wrote in 1907, "All the teaching of Jesus and all his thinking centered about the hope of the kingdom of God. His moral teachings get their real meaning only when viewed from that center." Christians came to understand that the social order was not necessarily divine—that it was riddled with sin—and that they could fix earthly structures to more fully resemble God's desire for humanity to "live rightly with their fellow-men and to constitute a true social life."[1]

The kingdom is a powerful metaphor in Christian history, going back to Jesus's own preaching: "Repent, the kingdom of heaven is at hand." For many centuries, however, Christians understood the kingdom as heaven—the place you go to after you die. Thus the kingdom was fundamentally unapproachable, as distant as an earthly throne room was to a peasant. In the modern period, however, as God's location moved, so did that of the kingdom. God's realm drew ever closer, and the kingdom seemed to be "at hand." Christians developed an intense interest in Christ's second coming, and many believed that the Lord's return was nigh. In the nineteenth century they developed a plethora of kingdom theologies, speculating on everything from the idea of the rapture (an event in which Jesus would take the faithful away from the war-convulsed earth before the kingdom arrived) to building God's kingdom through the social order. However they interpreted it, modern Christians took Jesus's prayer "Thy Kingdom Come" and made it their own work. They might not have known entirely where God was, but they increasingly believed that God's realm was with them.

Tolerance

In 1996 I covered the Republican National Convention on behalf of the *New York Times* regional newspapers. As a religion writer, I attended a variety of events featuring leaders from the Religious Right. Walking toward one gathering, that of the controversial antiabortion group Operation Rescue, I noticed a person proudly wearing a T-shirt bearing the phrase Intolerance Is a Beautiful Thing on the front. When he turned around, the shirt boasted a litany of intolerant Christians: Jesus was Intolerant of Pharisees, St. Paul was Intolerant of Homosexuals, Mother Teresa was Intolerant of Abortion, and so forth. As an Episcopalian, I found this bizarrely impolite if not theologically shocking. My secular colleagues thought it par for the course.

Ever since Christianity became the majority religion in Europe, the church found toleration a difficult virtue to practice. Indeed, well through the Reformation, some decided that toleration ranked as heresy and that the irenic were "mortal enemies of the Christian religion" subject to punishment.[2] In 1560 a Parisian crowd attacked one Robert Delors when he pleaded for empathy on behalf of a Protestant facing public execution. For his trouble, Delors was arrested by Catholic authorities and executed on charges of blasphemy.[3] And, of course, Delors was not the only one. For 150 years following the Reformation, when Christian diversity broke forth in new and unexpected ways, the blood of Protestants and Catholics flowed in the streets of Europe as everyone tried to kill everyone else in the name of Jesus, theological purity, and the one true church.

As a historian, I do not think that Christian failures regarding toleration (necessarily) arose from some moral flaw in Christians themselves. Rather, I suspect that intolerance was largely a function of historical circumstance. As one Dutch historian writes, "To those who lived through Europe's reformations, the idea that Christians might forevermore be divided by faith was unimaginable." He continues,

> After all, from their perspective, the unity of Western Christendom had been a basic principle and continuous fact for more than a millennium. Its shattering seemed nothing short of catastrophic. "Tis all in pieces, all coherence gone," wrote John Donne, lamenting the collapse of an ancient, comforting cosmology. . . . Nothing, not even the discovery of the Americas or the moons around Jupiter, caused Europeans more profound shock than their new religious divisions.[4]

However difficult they found these new realities, Western Christians were forced to adjust to them throughout modernity. They had to come to terms, first, with Christian diversity; second, with Christian-Jewish-Muslim (or "Abrahamic") diversity; and third, with the diversity of Eastern and new religions—processes of adjustment that are ongoing today.

During the early modern period several strategies developed to deal with religious diversity: creating a comprehensive national church (such as the Church of England), making a distinction between public and private practices of faith (such as "secret" Catholic churches in the Protestant Netherlands), or allowing safe passage for adherents to move between Catholic and Protestant towns for worship (as in Austria).[5]

No doubt one of the most imaginative renderings of toleration in early modern Europe is the Church of St. Martin's in Biberach, Germany. There, in 1548, Protestant and Catholic townspeople created a *Simultankirche*, a "simultaneous church." The church has two naves, a Lutheran one and a Catholic one. From one direction the church appears Protestant in its depiction of biblical scenes and the life of Jesus; from the other it appears Roman Catholic, decorated with its panoply of church fathers, saints, popes, and the Virgin Mary.[6] The arrangement originally developed because the Catholic emperor lacked the military resources to rid the town of its Lutherans; he had already stretched the army thin fighting other religious battles. Thus, for the absence of imperial troops, Biberach emerged as a biconfessional city.

In 1649 city fathers worked out a schedule of services for the church: Catholics used the building from 5:00 to 6:00 a.m., Lutherans from 6:00 to 8:00, Catholics again from 8:00 to 11:00, Lutherans back from 11:00 to 12:00, and Catholics holding their last Sunday service from 12:00 to 1:00. The same church bells called both communities to worship. Unlike other cities in Europe, Protestant and Catholic neighbors passed one another in the church doors on the way to their sacred services. "Thus," writes historian Benjamin Kaplan, "were Protestant and Catholic Biberachers required to share a building charged with symbolism. . . . It required opponents to face one another, acknowledge publicly one another's existence, share resources, and cooperate." Regular people learned the art of accepting differences—skills they translated into the political arena regarding issues of citizenship, intermarriage, and inheritance. They learned to let "God's house be used by God's enemies," eventually finding their way to peaceful coexistence and outright toleration.[7]

From such modest and difficult circumstances, modern Christians eventually learned that killing one's neighbors was not very, well, Christian. As the modern period unfolded, impulses toward comprehension resulted in a variety of political experiments regarding religious toleration—one thread of which resulted in the American practice of separation of church and state. Although the Operation Rescue brigade may not have gotten the message, most Western Christians agree today that tolerance, not intolerance, is a beautiful thing.

Equality

Several years ago a famous theologian gave a speech attacking modernity. He railed against the failings of the Enlightenment, depicting all Christian theology between 1650 and 1950 as hopelessly wrongheaded and unbiblical. He especially criticized ideals of toleration, equality, and human rights as secular values that had somehow muddled the practice of Christian virtue. In the audience immediately in front of me sat a black colleague, a learned woman I knew only by reputation. She looked increasingly uncomfortable with this man's analysis, until she leaned over to the woman next to her and said in a loud whisper, "I wouldn't be sitting here if it weren't for the Enlightenment."

The woman was, in a sense, correct. Like toleration, the idea of equality was not considered a virtue for much of Christian history. A few verses in the New Testament—like Galatians 3:28, "There is no longer Jew or Greek, there is no longer slave or free, there is no longer male or female; for all of you are one in Christ Jesus"—lay fallow in scripture for many centuries before anyone cared to water the seeds of equality planted in that verse. In the centuries following the Reformation, however, Protestant women started to point out the inconsistency of male pastors proclaiming spiritual liberty from Roman Catholicism yet still condemning women to silence in church. Margaret Fell, an early Quaker preacher, wrote the first full biblical exegesis supporting women's public spiritual leadership in the 1660s. And thereafter, tracts, pamphlets, and books appeared with increasing regularity through modern Christianity arguing for equality between the sexes. During the Enlightenment, Christians interpreted scriptures in new ways that—finally—allowed for social equality and human rights.

Sexual inequality was not, however, the only inequality experienced by Christian people. As modernity unfolded, Western Christianity moved out of its exclusively European context, encountering native peoples in the Americas, Africans in both Africa and at home as slaves, and Asian people on voyages of exploration. Europeans were frankly shocked when some of those they met were already Christian (Roman Catholics maintained tenuous mission endeavors during the Middle Ages; Eastern Orthodox churches had been continuously present in some parts of the world since ancient times), and they realized that those Christians had different cultures and skin colors than their own.[8] Thus modern Christianity displayed contradictory tendencies: some Christians literally invented the concept of race in order to justify oppression of persons of color while at the same time other Christians tried to interpret Jesus's words as the promise of a kingdom of full equality for all peoples.

On September 21, 1832, Maria Stewart (1803–1879) stood before an audience in Boston's Franklin Hall addressing them on the evils of slavery. She was the first woman—ever—to publicly address an abolitionist gathering. And she was an African American.

Stewart was born in Hartford, Connecticut; orphaned at five, she was bound to a clergyman's family where her sole education came from Sabbath schools. She left that family at age fifteen and became a domestic servant. Maria married in 1826, and her husband died only three years later, leaving her without income or property. In the two years following his death, Maria experienced a period of spiritual intensity. "I was," she wrote, "brought to the knowledge of the truth as it is in Jesus in 1830." A year later she made a public profession of her faith.[9] Shortly after this conversion, Maria Stewart heard God's call to her: "'Who shall go forward, and take off the reproach that is cast upon the people of color? Shall it be a woman?'" Maria responded, "If it is thy will, be it even so, Lord Jesus!"[10]

Before launching her public speaking career, Stewart wrote "Religion and the Pure Principles of Morality," an essay that links women's rights with freedom from slavery and argues for equality on the basis of both Christian scripture and Enlightenment principles. Many Christians used the Bible to enforce inequality, often quoting passages such as Ephesians 5 to remind women to "submit to their husbands" and "slaves, obey your masters." Yet Maria Stewart did not find submission and obedience in God's word; rather, God created all men and women—regardless of color or social status—as equal. From her perspective, religious doctrine and political democracy were of a piece. "All nations of the earth are crying out for Liberty and Equality," she stated. "This is the land of freedom. The press is at liberty. Every man has a right to express his opinion." Stewart continued,

> Many think, because your skins are tinged with a sable hue, that you are an inferior race of beings; but God does not consider you such. He hath formed and fashioned you in his own glorious image, and hath bestowed upon you reason and strong powers of intellect. . . . He hath crowned you with glory and honor; hath made you but a little lower than the angels; and according to the Constitution of these United States, he hath made all men free and equal.[11]

For Maria, practicing liberty and equality constituted the "pure principles" of "religion and morality" and serve as the only basis for a just and godly state. "Why then," she asked, "should man any longer deprive his fellow-man of equal rights and privileges?" Citing the spread of democracy around the world, Maria said pointedly, "It is the blood of our fathers, and the tears of our brethren that have enriched your soils. AND WE CLAIM OUR RIGHTS."

Historians have often noted that without the Enlightenment's political categories, it was very difficult to extract ideals of equality and human rights from traditional interpretations of the Bible. But as the modern era unfolded, women and African Americans, not formally schooled in those traditional readings of scripture, often rejected interpretations that denied them full participation in both church and society. When they sensed the call of God to do so, women like Maria Stewart willingly proclaimed a Jesus who would set free the captives of race, gender, and poverty, and she did so on the basis of their experience, the Bible, and Enlightenment political ideals. Since the mid–1700s, this interpretative move had been an impulse in the Christianity of African Americans and some women, but after the American Revolution the tendency to read scripture with an eye toward political liberation both widened and deepened.

Thus, starting in the eighteenth century and for the next two hundred years, some Christians made the case for full equality of all peoples and races on the basis of the Bible and the Constitution. Throughout modernity antislavery leaders like William Lloyd Garrison and Frederick Douglass would pave the way for Martin Luther King Jr. And women's rights activists would argue for equal education, voting rights, and ordination from Abigail Adams and Elizabeth Cady Stanton to Hillary Clinton.

But few grasped the innate connection between the rights of all excluded people as well as did Maria Stewart. She was not completely alone in her calls for inclusion; she was, however, a prophetic voice by virtue of combining the two movements of racial and gender equity into one. As such, she was a pioneer, along with Phillis Wheatley, Sojourner Truth, and Harriet Tubman, in claiming her powerful role as a black woman who proclaimed God's liberty to those most excluded by mainstream society.

Freedom

In her speech to the Democratic National Convention in August 2008, Senator Hillary Clinton invoked Harriet Tubman (ca. 1820–1913) as an example of political fortitude to a wildly cheering crowd:

> If you hear the dogs, keep going. If you see the torches in the woods, keep going. If there's shouting after you, keep going. Don't ever stop. Keep going. If you want a taste of freedom, keep going.[12]

Harriet Tubman probably never said exactly those words, but she was the most famous and successful conductor on the nineteenth-century Underground Railroad.

The Underground Railroad was not a real railroad. Rather, it was an underground resistance movement for freedom from slavery, and it was empowered by a radical version of Christian faith. In the early nineteenth century people from a variety of denominations formed a network of safe houses and churches as an escape route for slaves from the American South to freedom. Along the routes "conductors" provided slaves with guidance, food, and safe passage to Northern free states or Canada.

Harriet Tubman was born into slavery in Dorchester County, Maryland. Although she escaped to Philadelphia in 1849, her family remained slaves in Maryland, and Harriet felt compelled to rescue them. "I was free," she said later, "and they should be free." Fortified by personal experience and by a deep mystical awareness of God's presence, Tubman believed that she should go back to help free others. Warned that her niece Kessiah was to be sold, Tubman covertly returned to Maryland, where she arranged for the young woman to escape. This began Tubman's career as a daring conductor on the railroad, a woman on whose head authorities placed bounties totaling around $40,000. For eleven years she returned again and again to Maryland, personally freeing more than seventy slaves. Each time she risked her own life to help others escape. She claimed that God personally directed her journeys with spiritual premonitions along the way. "I was a conductor of the Underground Railroad," she would later state, "and I can say what most conductors can't say—I never ran my train off the track and I never lost a passenger." People nicknamed her "Moses."

One of the young men whom Tubman freed was Samuel Green Jr., who made it from Maryland to Canada in 1854. Young Green was a slave, the son of a freed slave, Samuel Green (ca. 1802–?), and his wife, Kitty. The elder Green may have been freed because of exemplary character or because a sympathetic owner discerned that Samuel Green had a call to the ministry. Upon leaving slavery, Green became a Methodist lay preacher and licensed exhorter, popular in the black Methodist congregations throughout Dorchester County, in the same area where Tubman was born. Eventually Green was able to purchase his wife from slavery, but not his children. Local people held him in high esteem, "an inoffensive, industrious man; earning his bread by the sweat of his brow . . . without exciting a spirit of ill will in the pro-slavery power of his community." Described as intelligent and literate, Green was viewed by a white pastor as "exceedingly useful" among black Christians, where "in their meeting-houses he preached to them the word of life."[13]

When his son escaped an exceptionally cruel master, however, local Maryland authorities began to suspect that the Reverend Green was involved in the Underground Railroad (a fact that Harriet Tubman confirmed in an 1897 interview). Those suspicions, combined with a trip that the elder Green made to Canada to visit his son, led to Green's arrest on April 4, 1857, on the grounds of "holding correspondence with the North." When the sheriff searched Green's house, he found, among maps to Canada, a copy of *Uncle Tom's Cabin*, the infamous (to Southerners, at least) antislavery book by Harriet Beecher Stowe. Green was brought to trial for both abetting slaves and for owning the "inflammatory" book. The first charge proved difficult to prove, but the second was not. The court found him guilty of possessing an "abolition pamphlet" and committed him to prison for ten years. The local paper, the *Easton Gazette*, reported that "Green was convicted simply and solely for having 'Uncle Tom's Cabin' in his possession." The proslavery paper then laid blame for Green's plight on the abolitionists, whose books stirred "happily contented slaves toward the troubles of freedom."[14]

Because of the danger involved, Samuel Green left little in the way of written records. Despite the fact that he could both read and write, no evidence of his involvement in the Underground Railroad remains. However, it is not hard to imagine the threat posed to the slaveholding community of a minister reading *Uncle Tom's Cabin.* Green influenced hundreds of slaves, a good number of whom had already escaped to freedom, led by Mrs. Tubman's visions of God. The last thing that Dorchester County appeared to need was an abolitionist Methodist preacher. One of Green's fellow Methodists, the Reverend John Dixson Long, told the story in blunt terms: "The slaveholders of Dorchester County thirsted for an object upon which to vent their rage [following a spate of slave escapes]; hence, poor Green's arrest and conviction."[15]

On May 18, 1857, Green entered the Maryland State Penitentiary, a facility noted for inhumane conditions. Almost immediately abolitionists made his situation a cause célèbre by insisting that Samuel Green be pardoned. Five years into Green's sentence, Governor Bradford finally granted him freedom on the condition that he leave Maryland. Samuel Green reunited with Kitty, and the couple made their way to Canada. On the trip he preached to various antislavery meetings, including one with noted abolitionist William Lloyd Garrison.

Green also met Harriet Beecher Stowe at her home in Hartford, Connecticut. Stowe recorded the episode in the newspaper *The Independent:*

> There came a black man to our house a few days ago, who had spent five years at hard labor in a Maryland penitentiary for the crime of having a copy of Uncle Tom's Cabin in his house. He had been sentenced to ten years, but on his promise to leave the state and go to Canada, was magnanimously pardoned out. Everybody cheated him of the little property he had . . . and so he left Maryland without any acquisition except an infirmity of the limbs which he had caught from prison labor. All this was his portion of the cross; and he took it meekly, without comment, only asking that as they did not allow him to finish reading the book, we would give him a copy of Uncle Tom's Cabin—which we did.[16]

In 1862 or 1863, Green apparently settled somewhere near his son in Salford, Ontario, where, it can be presumed, he finally finished *Uncle Tom's Cabin*. The road to freedom can, indeed, be a long one. You just have to keep going.

Community

During the 2008 presidential primaries a conservative talk-show host attacked the Democratic candidates' health-care plans as "socialized medicine," echoing a line of attack used to great effect in 1993 to derail President Clinton's attempt to reform American health care. Some fifteen years later these words sounded oddly antique. Socialized medicine? Was he worried about socialism? Certainly hosts of younger Americans barely remember—much less fear—a thing called socialism.

Nineteenth-century Christians stood on the other side of this historical divide. Many of them had never heard of socialism either. But that was because it was a new political idea, a critique sprung from the excesses of capitalism—the idea that society could be engineered to be more humane and fair on the basis of systemic economic equality. Christians who were acquainted with socialist political philosophy found its ideals attractive and strangely reminiscent of Jesus's teachings on wealth and poverty and the practices of the early church. For a time, Christian socialism attracted large numbers of thoughtful believers in North America and Europe.

"In the socialist state, as I conceive," wrote Vida Scudder in 1891, "material wealth will be distributed on the basis, not of service, but of need." Although "absolute equality" was not realistic, she saw a society in which "there will be no more violent extremes of riches and poverty, luxury and degradation. Those at the bottom will no longer need to strain every nerve lest the fiend starvation overtake them; those at the top will no longer be allowed to roll themselves in vast heaps of wealth. . . . At both ends, disproportion will be cut away."[17]

Vida Scudder (1861–1954), a professor of English literature at Wellesley College, was born in India to Congregationalist missionary parents. Her father died when she was still small, and her mother returned to the United States to raise their only child. In her final book, written three years before her death, Vida looked back on this time in her life: "How complacent was the middle class civilization of my New England girlhood! Especially was this true of the comfortable people with whom my lot was cast."[18] That memoir, titled *My Quest for Reality,* records her search for meaningful faith. The first step toward spiritual adventure took place when Vida was fourteen. Her mother joined the Episcopal Church, and Vida encountered the romantic Anglo-Catholic high-church piety, which inspired her or, as she said, it allowed her "to breathe the air I craved."[19]

Scudder's primary theological influence was F. D. Maurice (1805–1872), a British Unitarian who had likewise converted to Anglicanism. In 1848 Maurice had founded an organization of Christian socialists in the Church of England by wedding New Testament principles with social radicalism. Following her interest in Anglican theology, Vida Scudder became one of the first women to study at Oxford University. There she was intellectually attracted to the theological gadfly John Ruskin, whose lectures both heightened her appreciation for art and deepened her sense of responsibility for the poor. As a young woman, she came to believe Christian socialism fulfilled the words of Jesus's prayer: "Thy kingdom come." After university she took up a teaching post at Wellesley, a school that welcomed her expertise in English poetry but was "not ready for her politics."[20] For years she would struggle with academic authorities who tried to—alternatively—force her to resign or silence her regarding socialism.

But Scudder could not be silenced, believing as she did that spirituality and politics were intimately connected in the work of Christ. She was not, however, a traditional socialist. Rejecting secular socialism as dry and mechanical, she favored a romantic—and even medieval—vision of Christian communalism. Vida believed that modern faith was too individualistic and "that personal conversion is thwarted and inert unless it demands corporate transformation."[21] Her spirituality called her to community, both to that of the church and to the reform of human society.

In 1889 Scudder joined the Society of the Companions of the Holy Cross, a new monastic order for Anglican women founded by her friend Emily Morgan. In a 1911 letter Morgan summed up this vision of Christian society:

> To seek first the Kingdom of God and His Righteousness is to know that there is no such thing as a human problem or a vital question in relation to society without God. Any work we may do for humanity is vitalized only because God was made flesh and dwelt among us. Through the Incarnation of the Son of Man we feel every social problem, every injustice. . . . Those who fight for social justice with no recognition of a God once made man fight an uncertain battle.[22]

The Companions of the Holy Cross based social action on the person of Christ and his suffering on the cross. They read this kingdom vision most especially through the life of St. Francis, the saint whom they felt most fully embodied God's reign.

Thus Scudder envisioned a society based on political socialism and classical devotional practices. To her the kingdom resembled an extended monastic community in which men and women were freed from both extreme want and extreme greed and were shaped instead by spiritual disciplines so they might dedicate their lives to the "holy work" of art, philosophy, and science. To her, both the poor and the rich needed to be freed from the demands of outward life, those "shackles that bind down to the earth the free spirit of man," in order to pursue the kingdom of God within.[23]

Vida Scudder knew that this vision was utopian and ultimately not terribly realistic. However, she insisted that Christians should press toward this goal, where "the world glistens with radiant possibilities."[24] Certainly, Scudder understood the tension between the actual and the ideal in her own life. Caught in the world of her own elite family and Wellesley College (as one historian says, Scudder frequently "gave heartburn to Wellesley administrators"),[25] she sought communities that modeled her understanding of the kingdom. One such community was Adelynrood, a rural semimonastic house in Massachusetts where the Companions of the Holy Cross gathered for retreats, prayer, and friendship. There she found "spiritual union with others, and the privacy I desired. . . . Nearly all my tenderest relations would be found or formed within it."[26]

The other community was Denison House, a settlement house—a sort of neighborhood center where residents served the poor directly—in urban Boston, where Scudder frequently spent her summers. In 1889 Scudder organized the College Settlements Association, which enlisted privileged students to live among the poor as a way of imitating Christ. Two weeks before Jane Addams opened the more famous Hull House in Chicago, Scudder's students launched a settlement house in New York City and would eventually found Denison House in Boston. Although settlements were originally intended as educational centers for the new social sciences, where people could learn ways to alleviate poverty, Scudder believed they should be more than academic experiments. She imagined them as "centers of revelation," urban communities that combined spirituality and social justice.[27]

Thus Vida Scudder constructed a life around three poles—the intellectually satisfying life of a college professor, the spiritually enriching life of the Companions of the Holy Cross, and the socially challenging life of the settlement movement. Students, sisters, and socialists: in their company, Scudder experienced God in community, a foretaste of the kingdom to come. Although she was wrong in expecting that political socialism would win the day, she rightly maintained that the spiritual dimensions of Christian community, including both prayer and service, offered a distinct alternative to consumerist society. To her the kingdom of God passed "beyond theory" to become a "definite venture of faith," a social journey where she sought "less to know the doctrine than to live the life."[28] Her politics may sound antiquated, but its essential idealism—idealism found throughout church history—sounds remarkably like Christian hope.

Progress

A few years ago a Pennsylvania community was roiled in controversy regarding evolution. After a speech in a liberal Protestant church, an elderly gentleman stood up and addressed the audience. "I'm terrified that creationists might win in the local school board election," he stated. "The argument between evolution and creation is the most important issue Christians face today. Science is the front line of the culture war. Without evolution, there is no progressive Christianity." He continued on for a few minutes, getting more emotional with every word. Finally, unable to finish, he sat down. The audience was surprised; some obviously agreed with him while others felt merely uncomfortable. To him, however, the world hung on accepting the idea of evolution.

Although the debate between evolution and creation is most often framed as a scientific one, nineteenth-century Christians saw things somewhat differently. For them Darwinism functioned as a way of interpreting the universe, a theory that worked as a philosophical girder of reality. It entailed far more than thinking that human beings were somehow related to monkeys. Rather, evolutionary theory posited a worldview based on the idea of progress—an idea that differed from earlier views that creation was a fixed reality.

In the first decades of the nineteenth century, European and North American Christians began to explore ideas of growth and development related to human life and culture.

Medieval people had believed that the universe was static, a never-changing world with an established order of things descending from an eternal God. During modernity people noticed that the world was more dynamic than they had previously thought—that people, cultures, and social structures changed through time. Modern people further assumed that growth implied progress and that what occurred later in time was somehow better as well. Since recent developments built on the insights and patterns of older ones, newer practices and knowledge moved beyond the limits and mistakes of the past. Thomas Jefferson summed up this impulse when he wrote to John Adams in 1821, "I like the dreams of the future better than the history of the past."

When Charles Darwin offered his theory of natural selection in 1859, that species adapted over time in a process of natural evolution, the suggestion fell upon fertile intellectual ground. If human history had developed, why not human beings as well? In many ways Western Christians were prepared for the possibility that creation had been an organic process somehow initiated by God rather than a six-day miracle that, by the middle of the nineteenth century, was beginning to appear implausible on the basis of scientific evidence.

Some Christians, that is.

Princeton Seminary professor Charles Hodge clearly understood that Darwinism posed a problem for Christians who wanted to retain the idea of history as an unchanging order. "Natural selection," he wrote, "is a selection made by natural laws, working without intention and design." Evolution lacks divine intelligence and functionally "banish[es] God from the world." An absent God, Hodge insisted, was no God. Hodge did not tackle Darwinism on the basis of science; rather, he attacked evolution as a philosophy. Darwin denied the idea of "final causes," that there exists a supernatural intelligence guiding the natural world. "The denial of design in nature," he argued, "is virtually the denial of God." To Hodge, evolution was a fundamental challenge to Christian theology. "What is Darwinism?" he asked rhetorically. "It is Atheism."[29]

Other Christians accepted Hodge's analysis but rejected his conclusion. Yes, they argued, evolution does change the organizing principle of Christian theology. But they insisted that emerging ideas of progress were not antireligious. Darwinism is not atheism, they argued; it is only a new way of understanding God and human experience. "Liberal theology," states historian Robert Bruce Mullin, "not only accepted the idea of evolution, but embraced it as the foundation for understanding reality."[30] Belief in evolution and belief in progress merged, and Christians gained a new confidence that they were the agents of social development. God's kingdom was an organic reality, not a supernatural one, which they could bring about by enacting Jesus's teachings.

No one summed up this better than Harry Emerson Fosdick (1878–1969), a liberal Baptist preacher best known for his famous 1922 sermon, "Shall the Fundamentalists Win?" That same year Fosdick published a book titled *Christianity and Progress*, which summarized an evolutionary view of God's reign. After examining the changes wrought in the nineteenth century regarding progress, Fosdick argued, "The climactic factor was added which gathered up all the rest and embraced them in a comprehensive philosophy of life. Evolution became a credible truth. . . . It spread its influence out into every area of human thought until all history was conceived in genetic terms." Therefore, Fosdick claimed, "Growth became recognized as the fundamental law of life."[31]

Until this principle was understood, Fosdick believed, people lived without hope. After all, in a static universe change could occur only when God intervened. Thus the kingdom was primarily a supernatural reality—waiting in heaven—until God acted to do justice through some sort of apocalyptic event. People could do nothing but wait and beseech God to bring about the kingdom. According to Fosdick, progressive Christianity was a religion of hope. Men and women participate in the unfolding of God's reign in the world. This view inspires hope that faith can better humanity and correct injustice. We do God's work.

Fosdick was no fool. He did not see progressive Christianity as a smooth path to modernist perfection. "The course of human history is like a river," he wrote; "sometimes it flows so slowly that one would hardly know it moved at all; sometimes bends come in its channel so that one can hardly see in what direction it intends to go; sometimes there are backeddies so that it seems to be retreating on itself." Human history happens in fits and starts, "a fight, tragic and ceaseless, against destructive forces." The progress of God's kingdom in the world would not be easy. "The world needs something more," Fosdick insisted, "than a soft gospel of inevitable progress."[32]

The missing piece, according to him, is that humankind is not subject to some blind force of evolutionary progress. Rather, people need a "spiritual interpretation of life." How do we know that history is a river and not a whirlpool? Faith, Fosdick said, gives Christians the ability to "tell that the river of human history is flowing out toward the kingdom of God." Thus religion is more than a "frill." Rather, it acts as the primary way of interpreting scientific facts—spirituality is *the* capacity that transforms human *existence* into human *life* (emphasis his). Our "deepest need," he says, "is spiritual power, and spiritual power comes out of the soul's deep fellowship with the living God."[33] Faith made evolution make sense.

Far from excluding God from the world, a progressive vision thus invites God in. For, as Fosdick insists, evolution understood mechanically lacks the essential component of spiritual meaning and cannot ultimately enliven hope. Thus, to him, "religion is indispensable." Without it progress builds its "civilization upon sand, where the rain descends and the floods come and the winds blow and beat upon the house and it falls and great is the fall thereof."[34]

Fosdick warned his liberal readers that secular progress alone was not enough, that it had "unsettling effects" that could alternately spawn a "reactionary dogmatism" or could stagnate into a fetid pool. The way, therefore? Progressive spirituality. "While change is there, it is not aimless, discontinuous, chaotic change." It is neither atheism nor secularism. It is "a path which can be traced, recovered in thought, conceived as a whole." Thus the "rock" upon which wise ones build the house is the rock of spiritual progress, and "the stability is in the process itself, arising out of the abiding relationships of man with the eternal."[34]

Ecumenism

In 1980 I attended a mission conference in Edinburgh, Scotland. The meeting celebrated the seventieth anniversary of the 1910 Edinburgh Missionary Conference, an event that most historians agree was the most significant gathering of Christian missionaries ever held. The theme of the original conference was "The Evangelization of the World in This Generation." It marked the culmination of missions in the nineteenth century, dubbed by Christian historians as the Great Century, and simultaneously initiated the twentieth-century ecumenical movement to unite Christian churches.

A group of American evangelicals, mostly from southern California, organized the 1980 conference. Other than location, there seemed to be no actual link between the original meeting and the 1980 one. The 1980 meeting also promoted mission and was titled "A Church for Every People by the Year 2000," but nary a word was spoken about the ecumenical legacy of Edinburgh 1910. As the twentieth century progressed, American Protestants severed missions from ecumenical endeavor. Those Protestants who embraced conservative theology retained the passions of evangelization; those who followed a more liberal theology picked up the hope for ecumenism. During the late nineteenth and early twentieth centuries, American Protestantism was roiled in controversy between conservatives and liberals, a generation of church conflict known as the fundamentalist-modernist controversy.

The fundamentalist-modernist controversy was, not surprisingly, the culmination of historical modernism. As many millions of Christians embarked on quests to understand God and the faith in new contexts, many millions also rejected the idea that such new contexts mattered at all. After all, fundamentalists insisted, the faith was "once delivered to the saints" (Jude 1:3b) and stood firmly as "that old-time religion." Thus the fundamentalist-modernist controversy might be seen as a quarrel between questers and standers, and their argument rocked all the major Christian denominations. The events of those days were so painful that they still mark American religion, with the heirs of both sides of the fight still theologically isolated from one another and harboring grudges.

In the seventy years following that first Edinburgh Conference, the old synthesis had split, leaving conservative and liberal Protestants to claim different parts of the Edinburgh legacy. Conservatives, like the people who planned the Edinburgh 1980 meeting, looked back to the 1910 conference as the greatest missionary gathering in Christian history. Liberals, by contrast, regarded Edinburgh as the first expression of the twentieth-century quest for Christian unity.

The word *ecumenical* comes from a Greek word meaning "the whole inhabited world." As the twentieth century dawned, the word took on new meanings—a longing for Christian unity. The movement toward unity emerged among nineteenth-century missionaries who knew firsthand the problems of competition and theological confusion generated by Christian denominations on the mission field. The Edinburgh consultation was convened in order to foster greater cooperation between churches in mission work. At the beginning of the modern mission movement, evangelism and ecumenism were seen as interconnected; the Christian message could not be rightly presented unless it somehow reflected Jesus's prayer that his followers would be one (John 17:11).

Charles Clayton Morrison was the editor of the *Christian Century* magazine and attended the Edinburgh conference. On June 20, 1910, he described the many representatives of the denominations gathered. "It is a great assemblage of the church's greatest men," he reported. "But all are on the same level. Germans, French, Americans, Englishmen, Scandinavians, Japanese, Chinese, Hindus, Africans—all are here and mingle together in an easy equality."[36] Morrison quoted Lord Balfour, the Scottish secretary in the British government, as saying, "The hope has sprung up in my mind that unity if it begins on the mission field will not find its ending there. . . . Surely there is much more that should unite us than keep us apart." Conferees listened to speeches centered on the theme "The Missionary Message in Relation to Non-Christian Religions," with presentations made by a Chinese Christian and an Indian doctor who had converted from Hinduism to Christianity. Calling the meeting "unparalleled," Morrison observed, "The theme of Christian unity is running through the whole conference like a subterranean stream. . . . It is almost the exception for a speaker to sit down without deploring our divisions. The missionaries are literally plaintive in their appeal that the church of Christ reestablish her long lost unity."[37]

At the center of everything was John R. Mott (1865–1955), an American Methodist layperson. Born in humble circumstances, Mott grew up in Iowa as the son of a lumber merchant. A talented student, he enrolled at Upper Iowa University, where he proved his skills in debate and rhetoric and eventually transferred to Cornell University to major in law. At Cornell he attended a lecture by C. T. Studd, a well-known cricket player who had converted to Christianity. Studd challenged his audience: "Seekest thou great things for thyself? Seek them not. Seek ye the Kingdom of God."

The words impressed Mott. He gave up ambitions for the law in favor of Christian work. The following summer he represented Cornell's Young Men's Christian Association at its first international student conference in Northfield, Massachusetts. The meeting proved momentous when one hundred young men, including John R. Mott, pledged their lives to foreign missions. Although Mott would neither become ordained nor be a missionary, he served the YMCA for twenty-seven years, recruiting others to give their lives to Christian service. Historians estimate that more than twenty thousand students entered mission work at his behest. His unique ministry took him to every corner of the earth, and surely Mott was "the most widely traveled and universally trusted Christian leader of his time."[38]

Mott, however, was not an earlier version of Billy Graham. He did not lead tent revivals, found an evangelistic association, or create a missionary board. Instead Mott dedicated himself to serving existing denominations and expanding their global understanding with the ever-present hope for Christian unity. Not only did Mott seek to unify Protestant Christians for the sake of God's kingdom, he also reached out to Roman Catholics and Orthodox Christians, trying to secure their cooperation and friendship in the expanding work of the YMCA. These efforts eventually resulted in the establishment of the World Council of Churches, of which Mott is remembered as its "father," and he served as one of its provisional presidents.

In 1946 Mott won the Nobel Peace Prize for promoting unity through human understanding. In his last public speech Mott modestly commented, "While life lasts, I am an evangelist."

He was not, however, a fire-and-brimstone evangelist threatening hell to the unconverted heathen. He was an evangelist for peace, church unity, and a kingdom where all people would be one in Christ. For him, as for many nineteenth-century Christians, the two—evangelism and ecumenism—were one in a quest to embody God's reign of love.

Pluralism

In June 2008 the U.S. Religious Landscape Survey reported that 70 percent of Americans believe that "many religions can lead to eternal life," including strong majorities of both Protestants and Catholics. "It's not that Americans don't believe in anything," said Professor Michael Lindsay of Rice University, "it's that we believe in everything. We aren't religious purists or dogmatists."[39] Lindsay went to argue that new cultural conditions have fostered a climate of religious toleration: "If you have a colleague who is Buddhist or your kid plays with a little boy who is Hindu, it changes your appreciation of the religious 'other.'"[40] Commenting on the widespread acceptance of pluralism found by the survey, *Time* magazine's David Van Biema claims, "The new poll suggests a major shift, at least in the pews." Such broad tolerance seems a departure from much of Christian history, as Van Biema quips that the laity have accepted "a new polyglot heaven."

Although religious toleration may just now be registering in surveys, Christians have been exploring the territory of religious pluralism since the nineteenth century. In 1893, seventeen years before the Edinburgh Conference, the World's Parliament of Religions met to showcase the diversity of global faiths in conjunction with the Chicago World's Fair. More than a million invitations were sent to representatives of the world's religions to "pool their accumulated spiritual wisdom."[41] The majority of speakers were Christians, with most being Protestants, but Jews, Muslims, Hindus, Buddhists, Confucians, and many others participated in more than two weeks of meetings. Many observers of the World's Fair considered the Parliament the highlight of the Chicago exhibition, and newspapers enthusiastically reported on the spiritual spectacle.

When the World's Parliament of Religions opened, Charles Bonny reminded participants that the hope for the gathering was that "it will become like a new Mount Zion, crowned with glory and marking the actual beginning of a new epoch of brotherhood and peace." He continued, "We seek in this Congress to unite all Religion against irreligion; to make the gold rule the basis of this union; and to present to the world the substantial unity of many religions."[42]

Historians have long noted that the event was designed to privilege a liberal version of Christian religion, showcasing it as the culmination of human spiritual development and the bond of true unity. But something unexpected occurred. Instead of Christian voices dominating the meeting, other representatives caught the public imagination. "Judging by the reaction of the press and those who attended the Parliament," writes one historian, "the man who stole the show was the Hindu 'monk' Vivekananda."[43]

Swami Vivekananda (1863–1902) was born as Narendranath Dutta in Calcutta, India, to middle-class parents. Well educated and philosophically trained, he became a Hindu monk who wandered his native land seeking knowledge, and he earned fame as a holy man. Eventually Westerners learned of his reputation, and he was invited to the World's Parliament of Religions. When he rose to address the Chicago crowd, more than seven thousand people in the audience cheered him for three minutes. "I am proud," he announced, "to belong to a religion which has taught the world both tolerance and universal acceptance. We believe not only in universal toleration, but we accept all religions to be true." He went on to claim the truth as found in the Bhagavad Gita:

> "Whosoever comes to Me, through whatsoever form, I reach him; all men are struggling through paths which in the end lead to me." Sectarianism, bigotry, and its horrible descendant, fanaticism, have long possessed this beautiful earth. . . . But their time has come; and I fervently hope that the bell that tolled this morning in honor of this convention may be the death-knell of all fanaticism, of all persecutions with the sword or with the pen, and of all uncharitable feelings between persons wending their way to the same goal.[44]

Vivekananda introduced himself to a Western Christian audience by claiming that Hinduism, with its emphasis on unity and universalism, most perfectly demonstrated the goals of the conference. Hinduism, not Christianity, was the "universal religion," the spiritual place in which "all the streams of faith would meet."[45]

It may seem odd to include a Hindu monk in a history of Christianity, but the enthusiasm that greeted Vivekananda represents an early version of a Christian acceptance of and accommodation to other religions that a Pew poll would find more widespread a century later. At the time, Minnie Andrews Snell, a Christian attending the Parliament, recorded her observations as a poem by a fictitious "Aunt Hannah":

> Then I heered th' han'some Hindu monk, drest up in orange dress,
> Who sed that all humanity was part of God—no less,
> An' he sed we was not sinners, so I comfort took once more,
> While the Parliament of Religion roared with approving roar.
> Must I leave all this sarchin' 'tel I reach th' other side?
> I'll treat all men as brothers while on this airth I bide,
> An' let "Love" be my motto, 'tel I enter in th' door.
> Of that great Religious Parl'ment, where creeds don't count no more.[46]

The Parliament marked a watershed in Christian spirituality as it introduced, on a popular level in the West, the questions of religious pluralism. It opened the Christian imagination to the possibility that Christianity may not be superior to other faiths and that it may be one religion among many. Following his success in Chicago, Vivekananda went on a two-year speaking tour in which he introduced Americans to the practice of yoga—an evangelistic success if ever there was one. Thus the modern quest, which began with questions of religious tensions between Protestants and Catholics in Germany, culminated with the World's Parliament of Religions in Chicago. As the new century opened, Christians began to suspect that the kingdom might be inhabited by more than just one God. It had been quite a journey.

The Recent End

In August 1945 modernity came to a frightening end when the United States exploded two atomic bombs over Japan to end World War II. When the first bomb was tested in New Mexico, J. Robert Oppenheimer, one of the atomic scientists, quoted the Hindu Bhagavad Gita upon viewing the mushroom cloud: "I am become Death, the shatterer of worlds." Modernity had opened with the hope that wars could be ended; it closed with the fear that war could end everything. Many Christians thought the atomic bomb was the end of the world; others hoped it might be some sort of new spiritual beginning. "But nearly all agreed," writes historian Patrick Allitt, "that they were standing at one of the crossroads of history, faced with choices that would have consequences not only in the everyday world but for the future of their entire civilization."[47]

A little more than a year earlier, a young German Lutheran pastor named Dietrich Bonhoeffer (1906–1945) sat in a Nazi jail under arrest for suspected involvement in the plot to assassinate Adolph Hitler. Bonhoeffer was best known for his 1937 book, *The Cost of Discipleship*, in which he reflected on following the way of Jesus that "will liberate mankind from man-made dogmas, from every burden and oppression, from every anxiety and torture which afflicts the conscience." Pastor

Bonhoeffer was distressed that churches had cheapened the faith, that Christianity seemed to be too easy, a way marked by social respectability rather than a profound commitment to practice Jesus's command to love God and love our neighbors. He called for a return to "costly grace." As he explained, "It is grace because it calls us to follow Jesus Christ. It is costly because it costs a man his life."[48]

In the years following those words, they became increasingly real for Bonhoeffer. He watched the Nazis gain power in his beloved homeland, and he witnessed his own church bless the new National Socialist state. German Christians capitulated to the vision of an Aryan utopia and allowed, both tacitly and actively, Hitler to commit his atrocities on the world. Bonhoeffer had always resisted Hitler, and in the early 1930s he might have escaped Nazi Germany completely by remaining at his teaching post at Union Theological Seminary in New York. But Bonhoeffer saw the darkness gathering in Europe and chose to return home and stand with and for Christ in the midst of war. There he worked on behalf of the Confessing Church, a movement that refused to support the state, and helped to establish a semimonastic community to train pastors for the new church.

The Gestapo distrusted Bonhoeffer and forbade him from lecturing, writing, or making speeches. On April 5, 1943, they arrested him. Two years later, on Sunday, April 8, 1945, after leading fellow prisoners in worship, Nazi authorities took him away to be hanged.

Halfway through his imprisonment, on April 30, 1944, Bonhoeffer wrote to a friend that a question had been occupying his attention: "What *is* Christianity, and indeed, what *is* Christ, for us today?" Citing the apocalypse of the war, he wondered if Christianity was "over" as a religion, and maybe, he suggested, that all religion (as a "historical and temporary form of human self-expression") itself was dying. Modernism had begun so triumphantly; now that spirit of optimism lay in the charred remains of Western civilization. Bonhoeffer thought religion no longer made any sense and that it may have been the "garment of Christianity." He asked, "What is a religionless Christianity?"

For more than sixty years, theologians have been arguing over what Bonhoeffer meant by "religionless Christianity." In the 1950s and 1960s, it seemed almost foolish to suggest that the pattern, or forms, of traditional Christianity might be failing. After all, in the twenty or so years following World War II, Christian denominations in North America and Europe reached dizzying heights of membership, money, and influence, a kind of modern reconstruction of Christendom. But as soon as Christian power reached this twentieth-century zenith, it started a surprisingly quick slide into decline and cultural marginality. By the 1990s, it became commonplace in the West to say that one was "spiritual but not religious," a phrase that surely echoes Bonhoeffer's prediction of religionless Christianity.

Bonhoeffer may have perceived that Christianity was on the verge of great change—on the scale not seen since the Protestant Reformation. In his elusive phrase, he was trying to describe the passing of the Christian "pattern" of church that would give way to a more vital form of Christ-life shaped by spiritual practices of prayer, hospitality, and forgiveness, and that must be experienced profoundly in the world.

Religionless Christianity would not be primarily a religion of salvation where human beings would escape the suffering of the world. Rather, he said, "God is the 'beyond' in the midst of our life."[49]

Bonhoeffer did not live to finish his reflections on religionless Christianity, but the task he began to refashion the faith after modernity had only just begun.

PART V

THE RIVER

Contemporary Christianity 1945–Now

THIRTEEN

The River

In the spring of 1985, when I was a student at Gordon-Conwell Theological Seminary, a conservative evangelical school north of Boston, Massachusetts, Henri Nouwen, the well-known Roman Catholic author, was teaching a class at Harvard Divinity School called An Introduction to the Spiritual Life.

I knew Nouwen only through a small book, *Reaching Out: The Three Movements of the Spiritual Life*, which had been given to me by a friend when I graduated from college in 1981. When I opened the present I thought it a little odd. My friend was a conservative missionary, yet he gave me a book by a Catholic priest? I flipped the pages. The book opened with a question, "What does it mean to live a life in the Spirit of Jesus Christ?" Ruminating on the loneliness, fear, and struggles of living in the contemporary world, Nouwen went on to say, "This book does not offer answers or solutions but is written in the conviction that the quest for an authentic Christian spirituality is worth the effort and the pain, since in the midst of this quest we can find signs offering hope, courage, and confidence."[1] At twenty-two, I wanted answers, but I suspected that somehow Nouwen was right. Living like Jesus was not going to be easy. From the first paragraph, I was hooked.

More than two hundred students enrolled in Nouwen's Harvard course. I was not one of them, I am sorry to say. I had to take a different class offered at the same time. In some ways I was glad to have an excuse to beg off this class. Some of the professors back at Gordon-Conwell looked with suspicion on their students who wanted to take Nouwen's course; they did not want evangelical students to be studying with a Roman Catholic priest at a liberal, pluralistic seminary. A number of my more theologically rebellious friends, however, signed up for the Harvard class anyway, attracted by Nouwen's books and his reputation as a teacher of spiritual practices. When my schedule allowed, I would sneak down to Cambridge with them to sit in on Nouwen's lecture for a day.

In a packed lecture hall Nouwen taught his students how to actually live "the life of Jesus" by introducing us to the wide stream of Christian traditions, from desert monasticism to Orthodox icons, from medieval mysticism to Latin American liberation theology. He breathed church history, trusting that these ancient practices could change our lives and the life of the world, and he communicated this to us by combining "the passion of an evangelical preacher and the heart of a Catholic saint."[2]

More astonishing perhaps than Nouwen himself were the students. We came from all over the Boston area, from every seminary, church, and denomination across the theological spectrum. As I walked into the lecture hall I remember feeling a little afraid of being in the same room with the trendy-looking Harvard students, the somber, black-clad Roman Catholic priests, and the bearded Orthodox clergy. The students were black and white, male and female, rich and poor, liberal and conservative, gay and straight—with a few transgendered folks thrown in. I wondered: Were all these people even Christians?

An odd thing happened as Nouwen lectured. Everything we thought was so important about our doctrines began to slip to the background; it was as if the room actually shifted as new, more urgent concerns of faith and compassion came to the fore. One of the graduate students remembered,

> The normal rules of academic engagement seemed to be suspended as long as he was nearby. Students began to speak more openly; outsiders mingled freely, and everyone shared their insights back and forth, prayed and sang together, and occasionally even became tearful, a rare sight anywhere at Harvard. In this atmosphere somehow everyone's thoughts and feelings mattered, regardless of their views or their intellectual credentials.

We came together; all the diverse people in that room actually created a spiritual community. Another student remarked that Henri Nouwen's most important contribution to Harvard was "his practice of ecumenism, an ecumenism of the heart that seeks unity beyond conventional social and religious boundaries. . . . Henri showed Harvard what ecumenism, in the true, original sense, is actually about."

For those of us fortunate enough to be there, whether for an hour or an entire semester, Nouwen offered us an experience of a different kind of Christianity—a way of life based in the practice of friendship, hospitality, prayer, and forming community, all centered on the loving presence of Jesus Christ through worship and service to the poor. It was clear that he was trying to build a community, to teach through example that it is truly possible for Christians to overcome divisions around a "common table that excluded no one." Reflecting back, one of his students commented on this lesson:

> Henri respected the pluralism around him less ideologically (e.g., through revisionism and relativism) than in recognizing the variety of God's beloved people (e.g., embattled Sandinistas, Haitian children, the handicapped) and offering them love and life in Christ. Especially in the spring 1985 course, he reached beyond professed "tolerance" to offer the biblical grace of "hospitality."

Another simply remembers that Nouwen seemed like "an injection of real Christianity into a staid New England institution."

Although I was on the edge of all this activity, it overwhelmed the prejudices of my small world. In 1985 the ice of theological rigidity and frozen hearts broke—and God's river flowed over its banks into Harvard Square.

IN THE UNITED STATES it has become commonplace to speak of how divided our society is, a fifty-fifty nation permanently roiled in a culture war of conservatives and liberals. Indeed, historian Patrick Allitt argues that since 1945 American Christianity has become increasingly politicized with "sharply divided" constituencies.[3] Modernity had, at its core, the presupposition that people could know religious truth—and that truth was singular, one truth for all. Thus the modern Christian quest assumed that all right-thinking—or right-praying—believers could and would eventually wind up with the same opinions. Modern Christianity therefore resulted in a host of conflicts between truth claims, everyone contending to be right.

One of the most difficult of those arguments occurred around the turn of the twentieth century, when many Christian denominations split between fundamentalists and modernists. Over two generations this two-party religious squabble pitted conservatives against liberals in a battle for American souls. Churches, seminaries, and denominations split, resulting in a proliferation of new churches in a society already chock-full of religious brands. North American and European missionaries exported their denominations—along with their theological quarrels—to the emerging churches in Asia, Africa, and South America. By 1900 Christianity was both more global than ever before and even more fractured and divided than it had previously been. Modern Christianity, which began with a split between Protestants and Catholics, ended with a multitude of schisms and bitter theological arguments between Christians over the basic tenets of their faith. Many historians read the latter part of the twentieth century as a continuation of this story. Social tensions abound because religion is more diverse and more politicized than ever, hardening ideological walls of separation between people.

Such an interpretation, however, may depend upon whose voice one listens to.

In his *Quest*, Albert Schweitzer reflected on the modern search for Jesus and his kingdom, with its attendant dream of oneness: "So long as we are of one will among ourselves and with him in putting the kingdom of God above all else, serving it with faith and hope, there is fellowship between him and us and with men of all races who have lived and still live guided by the same idea."[4] But Christians, it appeared, were far from being guided by the "same idea."

Traditional sectarian divisions were complicated by the theological arguments between liberal and conservative Christians. Liberal Christianity, Schweitzer argued, had successfully navigated modern thought but had so accommodated itself to the spirit of the age that it may have "unstrung the bow" and teetered on becoming a "mere sociological instead of religious force"; conservatives, by implication, had proved themselves irrelevant by refusing to engage with modern questions, and they barely figured in Schweitzer's discussion.[5] In the process partisan Christianity lost any real sense of connection to Jesus, the "One unknown."

Schweitzer depicted the Christianity of his day as "two thin streams [that] wind alongside each other between the boulders and pebbles of a great river bed," following separate ways. No ideology, theology, or feat of ecclesiastical engineering could bring Christians back together. But Schweitzer wondered if there might come a different day: "When the waters rise and overflow the rock, they meet of their own accord."

> This is how the conservative and liberal forms of religion will meet, when desire and hope for the kingdom of God and fellowship with the spirit of Jesus again govern them as an elementary and mighty force, and bring their world-views and their religion so close that the differences in fundamental presuppositions, though still existing, sink, just as the boulders of the river bed are covered by the rising flood and at last are barely visible, gleaming through the depths of waters.[6]

His words strangely echoed Hildegard of Bingen's medieval vision of a time when "rivers of living water are to be poured out over the whole world, to ensure that people, like fishes caught in a net, can be restored to wholeness."[7] But neither medieval Hildegard nor modern Albert Schweitzer could truly imagine such a time might actually come.

Sociologists, philosophers, and historians now agree—in surprisingly uniform fashion—that the West has entered some new stage of modernity, hypermodernity, or postmodernity. In the decades since 1945 Western society and culture—and the Christian religion along with it—have been transformed not in degree but in kind. Nothing is as it was. Sociologist Zygmunt Bauman refers to the contemporary condition as "liquid modernity," where everything "solid" has melted away. He describes "fluidity" as the "leading metaphor for the present stage of modernity."

> Fluids travel easily. They 'flow', 'spill', 'run out', 'splash', 'pour over', 'leak', 'flood', 'spray', 'drip', 'seep', 'ooze'; unlike solids, they are not easily stopped—they pass

> around some obstacles, dissolve some others and bore or soak their way through others still. From the meeting with solids they emerge unscathed, while the solids they have met, if they stay solid, are changed—get moist or drenched.

This situation leaves each individual in a state of radical dislocation struggling to find (if at all possible) some "new narrative" for life.[8]

In each period of Christian history particular images or orientations seem to capture the spirit of the faith. Through time Christianity could be described as the way, a cathedral, the word, or a quest. Some scholars want to depict contemporary Christian faith as a quarrel. But I prefer to think of it as a river, water rising and overflowing its banks. A fluid faith.

SINCE 1945 THE river has been rising. With the dropping of the atomic bomb, the old dams broke and water started flowing in every direction. The last vestiges of Christendom disappeared in the West; religious pluralism grew in industrialized countries; new patterns of spirituality and supernatural forms of faith emerged; Christianity expanded to South America, Africa, and parts of Asia in ways no one could have imagined; and a renewed geopolitical conflict exploded between Christianity and Islam. At the end of World War II no historian, sociologist, theologian, or philosopher could have predicted any of this.

Many individual Christians contributed to the rising water of the twentieth century: Dorothy Day, an American convert to Roman Catholicism, who dedicated her life to social justice for the oppressed; Dietrich Bonhoeffer, a German Lutheran theologian, who argued for "costly grace" and was executed by the Nazis; C. S. Lewis, a British university professor, who proffered a simple and unifying description of Christian doctrine; Howard Thurman, an African American theologian, whose vision of the "beloved community" shaped Martin Luther King Jr.; Thomas Merton, a Roman Catholic monk, who renewed interest in the practice of contemplation; Oscar Romero, a Latin American archbishop, who embodied God's love for the poor and was martyred while celebrating the Eucharist; Verna Dozier, an African American Episcopal laywoman, whose theology of "the dream of God" inspired new interest in the church as an agent of God's reign; Madeleine L'Engle, an American writer, whose poetry and fiction sparked the Christian artistic imagination; and, of course, Henri Nouwen.[9]

These Christians pushed away obstacles that constricted the flow of faith, creating wide channels for God's spirit. Although they were very different, together they suggest that a new sort of Christianity is rising with the waters.

WHAT MIGHT THIS new Christianity look like? Instead of retracing the lives of the famous to understand contemporary Christianity, I gathered some friends and colleagues, with one exception all born since 1950, and asked them to describe the river of faith as they experience it. They are pastors, poets, writers, parents, teachers, and businesspeople. I hoped they might help me discern where the currents are taking us.[10]

Christianity as Navigation

"I became a Christian back in 1980–1981, much to the horror of my former hippie mother," recalls Aaron McCarroll Gallegos, a Web producer who lives in Toronto. "Just after letting her know I had become a Christian, we were watching TV together when Jerry Falwell appeared, saying that according to the Bible, the punishment for homosexuality was death by stoning. My mom, who had recently come out of the closet as a lesbian, slugged me hard on the shoulder and screamed, 'Is that what you believe?'"

Aaron was horrified. "No, Mom! No!" he shouted. "I'm not *that* kind of Christian! The Jesus I know is all about love, not hate!" He confesses, "In many ways my spiritual journey ever since has been an attempt to live that statement out in all aspects of my life."

Aaron's story illustrates something that many Christians feel today—an ambiguity, perhaps even a fear, about their identity in Christ. This is not, as Aaron pointed out to his mother, internal to his own experience of Jesus—he loves Jesus—but rather relates to the larger culture. Kathy Staudt, a poet who lives in Maryland, says, "Often I'll say that I believe in a generous, openhearted Christianity." That leads, she says, to "longer conversations" as to "the importance of Jesus in my life." Teresa Thompson Sherrill, a Mennonite pastor in Japan, explains simply that she is "the kind of Christian who loves Jesus."

Through many generations in the West, people did not ask if their neighbors were Christians. They assumed that they were. Americans and Europeans had a relatively stable sense of religious identity related to their long history and to the church. As Christianity split, people labeled themselves Catholic or Protestant or Orthodox. Eventually, when they explained their religious identity, Christians would appeal to their denominational traditions, Episcopal or Methodist or Baptist, aligning themselves with particular doctrines, creeds, and practices.

In the late twentieth century, however, the very word *Christian* began to take on negative meanings, increasingly defined by its most narrow partisans. Carol Howard Merritt, a thirty-something Presbyterian pastor in Washington, DC, relates a common sense in more progressive Christian communities: "People in my congregation tell me that when others know that they are going to church, they always have to qualify it by saying, 'But it's not like that.'" Carol continues,

> There are some assumptions in our culture about what kind of person a Christian is, or what kind of person goes to church and still has the nerve to talk about it, and it is frustrating to be lumped in together with them. I've noticed that people who are deeply committed to Christianity will identify themselves as a "Christ-follower" or a "disciple of Jesus." You can almost see them stepping away from Christianity in their reply. It's their way of saying, "It's not what you think. I'm trying to do something different. I'm trying to be someone different."

That difference lies in defining Christian identity in terms of Jesus's love for the world. Of course, most all Christians say theirs is a religion of love and that Jesus taught love. But some contemporary believers, such as Lisa Domke, a pastor and mother in Seattle, ground their identity in Christ's love but a love that goes beyond sentiment or feeling. "I say that I am someone seeking to live in the world with love and humility," Lisa reports, "following God in the way of Jesus." Love is the active practice of Christian virtue. As Sky, a Seattle Baptist, relates, "Children know that love is behavior, not romantic words."

Young adult believers sometimes lack words to label their identity; as one thirty-something Christian said, "Facebook has places for 'religious views' and 'political views'; I never can seem to come to anything satisfactory for a label for either." Yet they are not ambivalent about being Christian. Indeed, some Christians are very comfortable defining themselves as adherents to a Christian way of life rather than as adherents to a particular doctrine or creed. "When someone asks me what kind of Christian I am," says Brent Bill, a Quaker writer, "I say I'm a bad one." He goes on to say, "I've got the belief part down pretty well, I think. It's in the practice of my belief in everyday life where I often miss the mark." Finally, he states, "I see myself as a pilgrim—traveling the faith path to the destination of being a good Christian—and into the eternal presence of God."

Although all these people belong to traditional churches, they explain their faith fluidly as a process or journey of learning to live more fully in God's love. In a very real way they navigate their identity by following Jesus's example and trying to enact his mercy in the world. To them, identity is not solid, but spiritual identity flows in the channels of faithful Christian practice of loving God and loving their neighbor.

Devotion: Stepping into the River

A college classmate shares his story of finally embracing Christianity through Alcoholics Anonymous: "The practices of the Twelve-Step Program have been the most compelling, meaningful, and helpful practices through which I have apprehended the grace of Jesus Christ." A graduate of an evangelical college and seminary, he feels that he never really understood faith until he went through the twelve steps. "I experienced the gospel of Jesus Christ in dramatic ways," he confesses. "I learned that God is wildly at work in healing, redemptive, saving ways that were *way* outside the confines of the evangelical church." Through AA's practices of self-awareness, honesty, forgiveness, and reconciliation, he found new life.

> The deepest and most important spiritual lessons I ever learned came from a circle of drunks, fighting desperately not to drink today, whom I initially viewed as low-life losers, and who ultimately came to be for me the oracles of God. The Twelve Steps in no way diminished my appreciation for the gospel of Jesus Christ—quite the contrary—I am more convinced than ever of the reality of the gospel story.

In other words, practices transformed him. Alcoholics Anonymous teaches addicts to "fake it until you make it." Translating this insight into Christian spirituality, if you act like a Christian, you might just become one.

My friend's story illustrates an important aspect of contemporary Christian spirituality. In order to understand it, you have to dive in and do it. Devotion means stepping into the river of God, moving with the love of Christ. "I am particularly fed by solitary prayer," says Jan Edmiston, a Presbyterian minister in Virginia. "I walk in my neighborhood and pray as I go. I occasionally go to the National Cathedral and sit alone to pray in a corner without much traffic. I journal. For the past two years I have found that blogging has become an important spiritual practice. I can barely get through the day without taking time to reflect this way."

In the 1990s sociologist Robert Wuthnow noticed that Christian spirituality was developing a new orientation toward practice—the things that Christian people do for the sake of God in the world.[11] While practices are both practical and tangible, they also involve reflection. As a result, much of generative Christianity has a surprisingly introspective quality, as Jan pointed out. "I hear a call to fasting and silence," twenty-something Jonathan Wilson-Hartgrove tells me, "in our culture of senseless noise and artificial abundance." Kathy Staudt, an Episcopalian, says contemplative prayer is a compelling spiritual practice, "gazing, waiting on God's presence." Sky relates the power of a contemplative prayer service at his Baptist church. "We share music, poetry, readings, prayers, and life journeys," he says, "in ways that have contemporary meaning to my life." Rebecca Schott, a Roman Catholic spiritual director and mother in Ohio, testifies, "The contemplative tradition has most deeply influenced my spiritual growth and my identity. My Christian action flows from my life of prayer." Aaron McCarroll Gallegos agrees: "An authentic prayer life has become one of the most important Christian practices for me. . . . Without a vital inner spiritual life, I believe it is almost certain that one will lose their way."

The focus of this is often found in the ancient liturgical practice of the Lord's Supper, or the Eucharist. In a sense the Eucharist is the North Star, the orienting point of prayer and the contemplative journey. Terry Martin, an Episcopal priest in New Jersey, says that "to participate in God's grace flowing between the members of the gathered community in such a concrete way is the most powerful spiritual experience I have ever had." Although he celebrates it as part of his calling, he confesses, "Sometimes it still takes my breath away."

Ann Holmes Redding, a former Episcopal priest in Seattle who is deeply influenced by Islamic practices as well, insists that this sort of spirituality finds its richest expression in the stuff of the world. "I like using my body in devotion," she says, "making communion real by participating with others; being in conversation about the Word; hearing what's up with my soul when I sing; opening my heart; feeling God's creation and human genius when I touch beads."

None of these people told me faith was best practiced alone. Although all craved inner vitality, they shared that practices were strengthened and enriched in the bodily presence of others. Rebecca in Ohio summed it up: "Life in community is central to my Christian living. I am fully committed to parish and community life and to the joys and challenges that brings."

As is the case with Christian identity, spiritual practices have taken on a fluid quality. Not the purview of experts, or completed actions that may be perfected, practices buoy up the Christian life.

Ethics: Universal Hospitality

Professor Joseph Stewart-Sicking always insists that devotion and justice are interwoven, that spirituality and social justice are of a piece. "I was a junior in college, and I had a scholarship that included weekly community service," he remembers. "I had chosen to be a pastoral assistant at an inner-city Roman Catholic parish."

> Among the pastoral visits, there was one constant: a house mass. To understand this mass, you must understand its setting—a public housing high-rise for the impoverished elderly and the severely mentally ill. Both marginalized groups were left to fight it out in one tower of neglect: amidst the gray institutional hallways were piles of trash, disturbed by various foul scurrying creatures. It was hell. I used to call one of the residents my Virgil, leading me through the torments to parishioners. She was a parishioner who lived on the seventh floor and offered her apartment for mass. Each week the priest and I would round up all the residents who wanted to come and set them all up in her somewhat cramped quarters, with the dining room table serving as an altar. It was a place of simple yet intensely genuine and beautiful prayer. I understood for the first time what God's beauty really looked like—the beauty of contemplation joined with service, all among the "least of these." I could see what it meant to feed people with the spiritual food of Christ's Body and Blood. And while I found a spiritual home in the Episcopal Church,

> these masses still stand at the heart of my understanding of Christian identity.

"I can't separate devotion from ethics," he says.

Joseph's story is a discrete example of what many Christians long for: a faith that moves into the world to make it new with God's beauty. The house mass illustrates this sense of justice, the "making right" of all things. There in a grimy urban building, surrounded by trash and vermin, a priest, a student, and some elderly and disabled residents make the Eucharist, or "thanksgiving." Their praise transcends and transforms the setting and in the process creates a community that embodies Jesus in the worst of circumstances. Although the liturgy is performed in a specific, local setting, it moves beyond the walls of the tenement toward the cosmos. The participants enact a universal story; the mass connects them across time and space, joining their lives with God and with others. For a brief moment, everything is different.

It is also a story of hospitality. The transformation is not about the supernatural magic of the mass. Rather, justice occurs around a table at someone's home. There bread and wine invite the outcasts, the marginalized, to God's table. Together these people—the ones society has abandoned—feast with Christ, the expansive host. God's welcome is the radical act. And the mass fulfills Jesus's vision of universal justice: "I was hungry and you gave me food, I was thirsty and you gave me something to drink, I was a stranger and you welcomed me" (Matt. 25:35).

That experience reshaped Joseph's life in two ways. First, it taught him that Christian devotion always has social consequences. He understands himself as a Christian as participating in "the alternative politics of those in love with Christ," and he says, "Faith is only understood through experiencing its witness." Second, he is also a priest, a person whom his church (Episcopal) authorizes to celebrate the Eucharist. The liturgical is ethical, he insists. In liturgy "we are given a glimpse of the reign of God that moves us in hope towards greater love of God and neighbor."

Over the last few years, as a researcher and writer, I have listened to thousands of North American Christians express the same longings to which Joseph testified. The practice of Christian ethics is subtly becoming a vision of justice through universal hospitality, in other words, that the whole world will be made right through the boundless welcome of all to God's table. Without the work of justice, somehow faith is dead. Teresa explained it in the words of Menno Simmons (sixteenth century):

> True evangelical faith cannot lie dormant.
> It clothes the naked.
> It feeds the hungry.
> It comforts the sorrowful.
> It shelters the destitute.
> It serves those that harm it.
> It binds up that which is wounded.
> It has become all things to all people.

In Seattle Anne Holmes Redding describes universal hospitality as "making connections of the heart across humanly devised lines of separation. Cooperating with God's healing work in self, other, community, and world. Hearing and responding to the groans of creation. Basically falling in love with all the 'wrong' folks. Helping Jesus be a bridge rather than a barrier."

Rebecca refers to this as "Cardinal Bernardin's 'seamless garment' model," with its "preferential option for the poor and an obligation to work to achieve justice and equality." Kathy Staudt describes it as closing "the huge gap between the rich man and Lazarus; helping those who feel outcast and unloved to know that they are greatly beloved." Terry puts it simply: "We must alleviate suffering. It is through our loving actions that we manifest hope and move with God to transform this world." Jason Byassee, a thirty-something Methodist, says that Christians must "feed the hungry, clothe the naked, visit the imprisoned, all taken in a frighteningly literal way." Justice is not a metaphor.

Part of universal hospitality is in the practice of befriending other religious traditions and practices, while remaining deeply grounded. Brent Bill thinks Christians need to engage in "theological hospitality," that we "should be open and welcoming . . . instead of starting with the theological differences that divide us." Of the people I interviewed, only four were members of the denomination to which they were born; three had no religious background at all until they became Christians. Although all were quite committed to their faith communities, they have been a mobile lot—a Presbyterian who became Roman Catholic, several fundamentalists who had become liberal Protestants, a Southern Baptist–turned Pentecostal–turned Presbyterian, a Wesleyan-Presbyterian-Mennonite, and a Roman Catholic who converted to the Episcopal Church.

Most interesting, perhaps, were the Christians who claimed some sort of multiple or blended identity, thus embodying practices of religious friendship in their own lives. Jason Byassee, who is proudly Methodist, is also a Roman Catholic. When he was a baby his Catholic grandmother had him secretly baptized in her church against the wishes of his "pagan" parents. When his parents had their own religious experience, they also baptized him—this time with the Methodists. "I've had a joint identity ever since," he jokes. "We're all church mutts these days."

Steven Toshio Yamaguchi interprets his Christian faith through the lens of Japanese culture, which encourages "listening more than talking, being attentive, respecting the other, saving face, and appreciating beauty and simplicity." Likewise, Aaron McCarroll Gallegos is a Chicano who celebrates his Native American heritage. "I've participated in many indigenous ceremonies," he says, "including sweat lodge, sacred pipe, and sun dance. For many Chicanos, including me, there is no contradiction between Christian practices and native ceremonies. Both paths together complete our cultural makeup." About half of the people reported that they were fascinated by or borrowed practices from Buddhism. Sky describes himself as a "Buddhist-Baptist" whose primary religious practice is Zen meditation. Like Jason Byassee, Anne Holmes Redding claims dual identity—but she is both Christian and Muslim and participates fully in both communities and sets of practices. "Becoming a Muslim," she once told me, "has made me a better Christian."

It might be easy to accuse these people of sloppy thinking or random choice, a thoughtless spiritual stew of postmodern goofiness. But that would not be the case. Their spiritual lives reflect considered choices; they are well aware of the theological implications of their actions. They remain deeply Christian while at the same time welcoming the insights and practices of a wide variety of religions. In their collective experience they are trying to express God's hospitality toward all. Justice demands that all divisions be overcome by Christ's love—divisions of economics, class, race, health, education, nationality, and religion. In addition, they insist that the Christian ethical vision includes environmental stewardship or creation care, suggesting that the divide between human beings and the rest of creation also needs to be healed, that nature has become a stranger to us—a stranger to be welcomed as part of God's universal hospitality.

Universal hospitality. Welcoming all to God's table. A river of justice. Or, as the prophet Isaiah envisioned long ago, "They will not hurt or destroy on my holy mountain; for the earth will be full of the knowledge of the Lord as the waters cover the sea" (Isa. 11:9).

JUST BEFORE THE Iraq war began Jonathan and Leah Wilson-Hartgrove went to that country with Christian Peacemaker Teams in an effort to model Christ's love on the eve of the American invasion. It was a terribly risky venture. When the war started they had to escape through the desert to safety in Jordan.

The team's caravan traveled over difficult roads as American bombs fell. The car ahead of the one carrying Jonathan and Leah crashed. Jonathan and Leah remember the horror of seeing their friends thrown from the car. They jumped out to tend their injured colleagues, unsure of how to proceed.

Just then some Iraqis stopped by the roadside. Seeing the wounded Americans lying in the ditch, they picked them up. Jonathan recalls, "They carried our bleeding friends to this town called Rutba. When we got there the doctor said, 'Three days ago your country bombed our hospital. But we will take care of you.' He sewed up their heads and saved their lives. When I asked the doctor what we owed him for his services, he said, 'Nothing. Please just tell the world what has happened in Rutba.'"

Jonathan continues, "The more we told that story after returning from Iraq, the more we realized that it was a Good Samaritan story. The Iraqis, who were supposed to be our enemies, had stopped by the roadside, pulled our friends out of the ditch, and saved their lives. God gave us a sign of his love and sent a Good Iraqi to teach us how to love our neighbors as ourselves. In so many ways my life has become a meditation on the Good Samaritan story that we lived in the desert. The radical hospitality of people who were supposed to be my enemies opened my eyes to God's love in the world."

The Christian story began two thousand years ago in a Middle Eastern desert. Although this chapter has been about overflowing water, eventually a new riverbed forms. Jonathan and Leah have never fully understood what they experienced in Iraq. But I think they experienced the place where, however briefly, the water receded. They may have glimpsed the future, the contours of a holy geography where the love of God and love of neighbor meet, where people actually follow Jesus's command to "Go and do likewise."

Epilogue

> What is past is prologue.
>
> —William Shakespeare, *The Tempest*

In April 2008 Matthew Felling of WAMU radio in Washington, DC, interviewed Dr. Gordon Livingston, a psychiatrist who for more than thirty years has been studying human happiness. Felling asked the predictable question: "What is it? What makes people happy?"

Livingston responded by listed three things: meaningful work, meaningful relationships, and a sense of hope for the future. The first two are, in many ways, self-explanatory. But hope for the future? How is that achieved?

"By having a realistic sense of history," Livingston responded. He insisted that seeing the past on its own terms—not through the romantic gaze of nostalgia—is intrinsic to human flourishing. Nostalgia, he declared, is the enemy of hope. It tricks people into believing that their best days are gone. A more realistic view of history, he insisted, envisions the past as a theater of experience, some good and some bad, and opens up the possibility of growth and change. Our best days are ahead, not behind. Hope for the future.

Some Christians believe our best days are behind us—that Western Christianity no longer commands the influence and respect it once did; that its churches are weakened, its message muted, and its imaginative sway on individuals and the culture diminished. In order to recapture its former glory, they insist, Christians must go back to some halcyon days when the church was orthodox, prayerful, and pure. The faith of our fathers will surely save us.

Of course, no one agrees exactly what constituted this golden age; what counts as orthodoxy, spirituality, and morality have varied wildly through the last two thousand years. Exactly what are Christians nostalgic for? The early church, with its martyrs and trinitarian formulations? Medieval Christendom with the glories of Aquinas and Chartres? The Reformation? Which one, then? The Calvinists? The Lutherans? The Anabaptists? The Anglicans? The Catholic Reformation? Perhaps the best days of the Christian faith were in the nineteenth century, when missionaries spread out over the entire globe. Or perhaps the best Christian world was in the 1950s, when churches were big and families were strong.

A People's History is not a nostalgia trip. In these pages I hope it is clear that no period of church history is superior to another. Rather, each time unfolds on its own historical merits, as Christians struggle to enact Jesus's command to love God and neighbor in a unique human context. As they wrestled with both their own world and with God, they developed particular practices of devotion and ethics. In turn, they passed these things on to their children and grandchildren, who made them anew. History builds on itself. We are simultaneously just like our ancestors and completely different from them. Thus Christianity becomes a story of accumulated human experience of God that reveals a certain kind of wisdom in the world: To love God and love one's neighbor constitutes the good life. Love is, as the apostle Paul wrote, the greatest of all things. Without love we are, as the good apostle said flatly, "nothing" (1 Cor. 13). Without love, Christianity is either a pretty bad joke or a twisted political agenda.

Big-C Christianity has often surrendered the pursuit of love in favor of the pursuit of its own power and perfection; Great Command Christianity grounds faith in love of God and neighbor. Because Great Command Christianity seeks not its own way, it has been harder to detect in history, but it is there. It is the undertow of those quiet souls—some named, many unnamed—who have made the world a better place, as Jesus so instructed. They testify, pray, offer hospitality, feed hungry people, and visit prisoners. They challenge the church, they preach peace, and they call for justice. They are relentlessly creative artists of tradition who experience, as Augustine said, "beauty ever ancient, ever new."[1] They insist that the best days for both the church and the world are ahead. They embody hope. For their trouble, they often have been branded dissenters, heretics, infidels, and witches. Occasionally, the church gets it right and makes them saints.

There is a palpable longing for hope and change these days. "From the perspective of the Bible," states Jim Wallis, "hope is not simply a feeling or a mood or a rhetorical flourish."

> Hope is the very dynamic of history. Hope is the engine of change. Hope is the energy of transformation. Hope is the door from one reality to another. Things that seem possible, reasonable, understandable, even logical in hindsight . . . often seemed quite impossible, unreasonable, nonsensical, and illogical when we were looking ahead to them. The changes, the possibilities, the opportunities, the surprises that no one or very few would even have imagined become history after they've occurred.
>
> Between impossibility and possibility, there is a door, the door of hope. And the possibility of history's transformation lies through that door. . . . Spiritual visionaries have often been the first to walk through that door, because in order to walk through it, first you have to see it, and then you have to believe that something lies on the other side.[2]

A People's History of Christianity is ultimately a history of hope—that regular people often "get it" better than the rich, the famous, and the powerful. We see the door. We can practice God's love and universal hospitality in a world of strangers. That is the tradition of the church—faith, hope, and love entwined, and the greatest of these is love.

When I was a college professor, at the end of every church history course I shared with my students my hope for their lives: "You have studied church history. Now it is your turn. Go make church history."

Acknowledgments

Many thanks go to the professors, writers, friends, and colleagues who make up the community of people who research and teach the history of Christianity and have influenced my understanding of church history, but most especially to Professor Curt Whiteman, who first introduced me to the subject in college, and to Richard Lovelace, Eleanor McLaughlin, George Marsden, Grant Wacker, Bruce Mullin, Russ Richey, David Steinmetz, Elizabeth Clark, and Ted Campbell. The dedication you all bring to telling the stories of the past is a gift to the academy, the church, and the world. No doubt many of you will recognize your influence on these pages, whether specifically cited or not. I know that some will disagree with the interpretations offered here. I hope that I've not stepped on too many professional toes; I ask your forbearance and forgiveness in advance for whatever historical missteps remain in this manuscript. Of all people, church historians surely recognize the challenges of writing a book like this.

My special appreciation to those colleagues whose general histories I found particularly helpful in this project. Each recounts the tale of Christianity on the basis of the best and most recent scholarship on the subject: Robert Bruce Mullin for *A Short World History of Christianity;* Mark Ellingsen for his two-volume history, *Reclaiming Our Roots;* David Chidester for *Christianity: A Global History;* Linda Woodhead for her *Introduction to Christianity;* Martin Marty for *The Christian World;* Barbara MacHaffie for her now-classic *Her Story: Women in Christian Tradition;* and Denis Janz and the entire editorial team of the ambitious and outstanding multivolume *People's History of Christianity* from Fortress Press.

This book began more than fifteen years ago as a church history course in my first teaching position at Westmont College in Santa Barbara, California. The students who populated my classes there were some of the most intellectually engaged and spiritually courageous people I have ever known. I remember you all with gratitude, and hope that you are "making church history." My thanks also go to my former students at Macalester College, Rhodes College, and Virginia Theological Seminary.

I no longer earn my living in academia, but in the world of professional authors and public intellectuals, a community of uniquely gifted people. I am most thankful to Phyllis Tickle, Marcus Borg, Brian McLaren, Barbara Brown Taylor, Jim Wallis, and Lauren Winner for their encouragement, support, and friendship. Anne Howard, Joseph Stewart-Sicking, Linnae Himsl Peterson, Kathy Staudt, Jonathan Wilson, and Howard Anderson are good friends who offered insights along the way. I particularly thank those who contributed to Chapter 13. As always, I thank the library staff at the Virginia Theological Seminary for their generous borrowing privileges. And I am grateful to the Wisconsin Council of Churches and *Christian Century* for inviting me to test drive this material at the Washington Island Forum in June 2008.

The people of HarperOne have stood by this project in its several incarnations and a multitude of adjusted deadlines, always believing in *A People's History* and pushing me to make it a better, bigger book. I especially thank Roger Freet, whose editorial companionship makes writing both intellectually rewarding and surprisingly fun. My sincere appreciation extends to Mark Tauber, Mickey Maudlin, Lisa Zuniga, and the rest of the Harper team for their commitment to telling the history of Great Command Christianity.

This book—and the hundreds of books and articles that I consulted for it—squatted in my family room for more than a year, effectively turning our favorite gathering place into a very messy library. My husband, Richard, and daughter, Emma, endured much as I struggled through two thousand years of Christian history. To them and my stepson, Jonah, I owe my heart, humor, and sanity. Thank you, Richard, for being my first, best reader always.

Emma, you are now eleven, and I have dedicated this book to you. As you journey toward adulthood, I give you these stories as a gift from your ancestors, tales of their wisdom to accompany you on your way. I pray that you continue to embrace Great Command Christianity and that throughout your life you will, as Jesus directed, "Go and do likewise." I am, as always, proud of you.

Diana Butler Bass

Alexandria, Virginia

Notes

INTRODUCTION: AFTER JESUS

1. Rowan Williams, *Why Study the Past? The Quest for the Historical Church* (Grand Rapids, MI: Eerdmans, 2005), 25.
2. Gustav Neibuhr makes this point in his *Beyond Tolerance: Searching for Interfaith Understanding in America* (New York: Viking, 2008), xii.
3. Jeff Sharlet, *The Family: The Secret Fundamentalism at the Heart of American Power* (New York: HarperCollins, 2008), 339–56, 364–69.
4. http://ebooks.adelaide.edu.au/s/shelley/percy_bysshe/s54cp/volume. Shelley, *The Revolt of Islam: A Poem in Twelve Cantos*, Canto 7, line 2850. Somewhat ironically perhaps, Shelley is using Islam—not Christianity—as an example of broken memory.
5. Danièle Hervieu-Léger, *Religion as a Chain of Memory* (New Brunswick, NJ: Rutgers University Press, 2000), 3.
6. Christopher Hitchens, *God Is Not Great: How Religion Poisons Everything* (New York: Twelve Publishers, 2007).
7. As an example, see Mark Noll, *The Scandal of the Evangelical Mind* (Grand Rapids, MI: Eerdmans, 1994).
8. Those Christians in "brand-name" denominations such as the Episcopal Church, the Evangelical Lutheran Church in America, the Presbyterian Church, USA, the American Baptists, the United Methodists,

Disciples of Christ, Reformed Church in America, and the United Church of Christ.

9. Jackson W. Carroll and Wade Clark Roof, *Beyond Establishment: Protestant Identity in a Post-Protestant Age* (Louisville, KY: Westminster/John Knox Press, 1993), 16–17.

10. Robert Bellah et al., *Habits of the Heart* (Berkeley: University of California Press, 1985), 153.

11. Phyllis Tickle, *The Great Emergence: How Christianity Is Changing and Why* (Grand Rapids, MI: Baker Books, 2008); E. J. Dionne Jr., *Souled Out: Reclaiming Faith and Politics After the Religious Right* (Princeton, NJ: Princeton University Press, 2008); Jim Wallis, *The Great Awakening: Reviving Faith and Politics in a Post-Religious Right America* (San Francisco: HarperOne, 2008); Diana Butler Bass, *Christianity for the Rest of Us* (San Francisco: HarperSanFrancisco, 2006); Hal Taussig, *A New Spiritual Home: Progressive Christianity at the Grass Roots* (Santa Rosa, CA: Polebridge Press, 2006); Marcus Borg, *The Heart of Christianity: Rediscovering a Life of Faith* (San Francisco: HarperSanFrancisco, 2003); Ian Markham and Martyn Percy, eds., *Why Liberal Churches Are Growing* (London: T & T Clark, 2006); Michael Schwartzentruber, ed., *The Emerging Christian Way* (Kelowna, BC: CooperHouse, 2006); Eric Elnes, *Asphalt Jesus: Finding a New Christian Faith Along the Highways of America* (San Francisco: Jossey-Bass, 2007); Tony Jones, *The New Christians: Dispatches from the Emergent Frontier* (San Francisco: Jossey-Bass, 2008). See also Alan Cooperman, "Evangelicals at a Crossroads as Falwell's Generation Fades," *Washington Post*, May 22, 2007, A1. Scholars and observers have been struggling with a name for this rebirth; *emerging, progressive, practicing, intentional, neotraditional, new paradigm, postmodern, postliberal, postdenominational, postpartisan,* and *transformational Christianity* are all terms used to describe the renewal of mainline and liberal churches and the creation of alternative forms of community (such as house churches and online churches).

12. This portrait is drawn most thoroughly by Marcus Borg in *Jesus: Uncovering the Life, Teaching, and Relevance of a Religious Revolutionary* (San Francisco: HarperSanFrancisco, 2006). But versions of this Jesus are widely shared throughout the progressive community, including its more evangelical quarters. See, for example, Shane Claiborne and Chris Haw, *Jesus for President: Politics for Ordinary Radicals* (Grand Rapids, MI: Zondervan, 2008).

13. Howard Zinn, *A People's History of the United States* (New York: HarperCollins, 2003), 686, 683.

14. Mary F. Bednarowski, "Multiplicity and Ambiguity," in *A People's History of Christianity*, vol. 7, *Twentieth-Century Global Christianity* (Minneapolis: Fortress Press, 2008), 11–16.
15. Williams, *Why Study the Past?*

CHAPTER 1: CHRISTIANITY AS A WAY OF LIFE

1. Some scholars will no doubt quibble with this assertion. Protestantism itself is a kind of restorationist religion. In the sixteenth century the Reformers argued that Roman Catholicism had obscured the true message of Jesus and that Catholic accretions must be purged in order to renew the church. This chapter argues only that the restorationist impulse was introduced to liberal American Protestantism through the stir caused by Schweitzer's *Quest*. This impulse should not be confused with the early nineteenth-century restorationist movement that resulted in the birth of several denominations, including the Mormons and the Disciples of Christ.
2. Not all Protestants agreed with Schweitzer's conclusions about the historical Jesus; indeed, much of the twentieth century roiled with arguments between liberals, who accepted historical criticism, and conservatives, who rejected (or selectively employed) it. But eventually most liberal and conservative Protestants accepted the idea of the search while arguing over specific findings.
3. Although critics have long noted a decline in liberal Protestantism, *all* institutional forms of Christianity—regardless of their theological stance—are in decline in Western countries. See Paul Heelas and Linda Woodhead et al., *The Spiritual Revolution* (London: Blackwell, 2005); U.S. Religious Landscape Survey, Report 1, "Religious Affiliation," http://religions.pewforum.org/reports#; George Barna, *Revolution: Finding Vibrant Faith Beyond the Walls of the Sanctuary* (Wheaton, IL: Tyndale House, 2006).
4. Vida Scudder, *Socialism and Character* (Boston: Houghton Mifflin, 1912), 346.
5. See Rodney Stark, *Cities of God* (San Francisco: HarperOne, 2007), 26ff. for a full—and colorful—description of the deplorable conditions of ancient Roman cities; quote on 29.
6. Stark, *Cities of God*, 30.
7. For a summary of the ancient attacks on Christianity, see Robert L. Wilken, *The Christians as the Romans Saw Them* (New Haven, CT: Yale University Press, 1984).

8. Justin Martyr, 1 Apol. 14, quoted in Rowan Greer, *Broken Lights and Mended Lives: Theology and Common Life in the Early Church* (University Park: Pennsylvania State University Press, 1986), 13.
9. The importance of Jesus's teaching here is underscored by its inclusion in all three of the synoptic Gospels. See also Matthew 22:23–33 and Luke 10:25–28. The Mark version is the earliest of the three Gospel versions; I used the Luke version in the introduction.
10. "Didache," Roberts-Donaldson translation, *Early Christian Writings*, http://www.earlychristianwritings.com/text/didache-roberts.html.
11. Robin Jensen, "Baptismal Rites and Architecture," in *Late Ancient Christianity*, ed. Virginia Burrus (Minneapolis: Fortress Press, 2005), 117–44.
12. See, for example, Diana Butler Bass, *Christianity for the Rest of Us: How the Neighborhood Church Is Transforming the Faith* (San Francisco: HarperOne, 2006); Marcus Borg, *The Heart of Christianity: Rediscovering a Life of Faith* (San Francisco: HarperSanFrancisco, 2003); Phyllis Tickle, *The Great Emergence: How Christianity Is Changing and Why* (Grand Rapids, MI: Baker Books, 2008).

CHAPTER 2: DEVOTION: THE LOVE OF GOD

1. David Kinnaman, with Gabe Lyons, *UnChristian: What a New Generation Really Thinks About Christianity . . . And Why It Matters* (Grand Rapids, MI: Baker Books, 2007), 21–40.
2. There is significant disagreement in the Islamic world as to whether suicide bombers can be considered martyrs. Mainstream Muslims believe that martyrdom consists in a nonviolent acceptance of persecution of an individual for the sake of his or her faith—not the active pursuit of death. In early Christianity and in the medieval church, Christian authorities and theologians had a very similar argument about what constituted martyrdom. Orthodox Christianity insists that martyrdom should be welcomed if the occasion arises, but that it should not be provoked, especially by violent acts. There are recorded instances in Christian history (during the Crusades, for example) when Christians failed to live up to their own theology and enacted martyrdoms akin to that of the contemporary Palestinian woman. See, for example, the "martyr-activists" of Cordoba in the 850s who instigated their own deaths to make a political point in Chris Lowney, *A Vanished World: Muslims, Christians, and Jews in Medieval Spain* (New York: Oxford, 2005), 55–63.
3. Perpetua, "The Martyrdom of Perpetua (203)," in *In Her Words: Women's Writings in the History of Christian Thought*, ed. Amy G. Oden (Nashville:

Abingdon Press, 1994). All quotes in this section are from this source. For an academic discussion of this account, see Ross S. Kraemer and Shira L. Lander, "Perpetua and Felicitas," in *The Early Christian World*, vol. 2, ed. Philip F. Esler (London: Routledge, 2000), 1048–68.

4. Barbara MacHaffie, *Her Story: Women in Christian Tradition*, 1st ed. (Philadelphia: Fortress Press, 1986), 36.
5. Irenaeus, *Against Heresies*, 5.21.1 and 5, pref.
6. Mark Ellingsen, *Reclaiming Our Roots: An Inclusive Introduction to Church History* (Harrisburg, PA: Trinity Press, 1999), 1:72.
7. Clement of Alexandria, *Exhortation to the Heathen*, 12, 9.
8. Stephanie Paulsell, *Honoring the Body* (San Francisco: Jossey-Bass, 2002), xiv, 8–9.
9. Paulsell, *Honoring the Body*, 3.
10. Irenaeus, *Against Heresies*, 4.20.7.
11. Barack Obama, "Call to Renewal Keynote Address," *Barack Obama, U.S. Senator for Illinois*, http://obama.senate.gov/speech/060628call_to_renewal.
12. It is rather difficult to tell if the Catechetical School was a learning academy based on the model of the Platonic Academy in Athens or if the Alexandrian school was a more informal gathering of teachers from the Museum who instructed new Christians in their homes.
13. Quoted in "An Introduction to the School of Alexandria," *Coptic Orthodox Church Network*, http://www.copticchurch.net/topics/patrology/schoolofalex/I-Intro/chapter1.html.
14. Everett Ferguson, ed., *Encyclopedia of Early Christianity* (New York: Garland, 1997), s.v. "Origen."
15. Steven Fanning, *Mystics of the Christian Tradition* (London: Routledge, 2001), 25.
16. *Oxford Dictionary of Christianity*, 3rd ed., edited by E. A. Livingstone (Oxford: Oxford University Press, 1997), s.v. "Allegory."
17. Origen, *On First Principles*, 4.16.
18. Origen, *On First Principles*, 4.18.
19. Ursula King, *Christian Mystics* (Mahwah, NJ: Hidden Spring, 2001), 34.
20. As far as anyone knows, Origen was the first Christian theologian to interpret Song of Songs in this way.
21. Origen, *The Song of Songs, Commentaries and Homilies*, trans. R. P. Lawson, *Ancient Christian Writers: The Works of the Fathers in Translation*, ed. J. Quasten and J. Plumpe (Westminster, MD: Newman Press, 1957), 23.

22. Athanasius, *Life of Anthony*, was one of the best-selling books of the fourth century.
23. Quoted in Fanning, *Mystics*, 29.
24. King, *Christian Mystics*, 43.
25. A very good book on the desert tradition is Roberta C. Bondi, *To Love as God Loves* (Philadelphia: Fortress Press, 1987).
26. Mary C. Earle, *The Desert Mothers: Spiritual Practices from Women of the Wilderness* (Harrisburg, PA: Morehouse, 2007), 8.
27. Quoted in Bondi, *To Love*, 25.
28. Quoted in Laura Swan, *The Forgotten Desert Mothers: Sayings, Lives, and Stories of Early Christian Women* (New York: Paulist Press, 2001), 60.
29. Roberta C. Bondi, *To Pray and to Love* (Minneapolis: Fortress Press, 1991), 12–13, 14.
30. Donald Schell, "The Dancing Saints," *God's Friends* 8, no. 2 (August 1997), http://godsfriends.org/Vol8/No2/Dancing_Saints.html.
31. University Hill Congregation, "Salt of the Earth: The Christian Seasons Calendar," http://www.thechristiancalendar.com.
32. David Frankfurter, "Beyond Magic and Superstition," in *Late Ancient Christianity*, ed. Virginia Burrus (Minneapolis: Fortress Press, 2005), 260.
33. *The Study of the Liturgy*, ed. Cheslyn Jones, Geoffrey Wainwright, and Edward Yarnold (New York: Oxford, 1978), 404.
34. Robert Bruce Mullin, *A Short World History of Christianity* (Louisville, KY: Westminster John Knox Press, 2008), 58–59.
35. There are many versions of Egeria's pilgrimage. These quotes are from Oden, ed., *In Her Words*, 78–79, and Mary Gerhart and Fabian Udoh, eds., *The Christianity Reader* (Chicago: University of Chicago Press, 2007), 356.
36. Quoted by John Abela, OFM, "Egeria: Some Background Information," *Basilica of the Holy Sepulchre*, http://198.62.75.1/www1/jhs/TSspegria.html.
37. Rita Nakashima Brock and Rebecca Ann Parker, *Saving Paradise: How Christianity Traded Love of This World for Crucifixion and Empire* (Boston: Beacon Press, 2008), 133, 84.
38. Dorothy Bass, *Receiving the Day* (San Francisco: Jossey-Bass, 2000), 87, 90, 96–97.

39. Matt Bai gives some insight into the emergence of *progressive* in his book, *The Argument: Billionaires, Bloggers, and the Battle to Remake Democratic Politics* (New York: Penguin, 2007).
40. And Jews, Muslims, and Buddhists too. See Robert Jones, *Progressive and Religious: How Christian, Jewish, Muslim, and Buddhist Leaders Are Moving Beyond the Culture Wars* (Lanham, MD: Rowman & Littlefield, 2008).
41. Quoted in Greer, *Broken Lights*, 45.
42. Gregory of Nyssa, *Life of Moses*, 1.8, 1.5.
43. Gregory of Nyssa, *Life of Moses*, 2.312, 2.316, 2.317.
44. Gregory of Nyssa, *Life of Moses*, 2.319, 2.320.

CHAPTER 3: ETHICS: THE LOVE OF NEIGHBOR

1. Rodney Stark, *The Rise of Christianity: A Sociologist Reconsiders History* (Princeton, NJ: Princeton University Press, 1996), 38, 78.
2. Quoted in Stark, *Rise of Christianity*, 81.
3. Stark, *Rise of Christianity*, 211.
4. John Chrysostom, Homily 25 on 1 Cor., http://en.wikisource.org/wiki/Nicene_and_Post-Nicene_Fathers:_Series_1/Volume_X.
5. Quoted in Amy G. Oden, ed., *In Her Words: Women's Writings in the History of Christian Thought* (Nashville: Abingdon Press, 1994), 60.
6. Quoted in Rowan Greer, *Broken Lights and Mended Lives: Theology and Common Life in the Early Church* (University Park: Pennsylvania State University Press, 1986), 119.
7. Harry O. Maier, "Heresy, Households, and the Disciplining of Diversity," in *Late Ancient Christianity*, ed. Virginia Burrus (Minneapolis: Fortress Press, 2005), 213–33.
8. For a good discussion of Priscilla, see Carolyn Osiek and Margaret Y. MacDonald with Janey H. Tulloch, *A Woman's Place: House Churches in Earliest Christianity* (Minneapolis: Fortress Press, 2006), 26–35.
9. Greer, *Broken Lights*, 131.
10. Quoted in Oden, ed., *In Her Words*, 174.
11. Greer, *Broken Lights*, 124.
12. Chrysostom, *Homilies*, 14.2, quoted in Greer, *Broken Lights*, 129.
13. Julian the Apostate, the last Roman emperor to conduct a persecution, said as much himself. See also Rodney Stark, *The Rise of Christianity:*

A Sociologist Reconsiders History (Princeton, NJ: Princeton University Press, 1996), esp. chap. 4, "Epidemics, Networks, Conversion," regarding the practice of hospitality toward the sick and dying.

14. Tertullian, *Apology* 39, 1989, quoted in Stark, *Rise of Christianity*, 87.
15. Quoted by Ted Mellor, "Traditional Values," *Anglo-Catholic Socialism*, http://www.anglocatholicsocialism.org/acsoc.html.
16. Quoted in Greer, *Broken Lights*, 120.
17. Quoted by Ted Mellor, "Traditional Values," *Anglo-Catholic Socialism*, http://www.anglocatholicsocialism.org/acsoc.html.
18. Quoted by Ted Mellor, "'Should We Not Make It a Heaven on Earth?' From a Homily by St. John Chrysostom on the Acts of the Apostles," *Anglo-Catholic Socialism*, http://www.anglocatholicsocialism.org/chrysos.html.
19. Quoted by Ted Mellor, "Traditional Values," *Anglo-Catholic Socialism*, http://www.anglocatholicsocialism.org/acsoc.html.
20. John Chrysostom, *Homilies on the Gospel of Matthew*, 46.3.
21. John Chrysostom, Homily 14 on Timothy, in *In Her Words*, ed. Oden, 105.
22. Reported in numerous sources, including David Chidester, *Christianity: A Global History* (San Francisco: HarperSanFrancisco, 2000), 187.
23. Some may protest that the Gospels and Acts mention soldiers who believed in Christ. While that is true, neither the Gospels nor Acts mentions what those soldiers did after their baptism in relation to their profession of faith and their vocations.
24. Quoted by Sojourners, "Sojomail," *Sojourners: Faith, Politics, Culture*, http://www.sojo.net/index.cfm?action=sojomail.display&issue=020925.
25. Lisa Sowle Cahill, *Love Your Enemies: Discipleship, Pacifism, and Just War Theory* (Minneapolis: Fortress Press, 1994), 41.
26. Tertullian, *Of the Crown* (ca. 201) http://www.tertullian.org/lfc/LFC10-11_de_corona.htm.
27. Tertullian, *On Idolatry*. Excellent discussion on Tertullian in Cahill, *Love Your Enemies*, 41–48.
28. *Anglo-Catholic Socialism*, http://www.anglocatholicsocialism.org/assoc.html.
29. Cahill, *Love Your Enemies*, 54.
30. Roberts-Donaldson English translation, *Epistle of Mathetes to Diognetus*, 5, *Early Christian Writings*, http://www.earlychristianwritings.com/text/diognetus-roberts.html.

31. Tertullian, *The Prescription Against Heretics,* trans. Peter Holmes, *Ante-Nicene Fathers,* vol. 3, *Latin Christianity: Its Founder, Tertullian,* ed. Allan Menzies, chap. 7 (Edinburgh: T & T Clark, n.d.), *Christian Classics Ethereal Library,* http://www.ccel.org/ccel/schaff/anf03.v.iii.vii.html.
32. A good discussion of Justin's and Tertullian's contrasting methods can be found in Mark Ellingsen, *Reclaiming Our Roots: An Inclusive Introduction to Church History* (Harrisburg, PA: Trinity Press, 1999), 1:49–55.
33. Rowan Williams, *Why Study the Past? The Quest for the Historical Church* (Grand Rapids, MI: Eerdmans, 2005), 34.
34. Verna Dozier, *The Dream of God: A Call to Return* (Cambridge, MA: Cowley, 1991).
35. And a set of views that basically abandoned the early church's emphasis on the imitation of Christ and deification—ideals that would continue in Eastern Orthodox Christianity.
36. All quotes in this section are from Augustine, *Enchiridion on Faith, Hope, and Love,* ed. Henry Paolucci (Chicago: Regnery Gateway, 1961), chap. 21.
37. Thomas Merton, Introduction to Augustine, *City of God* (New York: Modern Library, 1950), ix.
38. This section closely follows an earlier book of mine, Diana Butler Bass, *Broken We Kneel* (San Francisco: Jossey-Bass, 2002), 22–25.
39. Butler Bass, *Broken We Kneel,* 23.

CHAPTER 4: CHRISTIANITY AS SPIRITUAL ARCHITECTURE

1. Any English-speaking tourist who has taken a tour of Chartres since 1958 has likely had Miller as guide. Although I was unaware of it at the time, he is one of the world's foremost experts on Chartres's stained-glass windows and is an internationally famous lecturer. On February 11, 2001, NPR's Sara Chayles interviewed Miller for *All Things Considered,* http://www.npr.org/templates/story/story.php?storyId=1118434.
2. Regine Pernoud, *Those Terrible Middle Ages! Debunking the Myths* (San Francisco: Ignatius Press, 1977), 64.
3. This concept is a prominent aspect of Celtic spirituality.
4. Larry Rasmussen, "Shaping Community," in *Practicing Our Faith,* ed. Dorothy Bass (San Francisco: Jossey-Bass, 1997), 120.

5. Linda Woodhead, *An Introduction to Christianity* (Cambridge: Cambridge University Press, 2004), 90.
6. Quoted in Carl A. Volz, *The Medieval Church: From the Dawn of the Middle Ages to the Eve of the Reformation* (Nashville: Abingdon Press, 1997), 29.
7. Joan Chittister, *The Rule of Benedict: Insights for the Ages* (New York: Crossroad, 1996), 16.
8. Benedict, Prologue to the Rule of St. Benedict, in *The Christianity Reader*, ed. Mary Gerhart and Fabian E. Udoh (Chicago: University of Chicago Press, 2007), 469.

CHAPTER 5: DEVOTION: PARADISE RESTORED

1. In their book *Saving Paradise* (Boston: Beacon, 2008), Rita Brock and Rebecca Parker argue that the image of Christian life as paradise dominated the first Christian millennium. The Middle Ages were, therefore, an extended argument between "paradise" and violent visions of hell and death.
2. William Parker Marsh and Christopher Bamford, eds., *Celtic Christianity: Ecology and Holiness: An Anthology* (Edinburgh: Floris, 1991), 45.
3. Richard Woods, *Christian Spirituality: God's Presence Through the Ages*, rev. ed. (Maryknoll, NY: Orbis Books, 2006), 104.
4. Woods, *Christian Spirituality*, 104.
5. Quoted in Philip Sheldrake, *Living Between Worlds: Place and Journey in Celtic Spirituality* (Cambridge, MA: Cowley, n.d.), 61.
6. Oliver Davies, trans., with Thomas O'Loughlin, *Celtic Spirituality*, Classics of Western Spirituality (New York: Paulist Press, 1999), 155–90.
7. Quoted in Sheldrake, *Living Between Worlds*, 67.
8. Quoted in Sheldrake, *Living Between Worlds*, 67.
9. Stephen Neill, *History of Christian Missions* (New York: Penguin, 1981); Nora K. Chadwick, *The Age of the Saints* (London and New York: Oxford, 1961); George Hunter III, *Celtic Way of Evangelism: How Christianity Can Reach the West . . . Again* (Nashville: Abingdon Press, 2000).
10. Alejandro García-Rivera, "Aesthetics," in *The Blackwell Companion to Christian Spirituality*, ed. Arthur Holder (Oxford: Blackwell, 2005), 352.
11. Quoted in Alain Besançon, *The Forbidden Image: An Intellectual History of Iconoclasm* (Chicago: University of Chicago Press, 2000), 149.

12. Sharon Gerstel, "The Layperson in Church," in *A People's History of Christianity*, vol. 3, *Byzantine Christianity*, ed. Derek Krueger (Minneapolis: Fortress Press, 2006), 111.
13. Charles Barber, "Icons, Prayer, and Vision in the Eleventh Century," in *Byzantine Christianity*, ed. Krueger, 149–61.
14. From John of Damascus, *Apologia Against Those Who Decry Holy Images*, available at *ORB: The On-line Reference Book for Medieval Studies*, ed. Paul Halsall, *Internet Medieval Sourcebook*, http://www.fordham.edu/halsall/basis/johndamascus-images.html.
15. John of Damascus, quoted at "Seventh Ecumenical Council," *Orthodox Wiki*, http://orthodoxwiki.org/Seventh_Ecumenical_Council.
16. Quoted in García-Rivera, "Aesthetics," 351.
17. For a good historical summary of fixed-hour prayer, see Phyllis Tickle, *The Divine Hours: Prayers for Autumn and Wintertime* (New York: Doubleday, 2000), viii–xii.
18. Joan Chittister, *Wisdom Distilled from the Daily: Living the Rule of St. Benedict Today* (San Francisco: HarperSanFrancisco, 1991), 30.
19. Dorothy Bass, *Receiving the Day: Christian Practices for Opening the Gift of Time* (San Francisco: Jossey-Bass, 2000), 26.
20. Ulrike Wiethaus, "Christian Spirituality in the Medieval West, 600–1450," in *The Blackwell Companion to Christian Spirituality*, ed. Arthur Holder (Oxford: Blackwell, 2005), 115.
21. Eamon Duffy, *Marking the Hours: English People and Their Prayers, 1240–1570* (New Haven: Yale University Press, 2006), 5.
22. Duffy, *Marking the Hours*, 55.
23. The story of the Roberts family prayer book is in Duffy, *Marking the Hours*, 81–96; quotes on 91–92 and 96.
24. Shawn Madigan, ed., *Mystics, Visionaries, and Prophets* (Minneapolis: Fortress Press, 1998), 191.
25. Julian, *Showings*, 58, in Madigan, ed., *Mystics, Visionaries*, 200, 202.
26. Julian, *Showings*, 60, in Madigan, ed., *Mystics, Visionaries*, 204.
27. Julian, *Showings*, 63, in Madigan, ed., *Mystics, Visionaries*, 204, 206.
28. For a full exploration of maternal imagery for God, see Caroline Walker Bynum, *Jesus as Mother: Studies in the Spirituality of the High Middle Ages* (Berkeley and Los Angeles: University of California Press, 1982).
29. James Burge, *Heloise and Abelard: A New Biography* (San Francisco: HarperSanFrancisco, 2006), 56.

30. Abelard, *Sic et Non*, quoted in Burge, *Heloise and Abelard*, 54.
31. Abelard, Autobiography, quoted in Burge, *Heloise and Abelard*, 94. For an interesting rendering of their romance, see the 1988 film *Stealing Heaven*, directed by Clive Donner.
32. Burge, *Heloise and Abelard*, 137.
33. In one of the stranger aspects of their story, they named their son Astrolabe, after the medieval scientific and navigational instrument that enabled one to explore the stars, completely breaking with the tradition of naming Christian children after saints. It would be rather like naming a child Google today.
34. Quoted in Pelikan, *The Growth of Medieval Theology (600–1300)* (Chicago: University of Chicago Press, 1978), 127–28.
35. Quoted in Rita Nakashima Brock and Rebecca Ann Parker, *Saving Paradise: How Christianity Traded Love of This World for Crucifixion and Empire* (Boston: Beacon Press, 2008), 292.
36. Brock and Parker, *Saving Paradise*, 293.
37. Richard Holloway, *Doubts and Loves: What Is Left of Christianity* (Edinburgh: Canongate, 2001), 244.
38. John Shinners, ed., *Medieval Popular Religion, 1000–1500: A Reader* (Peterborough, ON: Broadview Press, 1997), 525.
39. "The Art of Dying Well," in Shinners, ed., *Medieval Popular Religion*, 525.
40. "Art of Dying Well," in Shinners, ed., *Medieval Popular Religion*, 526–35.
41. Amy Plantinga Pauw, "Dying Well," in *Practicing Our Faith*, ed. Dorothy Bass (San Francisco: Jossey-Bass, 1997), 167.

CHAPTER 6: ETHICS: WHO IS MY NEIGHBOR?

1. David Chidester, *Christianity: A Global History* (San Francisco: HarperSanFrancisco, 2000), 173, 171.
2. Stephen O'Shea, *Sea of Faith: Islam and Christianity in the Medieval Mediterranean World* (New York: Walker, 2006), 78.
3. Chris Lowney, *A Vanished World: Muslims, Christians, and Jews in Medieval Spain* (New York: Oxford, 2005), 189.
4. Lowney, *Vanished World*, 150.
5. Lowney, *Vanished World*, 161.
6. Lowney, *Vanished World*, 169.

7. Lowney, *Vanished World*, 171.
8. Lowney, *Vanished World*, 173.
9. George M. Marsden, *Fundamentalism in American Culture* (New York: Oxford, 1980); Barbara Rossing, *The Rapture Exposed: The Message of Hope in the Book of Revelation* (Boulder, CO: Westview, 2004).
10. Steven Fanning, *Mystics of the Christian Tradition* (London: Routledge, 2001), 83.
11. Mandalas are more common in Eastern religions than the faiths of the West. One author explains, "The word 'mandala' is from the classical Indian language of Sanskrit. Loosely translated to mean 'circle,' a mandala is far more than a simple shape. It represents wholeness, and can be seen as a model for the organizational structure of life itself—a cosmic diagram that reminds us of our relation to the infinite, the world that extends both beyond and within our bodies and minds"; see Bailey Cunningham, *Mandala: Journey to the Center* (New York: DK Publishing, 2003), quoted at http://www.mandalaproject.org/What/Index.html.
12. Barbara Newman, Introduction to *Hildegard of Bingen: Scivias*, trans. Columba Hart and Jane Bishop (Mahwah, NJ: Paulist Press, 1990), 21.
13. Quoted in Rita Nakashima Brock and Rebecca Ann Parker, *Saving Paradise: How Christianity Traded Love of This World for Crucifixion and Empire* (Boston: Beacon Press, 2008), 289.
14. Barbara Newman, *Sister of Wisdom: St. Hildegard's Theology of the Feminine* (Berkeley and Los Angeles: University of California, 1987), 239.
15. For Hildegard, this even included the Jews, whom she believed would convert to Christ in the end on the basis of love and not coercion—one of the more broadminded positions in medieval theology.
16. Miriam Schmitt and Linda Kulzer, eds., *Medieval Women Monastics: Wisdom's Wellsprings* (Collegeville, MN: Liturgical Press, 1996), 158.
17. Alan Cooperman, *Washington Post*, October 12, 2002.
18. The dates of the Crusades were: First Crusade, 1096–1099; Second, 1147–1149; Third, 1189–1192; Fourth, 1202–1204. The major crusades were supplemented by skirmishes and attacks throughout the time period, with minor crusades continuing until 1291. The best book about the Crusades is Christopher Tyerman, *God's War: A New History of the Crusades* (Cambridge: Harvard University Press, 2006).
19. Lisa Sowle Cahill, *Love Your Enemies: Discipleship, Pacifism, and Just War Theory* (Minneapolis: Fortress Press, 1994), 91.

20. Cahill, *Love Your Enemies*, 92.
21. Mark Jordan, "Thomas Aquinas," in *Empire and the Christian Tradition: New Readings of Classical Theologians*, ed. Kwok Pui-lan, Don H. Compier, and Joerg Rieger (Minneapolis: Fortress Press, 2007), 162.
22. Paul Waldau, *The Specter of Speciesism: Buddhist and Christian Views of Animals*, American Academy of Religion Academy Series (New York: Oxford University Press, 2002), 200–201.
23. Thomas of Delano, *First Life of St. Francis*, quoted in Brother Ramon, SSF, *Franciscan Spirituality: Following St. Francis Today* (London: SPCK, 1994), 134.
24. Lawrence Cunningham, *Francis of Assisi: Performing the Gospel Life* (Grand Rapids, MI: Eerdmans, 2004), 95.
25. Ramon, *Franciscan Spirituality*, 130.
26. Cunningham, 100–102.
27. Cunningham, 93.
28. The other slender thread being that of Celtic spirituality. See for example, Esther de Waal, *The Celtic Vision* (London: Darton, Longman, and Todd, 1988), and *A World Made Whole: Rediscovering the Celtic Tradition* (London: HarperCollins, 1991).
29. Quoted in Ramon, *Franciscan Spirituality*, 130.
30. Ramon, *Franciscan Spirituality*, 130.
31. A summary of these events can be found in James Dowd, "Grace–St. Luke's Rector Ends Turbulent Tenure," *Memphis Commercial Appeal*, September 29, 2007.
32. Cathy Cox and Virginia Brown, *Inside Stories: Ordinary Lives of Extraordinary Authenticity* (Memphis: self-published, 1999), chap. 10, p. 1.
33. Richard Woods, *Christian Spirituality: God's Presence Through the Ages*, rev. ed. (Maryknoll, NY: Orbis Books, 2006), 153.
34. Jo Ann Kay McNamara, *Sisters in Arms: Catholic Nuns Through Two Millennia* (Cambridge: Harvard University Press, 1996), 250.
35. Quoted in McNamara, *Sisters in Arms*, 252–53.
36. Quoted in Shawn Madigan, ed., *Mystics, Visionaries, and Prophets* (Minneapolis: Fortress Press, 1998), 168.
37. Mechthild of Magdeburg, *Flowing Light of the Godhead*, 5.4, 6.3.
38. Cox and Brown, *Inside Stories*, chap. 10, p. 3.
39. McNamara, *Sisters in Arms*, 245.
40. McNamara, *Sisters in Arms*, 251.

41. Rutba House Community, "New Monasticism," http://www.newmonasticism.org/who/who.php.
42. John van Engen, ed., *Devotio Moderna: Basic Writings* (New York: Paulist Press, 1988), 37.
43. Van Engen, ed., *Devotio Moderna*, 47.
44. "Edifying Lives," in van Engen, ed., *Devotio Moderna*, 122. The original document contains the stories of sixty-seven women. All the accounts following can be found in van Engen, *Devotio Moderna*, 121–36. Van Engen also translated "The Chronicle of the Brothers' House at Emmerich," a similar text of men of the New Devout, in *Devotio Moderna*, 137–52.
45. Van Engen, ed., *Devotio Moderna*, 45, 133.

CHAPTER 7: CHRISTIANITY AS LIVING WORDS

1. Steven E. Ozment, *The Reformation in the Cities: The Appeal of Protestantism to Sixteenth-Century Germany and Switzerland* (New Haven, CT: Yale University Press, 1975), 34.
2. Quoted in Hugh T. Kerr, ed., *A Compendium of Luther's Theology* (Philadelphia: Westminster, 1943), 11–12.
3. Richard Lischer, *The End of Words: The Language of Reconciliation in a Culture of Violence* (Grand Rapids, MI: Eerdmans, 2005), 56.
4. Lischer, *End of Words*, 62.
5. Frederick Herzog, "Reformation Today," *Christian Century*, October 27, 1982, 1078, http://www.religion-online.org/showarticles.asp?title=1349.
6. Matthew Fox, *A New Reformation: Creation Spirituality and the Transformation of Christianity* (Rochester, VT: Inner Traditions, 2006), 11–16, 17, 60.
7. Phyllis Tickle, *The Great Emergence: How Christianity Is Changing and Why* (Grand Rapids, MI: Baker Books, 2008); also Phyllis Tickle, "The Future of the Emerging Church," March 19, 2007, *Christianity Today*, http://blog.christianitytoday.com/outofur/archives/2007/03/the_future_of_t.html.
8. Eric Elnes, *The Phoenix Affirmations: A New Vision for the Future of Christianity* (San Francisco: Jossey-Bass, 2006); Marcus Borg, *The Heart of Christianity: Rediscovering a Life of Faith* (San Francisco: HarperSanFrancisco, 2003); John Shelby Spong, "A Call for a New Reformation," http://www.dioceseofnewark.org/jsspong/reform.html; Gretta Vosper, *With or Without God* (Toronto: HarperCollins Canada, 2008).

9. "Rick Warren's Second Reformation: Interview by David Kuo," *Belief Net*, http://www.beliefnet.com/story/177/story_17718_1.html.
10. James H. Gilmore and Joseph B. Pine, *Authenticity: What Consumers Really Want* (Cambridge: Harvard Business School Press, 2007), 148, emphasis theirs.
11. Diarmaid MacCulloch, *The Reformation: A History* (New York: Penguin, 2005), 76–77.
12. MacCulloch, *Reformation*, 98.
13. Quoted in Christianity Today, *Christian History & Biography*, "Erasmus," http://www.christianitytoday.com/history/special/131christians/erasmus.html.
14. MacCulloch, *Reformation*, 99–100, 99.
15. Quoted in Christianity Today, "Erasmus."

CHAPTER 8: DEVOTION: SPEAKING OF FAITH

1. Peter Matheson, "Reforming from Below," in *A People's History of Christianity*, vol. 5, *Reformation Christianity*, ed. Peter Matheson (Minneapolis: Fortress Press, 2007), 19.
2. Quoted in William Bouwsma, "The Spirituality of Renaissance Humanism," in *Christian Spirituality: High Middle Ages and Reformation*, ed. Jill Raitt (New York: Crossroad, 1987), 245.
3. Quoted in James D. Tracy, "Ad Fontes: The Humanist Understanding of Scripture as Nourishment for the Soul," in *Christian Spirituality*, ed. Raitt, 254.
4. Peter Matheson, *The Imaginative World of the Reformation* (Edinburgh: T & T Clark, 2000), 7ff., 125.
5. Brad shared this story with me more than a dozen years ago. I have reconstructed it from memory, and it should be considered a paraphrase.
6. Luther, in Marc Lienhard, "Luther and the Beginnings of the Reformation," in *Christian Spirituality*, ed. Raitt, 269.
7. Luther, in Hans Hillerbrand, *The Reformation: A Narrative History* (1964; repr. Grand Rapids, MI: Baker, 1970), 27.
8. Luther, in Hillerbrand, *Reformation*, 27.
9. Raymond A. Mentzer, "The Piety of Townspeople and City Folk," in *A People's History of Christianity*, vol. 5, *Reformation Christianity*, ed. Peter Matheson (Minneapolis: Fortress Press, 2007), 23.
10. Eamon Duffy, *The Voices of Morebath: Reformation and Rebellion in an English Village* (New Haven, CT: Yale University Press, 2001).

11. Elsie McKee, "The Emergence of Lay Theologies," in *A People's History of Christianity*, vol. 5, *Reformation Christianity*, ed. Peter Matheson (Minneapolis: Fortress Press, 2007), 214–15.
12. Katharina Schütz Zell, "Letter to the Suffering Women of the Community of Kentzingen," in *Church Mother: The Writings of a Protestant Reformer in Sixteenth-Century Germany*, ed. and trans. Elsie McKee (Chicago: University of Chicago Press, 2006), 50–56.
13. Katharina Schütz Zell, "Apologia for Master Zell," in *Church Mother*, ed. McKee, 62–82.
14. See Steven E. Ozment, *Protestants: The Birth of a Revolution* (New York: Doubleday, 1991), 45–66, and *The Reformation in the Cities: The Appeal of Protestantism to Sixteenth-Century Germany and Switzerland* (New Haven, CT: Yale University Press, 1975), 47.
15. This story is from Diana Butler Bass, *Broken We Kneel: Reflections on Faith and Citizenship* (San Francisco: Jossey-Bass, 2004), 45.
16. Don Saliers, "Singing Our Lives," in Dorothy Bass, ed., *Practicing Our Faith* (San Francisco: Jossey-Bass, 1997), 180.
17. Don Saliers and Emily Saliers, *A Song to Sing, a Life to Live: Reflections on Music as Spiritual Practice* (San Francisco: Jossey-Bass, 2005), 12, 37. Don Saliers teaches church music; Emily Saliers, his daughter, is a member of the Indigo Girls.
18. Madeleine Gray, *The Protestant Reformation: Beliefs and Practices* (Brighton, UK: Sussex Academic Press, 2003), 169.
19. Quoted in Matheson, *Imaginative World*, 43.
20. McKee, ed., *Church Mother*, 96.
21. "Durch Adams Fall ist ganz verderbt," trans. Francis Browne, November 2005, *Bach Cantatas Website*, http://www.bach-cantatas.com/Texts/Chorale045-Eng3.htm.
22. Matheson, *Imaginative World*, 25–48.
23. Calvin, in William Bouwsma, "The Spirituality of John Calvin," in *Christian Spirituality: High Middle Ages and Reformation*, ed. Jill Raitt (New York: Crossroad, 1987), 320.
24. Mentzer, "Piety of Townspeople," in *Reformation Christianity*, ed. Matheson, 31.
25. John Calvin, "The Catechism of the Church of Geneva," 1545, quoted in Gary A. Hand, *On Doctrine*, http://www.ondoctrine.com/2cal0504.htm.
26. Peter Matheson, "The Language of the Common Folk," in *A People's History of Christianity*, vol. 5, *Reformation Christianity* (Minneapolis: Fortress Press, 2007), 272.

27. Quoted in Matheson, *Imaginative World*, 127.
28. Quoted in Miriam Usher Chrisman, *Conflicting Visions of Reform: German Lay Propaganda Pamphlets, 1519–1530* (Atlantic Highlands, NJ: Humanities Press, 1996), 69.
29. Tony Jones, *The New Christians: Dispatches from the Emergent Frontier* (San Francisco: Jossey-Bass, 2008), 2.
30. Teresa of Avila, *The Life of Saint Teresa of Avila by Herself*, translation by J. M. Cohen (New York: Penguin, 1957). See also, Cathleen Medwick, *Teresa of Avile: The Progress of a Soul* (New York: Knopf, 1999), especially Chapter 8, "Cultivating Souls," 98–111.
31. Keith P. Luria, "Rural and Village Piety," in Denis Janz, ed., *Reformation Christianity* (Minneapolis: Fortress Press, 2007), 61–68.
32. Anne Winston-Allen, *Stories of the Rose: The Making of the Rosary in the Middle Ages* (University Park, PA: Pennsylvania State University, 1997), 118–119.
33. Luria, "Rural and Village Piety," 61

CHAPTER 9: ETHICS: WALKING THE TALK

1. Martin Luther, "Freedom," in *The Protestant Reformation*, ed. Hans J. Hillerbrand (New York: Walker, 1968), 4.
2. Luther, "Freedom," 4.
3. Luther, "Freedom," 6, 13.
4. Luther, "Freedom," 16, 21.
5. Scott H. Hendrix, *Recultivating the Vineyard: The Reformation Agendas of Christianization* (Louisville, KY: Westminster John Knox Press, 2004), 18.
6. Peter Matheson, *The Imaginative World of the Reformation* (Edinburgh: T & T Clark, 2000), 28–29.
7. Anne Locke, *A Meditation of a Penitent Sinner* (1560); http://www.ccel.org/node/3813. English has been modernized.
8. Luther, *Freedom of a Christian in the Protestant Reformation*, ed. Hans Hillerbrand (New York: Harper, 1968), 23.
9. Miriam Usher Chrisman, *Conflicting Visions of Reform: German Lay Propaganda Pamphlets, 1519–1530* (Atlantic Highlands, NJ: Humanities Press, 1996), 15.
10. Hendrix, *Recultivating the Vineyard*, 35.
11. Quoted in James M. Stayer, "The Dream of a Just Society," in *A People's History of Christianity*, vol. 5, *Reformation Christianity*, ed. Peter Matheson (Minneapolis: Fortress Press, 2007), 194–95.

12. Matheson, *The Imaginative World of the Reformation*, 54–55.
13. Quoted in Peter Matheson, ed., *Argula von Grumbach: A Woman's Voice in the Reformation* (Edinburgh: T & T Clark, 1995), 149.
14. Lotzer's story is told in George H. Williams, *The Radical Reformation*, 3rd ed. (Kirksville, MO: Sixteenth Century Journal Publishers, 1992), 151–55.
15. For the transformation of marriage through time, see Stephanie Coontz, *Marriage: A History* (New York: Viking, 2005).
16. Steven E. Ozment, *The Age of Reform (1250–1550): An Intellectual and Religious History of Late Medieval and Reformation Europe* (New Haven, CT: Yale University Press, 1980), 386.
17. Lyndal Roper, "Luther: Sex, Marriage, and Motherhood," quoted in Henry J. Cohn, *Case Study 9: The Impact of the Reformation on Women in Germany*, http://www.warwick.ac.uk/fac/arts/History/teaching/protref/women/WR0911.htm.
18. Diarmaid MacCulloch, *The Reformation: A History* (New York: Penguin, 2005), 653–54.
19. MacCulloch, *Reformation*, 661.
20. A. L. Maycock, *Nicholas Ferrar of Little Gidding* (Grand Rapids, MI: Eerdmans, 1980), 115.
21. Maycock, *Nicholas Ferrar*, 156.
22. This story is told in three places: Diana Butler Bass, *Christianity for the Rest of Us: How the Neighborhood Church Is Transforming the Faith* (San Francisco: HarperOne, 2006), 129–39; Diana Butler Bass and Joseph Stewart-Sicking, eds., *From Nomads to Pilgrims: Stories from Practicing Congregations* (Herndon, VA: Alban Institute, 2006), and Lillian Daniel, *Tell It Like It Is: Reclaiming the Practice of Testimony* (Herndon, VA: Alban Institute, 2006).
23. Quoted in Elsie McKee, "The Emergence of Lay Theologies," in *A People's History of Christianity*, vol. 5, *Reformation Christianity*, ed. Peter Matheson (Minneapolis: Fortress Press, 2007), 212.
24. See Elaine V. Beilin, ed., *The Examinations of Anne Askew* (New York: Oxford University Press, 1996).
25. Quoted in Timothy George, "The Spirituality of the Radical Reformation," in *Christian Spirituality: High Middle Ages and Reformation*, ed. Jill Raitt (New York: Crossroad, 1987), 344–45.
26. Beilin, ed., *Anne Askew*, 88, 152–55.
27. From the *Registers of the Consistory of Geneva*, quoted in Raymond A. Mentzer, "The Piety of Townspeople and City Folk," in *A People's*

History of Christianity, vol. 5, *Reformation Christianity*, ed. Peter Matheson (Minneapolis: Fortress Press, 2007), 42.

28. MacCulloch, *Reformation*, 591.
29. MacCulloch, *Reformation*, 591.
30. MacCulloch, *Reformation*, 596.
31. Mentzer, "Piety of Townspeople," 42.
32. MacCulloch, *Reformation*, 598, 599.
33. Hendrix, *Recultivating the Vineyard*, 109.
34. Urbanus Rheguius, quoted in Hendrix, *Recultivating the Vineyard*, 113.
35. Bert Friesen et al., eds., *Global Anabaptist Mennonite Encyclopedia Online*, s.v. "Dachser, Jakob (1486–1567)," http://www.gameo.org/encyclopedia/contents/D17.html.
36. Richard F. Lovelace, *Dynamics of Spiritual Life: An Evangelical Theology of Renewal* (Downers Grove, IL: InterVarsity Press, 1979), 13.
37. Peter Erb, ed., *Pietists: Selected Writings* (New York: Paulist Press, 1983), 3.
38. Philipp Jakob Spener, *Pia Desideria*, trans. Theodore G. Tappert (Philadelphia: Fortress Press, 1964), 53.
39. Lovelace, *Dynamics*, 34.
40. Spener, *Pia Desideria*, 115–17.
41. Spener, *Pia Desideria*, 53.
42. Spener, *Pia Desideria*, 95, 101, 96.
43. Quoted in Spener, *Pia Desideria*, 51; from Luther, "Epistle or Instruction from the Saint to the Church in Erfurt," 1522.

CHAPTER 10: CHRISTIANITY AS A QUEST FOR TRUTH

1. Marcus Borg, "An Appreciation of Albert Schweitzer," in Albert Schweitzer, *The Quest of the Historical Jesus*, ed. John Bowden (Minneapolis: Fortress Press, 2001), ix.
2. Charles Taylor, *A Secular Age* (Cambridge: Harvard University Press, 2007), 13–14, 3.
3. There are innumerable books on this subject. But the most helpful in my thinking include: Zygmunt Bauman, *Intimations of Postmodernity* (London: Routledge, 1992); Paul Heelas, *Religion, Modernity and Postmodernity* (Oxford: Blackwell, 1998); Albert Borgmann, *Crossing the Postmodern Divide* (Chicago: University of Chicago Press, 1992).
4. Anthony Giddens, *Modernity and Self-Identity: Self and Society in the Late Modern Age* (Stanford, CA: Stanford University Press, 1991), 14–15, 21.

5. Giddens, *Modernity and Self-Identity*, 21.
6. Schweitzer, *Quest*, 487.

CHAPTER 11: DEVOTION: THE QUEST FOR LIGHT

1. For a longer discussion of this question, see Diana Butler Bass and Joseph Stewart-Sicking, "Europe and North America since 1700," in *The Blackwell Companion to Christian Spirituality*, ed. Arthur Holder (Oxford: Blackwell, 2005), 141ff.
2. George M. Marsden, *Jonathan Edwards: A Life* (New Haven, CT: Yale University Press, 2003), 54.
3. Edwards's belief here has led some historians and theologians to speculate that he was a panentheist, one who believes that God is *in* all things—in distinction to a pantheist, who believes that God *is* all things.
4. Marsden, *Jonathan Edwards*, 156–57.
5. George Fox, "Journal," *Quaker Electronic Journal*, http://www.qis.net/~daruma/fox-ministry.html. On George Fox in the context of seventeenth-century spirituality, see Ted A. Campbell, *Religion of the Heart* (Columbia: University of South Carolina Press, 1991), 58–63.
6. Fox, "Journal."
7. Fox, "Journal."
8. Robert Barclay's *Apology for the True Christian Divinity* (1675), http://www.qis.net/~daruma/barclay.html#PROP%202.
9. Fox, "Journal."
10. Although women had frequently taken on the mantle of prophet, often to the consternation of the church, which sometimes led to imprisonment, charges of witchcraft, exile, or execution. See Anne Llewellyn Barstow, *Witchcraze: A New History of the European Witch Hunts* (San Francisco: HarperSanFrancisco, 1994).
11. Margaret Fell, *Women's Speaking Justified* (ca. 1666) at Quaker Heritage Press, http://www.qhpress.org/texts/fell.html.
12. Phyllis Mack, *Visionary Women: Ecstatic Prophecy in Seventeenth-Century England* (Berkeley and Los Angeles: University of California Press, 1992), 127.
13. Quoted in Jo Ann Kay McNamara, *Sisters in Arms: Catholic Nuns Through Two Millennia* (Cambridge: Harvard University Press, 1996), 539.
14. Juana Inés de la Cruz, *El Sueño*, excerpts, quoted in Dorothy Disse, *Other Women's Voices*, http://home.infionline.net/~ddisse/juana.html#anchor129509.

15. Juana Inés de la Cruz, *Respuesta a Sor Filotea de la Cruz*, in *In Her Words: Women's Writings in the History of Christian Thought*, ed. Amy G. Oden (Nashville: Abingdon Press, 1994), 240.
16. Inés de la Cruz, *Respuesta*, 241–42.
17. Campbell, *Religion of the Heart*, 119.
18. John Wesley, "Journal of John Wesley: 'I Felt My Heart Strangely Warmed,'" Calvin College, *Christian Classics Ethereal Library*, http://www.ccel.org/ccel/wesley/journal.vi.ii.xvi.html.
19. Jerena Lee, *The Life and Religious Experience of Jerena Lee, A Coloured Lady, Giving an Account of Her Call to Preach the Gospel* (Philadelphia, 1836), in William Andrews, *Sisters of the Spirit* (Bloomington: Indiana University Press, 1986), 27–34.
20. Lee, *Life and Religious Experience*, 36, 42.
21. Donald Mathews, *Religion in the Old South* (Chicago: University of Chicago Press, 1977), 9, 14.
22. Mathews, *Old South*, 237–50.
23. Eugene R. Sheridan, *Jefferson and Religion* (Charlottesville, VA: Monticello Monograph Series, 1998), 9.
24. Sheridan, *Jefferson and Religion*, 18.
25. Quoted in Edwin S. Gaustad, *Sworn on the Altar of God: A Religious Biography of Thomas Jefferson* (Grand Rapids, MI: Eerdmans, 1996), 27.
26. Quoted in Sheridan, *Jefferson and Religion*, 18.
27. Quoted in Gaustad, *Altar of God*, 27.
28. Sheridan, *Jefferson and Religion*, 31, 37, 38.
29. Charles Taylor, *A Secular Age* (Cambridge: Harvard University Press, 2007), 222.
30. Taylor, *Secular Age*, 221–34.
31. Quoted in *Eerdman's Handbook to Christianity in America* (Grand Rapids, MI: Eerdmans, 1983), 164.
32. N. Graham Standish, *Becoming a Blessed Church: Forming a Church of Spiritual Purpose, Presence, and Power* (Herndon, VA: Alban Institute, 2005), 15.
33. Daniel G. Reid, ed., *Dictionary of Christianity in America* (Downers Grove, IL: InterVarsity Press, 1990), s.v. "Transcendentalism."
34. Philip Gura, *American Transcendentalism: A History* (New York: Hill & Wang, 2007), 70.
35. Gura, *American Transcendentalism*, 71.

36. Orestes Brownson, *New Views of Christianity, Society, and the Church*, quoted in Gura, *American Transcendentalism*, 77.
37. Ralph Waldo Emerson, "Nature" (1836), at Bill Uzgalis, *The History of Western Philosophy*, http://oregonstate.edu/instruct/phl302/texts/emerson/nature-emerson-a.html#Chapter%20I.
38. This paragraph closely follows Gura's argument on 48–49.
39. Catherine L. Albanese, *Nature Religion in America: From the Algonkian Indians to the New Age* (Chicago: University of Chicago Press, 1990), 81.
40. Horace Bushnell, "Christian Comprehensiveness," *New Englander* 6 (1848), an article from a magazine bound into a single volume, New Haven, Maltby, 81–111. Contemporary historian E. Brooks Holifield identifies Bushnell's essay as the key to his thought; see Holifield, *Theology in America* (New Haven, CT: Yale University Press, 2003), 452–66.
41. Bushnell, "Christian Comprehensiveness," 87.
42. Robert Bruce Mullin points out Bushnell's surprising charity toward Roman Catholicism in his book *The Puritan as Yankee: A Life of Horace Bushnell* (Grand Rapids, MI: Eerdmans, 2002), 102–4; see Bushnell, "Christian Comprehensiveness," 102–5.
43. Bushnell, "Christian Comprehensiveness," 105.
44. Bushnell, "Christian Comprehensiveness," 111.
45. David Van Biema, "Mother Teresa's Crisis of Faith," *Time*, Aug. 23, 2007, http://www.time.com/time/world/article/0,8599,1655415,00.html.
46. Jennifer Hecht, *Doubt: A History* (San Francisco: HarperSanFrancisco, 2003), 314; see especially chaps. 7 and 8.
47. Roger Lundin, *Emily Dickinson and the Art of Belief* (Grand Rapids, MI: Eerdmans, 2004), 43–45.
48. Hecht, *Doubt*, 425.
49. Lundin, *Emily Dickinson*, 168.
50. Quoted in Lundin, *Emily Dickinson*, 3.

CHAPTER 12: ETHICS: KINGDOM QUEST

1. Walter Rauschenbusch's 1907 *Christianity and the Social Crisis* was reprinted in a hundredth-anniversary edition as *Christianity and the Social Crisis in the 21st Century*, ed. Paul Raushenbush (San Francisco: HarperOne, 2007), 55.
2. Theodore Beza, quoted in Benjamin Kaplan, *Divided by Faith: Religious Conflict and the Practice of Toleration in Early Modern Europe* (Cambridge: Harvard University Press, 2007), 20.

3. Delors's story is found in Kaplan, *Divided by Faith*, 21.
4. Kaplan, *Divided by Faith*, 127.
5. All of these experiments are outlined in Kaplan, *Divided by Faith*, which is the best single-volume historical account of toleration available.
6. The artwork and dual nave architecture was completed in the 1740s, some two hundred years after the congregation formed. Pastors who have led congregations through building renovations may take some comfort in this!
7. Kaplan, *Divided by Faith*, 198–204, 211–17.
8. For this history, long forgotten by European Christians, see Philip Jenkins, *The Lost History of Christianity* (San Francisco: HarperOne, 2008).
9. Maria Stewart, "Religion and the Pure Principles of Morality: The Sure Foundation on Which We Must Build," Boston, October 1831, http://afroamhistory.about.com/library/blmaria_stewart_religion.html. All grammar, spelling, and emphasis are original.
10. Maria Stewart, "Lecture Delivered at the Franklin Hall," Boston, September 21, 1832, http://afroamhistory.about.com/library/blmaria_stewart_lecture_franklinhall.htm.
11. Maria Stewart, "Religion."
12. For the full speech, see "Transcript: Hillary Clinton" at http://www.politico.com/news/stories/0808/12869.html.
13. Quotes found in Richard A. Blondo, "Samuel Green: A Black Life in Antebellum Maryland" (Master's Thesis, University of Maryland, 1988), 19.
14. Quoted in Blondo, "Samuel Green," 35–36, 37.
15. Quoted in Blondo, "Samuel Green," 50.
16. Harriet Beecher Stowe, "Simon the Cyrenian," *The Independent* 14 (Jan.–Dec. 1862).
17. Vida Scudder, "Socialism and Spiritual Progress," *Andover Review* (July 1891), 50–51.
18. Vida Scudder, *My Quest for Reality* (Wellesley, MA: the author, 1952), 25.
19. Vida Scudder, *On Journey* (New York: Dutton, 1937), 43.
20. Gary Dorrien, *The Making of American Liberal Theology: Idealism, Realism, and Modernity, 1900–1950* (Westminster, KY: John Knox Press, 2003), 131.
21. Scudder, *My Quest*, 27.

22. Emily Malbone Morgan, ed. Vida Scudder, *Letters to Her Companions* (South Byfield, MA: Society of the Companions of the Holy Cross, 1944), 138.
23. Scudder, "Socialism and Spiritual Progress," 58–61, 62.
24. Scudder, "Socialism and Spiritual Progress," 62–63.
25. Dorrien, *American Liberal Theology*, 132.
26. Scudder, *On Journey*, 120.
27. Dorrien, *American Liberal Theology*, 132–33.
28. Scudder, *On Journey*, 119.
29. Charles Hodge, "What Is Darwinism," in Robert R. Mathison, ed., *The Role of Religion in American Life: An Interpretive Historical Anthology* (Lanham, MD: University Press of America, 1982), 188ff.
30. Robert Bruce Mullin, *A Short World History of Christianity* (Louisville, KY: Westminster John Knox Press, 2008), 207.
31. Harry Emerson Fosdick, *Christianity and Progress* (New York: Revell, 1922), 31.
32. Fosdick, *Christianity and Progress*, 45, 40.
33. Fosdick, *Christianity and Progress*, 49–85.
34. Fosdick, *Christianity and Progress*, 85.
35. Fosdick, *Christianity and Progress*, 208–9, 212–13.
36. Charles Clayton Morrison, "The World Missionary Conference," *Christian Century*, July 7, 1910, available at *Religion Online*, ed. Henry and Grace Adams et al., http://www.religion-online.org/showarticle.asp?title=471.
37. Morrison, "World Missionary Conference."
38. Kenneth Cracknell and Susan White, *An Introduction to World Methodism* (Cambridge: Cambridge University Press, 2005), 243.
39. Quoted in Neela Banerjee, "Survey Shows U.S. Religious Tolerance," *New York Times*, June 24, 2008, http://www.nytimes.com/2008/06/24/us/24religion.html?_r=1&hp&oref=slogin.
40. David Van Biema, "Christians: No One Path to Salvation," *Time*, June 23, 2008, http://www.time.com/time/printout/0,8816,1817217,00.html.
41. Linda Woodhead, ed., *Reinventing Christianity: Nineteenth-Century Contexts* (Aldershot, England: Ashgate, 2001), 84.
42. Quoted in Woodhead, *Reinventing Christianity*, 86.
43. Quoted in Woodhead, *Reinventing Christianity*, 88.

44. Vivekananda, "Response to Welcome," The Complete Works, http://en.wikisource.org/wiki/The_Complete_Works_of_Swami_Vivekananda/Volume_1/Addresses_at_The_Parliament_of_Religions/Response_to_Welcome.
45. Mullin, *Short World History of Christianity*, 227–28.
46. Minnie Andrews Snell, "Aunt Hannah on the Parliament of Religions," *Open Court* (October 12, 1893).
47. Patrick Allitt, *Religion in America Since 1945: A History* (New York: Columbia University Press, 2003).
48. Dietrich Bonhoeffer, *The Cost of Discipleship* (New York: Macmillan, 1963), 40, 47.
49. Dietrich Bonhoeffer, *Letters and Papers from Prison*, Eberhard Bethge, ed. (London: SCM Press, 1953), 90–95.

CHAPTER 13: THE RIVER

1. Henri Nouwen, *Reaching Out* (New York: Doubleday, 1975), 8.
2. For a series of reminiscences of Nouwen's Harvard class, see "A Spiritual Mentor's Lasting Influence," http://www.hds.harvard.edu/news/article_archive/nouwen.html. All quotes about Nouwen's course are from this article.
3. Patrick Allitt, *Religion in America Since 1945: A History* (New York: Columbia University Press, 2003), 263.
4. Albert Schweitzer, *The Quest of the Historical Jesus*, ed. John Bowden (Minneapolis: Fortress Press, 2001), 486–87.
5. Albert Schweitzer, *The Quest of the Historical Jesus* (New York: Macmillan, 1948, 1910 edition), 402–3.
6. Schweitzer, *Quest of the Historical Jesus*, ed. Bowden, 487.
7. Quoted in Rita Nakashima Brock and Rebecca Ann Parker, *Saving Paradise: How Christianity Traded Love of This World for Crucifixion and Empire* (Boston: Beacon Press, 2008), 289.
8. Zygmunt Bauman, *Liquid Modernity* (Oxford: Blackwell, 2000), 1–3.
9. For an interesting and helpful analysis of the kind of Christianity practiced by these people (and many others), see Gustav Niebuhr, *Beyond Tolerance: Searching for Interfaith Understanding in America* (New York: Viking, 2008).
10. Participants included: Anonymous, Brent Bill (b. 1951), Jason Byassee (b. 1974), Lisa Domke (b. 1968), Jan Edmiston (b. 1956), David (Sky) Enroth (b. 1943), Terry Martin (b. 1954), Aaron McCarroll Gallegos (b. 1961), Carol Howard Merritt (b. 1971), Michael Morrell (b. 1980),

Anne Holmes Redding (b. 1951), Rebecca Schott (b. 1958), Teresa Thompson Sherrill (b. 1959), Kathleen Staudt (b. 1953), Joseph Stewart-Sicking (b. 1973), Jonathan Wilson-Hartgrove (b. 1980), and Steven Toshio Yamaguchi (b. 1953).

11. Robert Wuthnow, *After Heaven: Spirituality in America Since the 1950s* (Berkeley: University of California Press, 1998).

EPILOGUE

1. Quoted in Jaroslav Pelikan, *The Vindication of Tradition* (New Haven and London: Yale University Press, 1984), 8.
2. Jim Wallis, *The Soul of Politics* (New York and Maryknoll, NY: New Press and Orbis, 1994), 238–40.

Index

Study Guide

INTRODUCTION: AFTER JESUS

1. Have you ever, as Bass addresses in her Introduction, felt that you needed to qualify your Christianity to others based on widespread assumptions of what being a "Christian" means in today's world?

2. Have you ever described yourself as "spiritual, but not religious?" If yes, what was the context of the situation? Do you actually feel this way or was it used as a way to avoid discussing your religious affiliation?

3. Do you agree with the statement that "Many Western people, even a good number of Christians, secretly agree with atheist Christopher Hitchens when he claims, 'Religion poisons everything.'" (page 7)? What is your most basic, visceral reaction to this statement?

4. Do you think that history is relevant to your day-to-day Christian life in the twenty-first century? Can you explain how the history of Christianity affects your daily or weekly religious routine? Or has history, as Bass contends, "ceased to exist"?

5. The two main focal points of this book are Jesus's Great Command to love God (devotion) and to love our neighbor (ethics)—a focus on tending devoutly to our inner lives while also doing good in the world. The author feels that this balance has been prominent in our past and is the key to our future. Do you agree? How do these two threads play out in your life now? Are you balanced or do you tend to put more importance on one over the other?

   Bible passages for further reflection:
   Luke 10:25–28
   Mark 12:28–34

PART I: THE WAY, EARLY CHRISTIANITY, 100-500

CHAPTER 1: CHRISTIANITY AS A WAY OF LIFE

1. According to *A People's History*, the first five centuries of Christianity have been studied and written about profusely over the last thirty years. The book offers many pieces of lesser known history, but what, specifically in Part I, surprised you most about the first five centuries of Christianity?

2. Do you believe that our current times mirror those of ancient Rome? In what ways are we alike and, perhaps more importantly, how do we differ?

3. Bass writes, "Throughout the first five centuries people understood Christianity primarily as a way of life in the present, not as a doctrinal system" (page 27). Is Christianity still seen this way by outsiders to the religion? Do you personally feel that your faith is an active and adventure-seeking way of life rather than a doctrinal-based practice?

   Bible passages for further reflection:
   John 14:1–6a
   Acts 9:2

CHAPTER 2: DEVOTION: THE LOVE OF GOD

1. It can be hard as modern people to relate to martyrdom as it existed in the first five centuries of Christianity. Bass writes, "As Christ had died for the love of humanity, so they too were called to die for a greater love than their earthly loves" (page 35). What would you consider a modern example of martyrdom in our society? Think not only on a national/international political or religious level, but also at the microcosmic level of your own daily existence—your neighborhood, your church, or your school or office.

2. A major part of the history of devotion in early Christianity focuses on the human relationship with our bodies. *A People's History of Christianity* discusses the practice of honoring the body, which should be considered a sacred gift. In your mind does this relate in some way to many modern cultures' body obsession? Does our society's lack of reverence for the body stem from a lack of faith or is it from a lack of knowledge of our history? Or do you think it is unfair to draw a connection between this ancient practice and our era's obesity and eating disorder epidemic?

3. On page 40, Bass references a criticism of President Barack Obama by evangelical leader James Dobson. How do you feel about Obama's take on the role of religion in politics? Do you agree or disagree with Dobson's critique? Why or why not?

4. The story of Origen is an interesting contrast between allegorical and literal interpretations of the Bible in the early third century. Are you surprised that an argument which is still so central to Christianity today was relevant in the third century? Do you read the Bible literally or allegorically? Will the illumination of history here have any effect on how you will interpret scripture in the future?

Bible passages for further reflection:
Matthew 19:16–21

CHAPTER 3: ETHICS: THE LOVE OF NEIGHBOR

1. The commandment to love our neighbors has remained a central part of Christianity through the ages, but has also proven to be one of the hardest tenets to observe. Consider the selfless acts of early Christians who stayed behind in plague-ridden cities to tend to the sick and dying. If the same circumstances presented themselves today, would you, as a Christian, stay behind to nurse the sick? How have you responded—and how can you continue to respond—to modern-day crises like AIDS, cancer, or recent flu epidemics? Is it necessary to put yourself in danger in order to love your neighbor as Jesus intended?

2. Contemporary values, at times, seem to be dynamically opposed to the Christian ideals of hospitality, living simply, and taking care of the poor. In the fourth century, John Chrysostom preached these ideals and was eventually banished for his vocalness. What parallels can you draw between the fourth century and today in regard to greed, money, and political power silencing the Christian ideals of hospitality? How does this relate to the popularity of today's "prosperity gospel"? Can both the prosperity gospel and true Christian hospitality co-exist?

3. The second century's Origen "pointed out the positive vision of a life of Christian peacemaking. He criticized the army as a society of 'professional violence,' pointing out that Jesus forbids any kind of violence or vengeance against another" (page 72). According to a 2001 survey of the U.S. military conducted by Population Reference Bureau, nearly 80 percent of U.S. military members identified themselves with some denomination of Christianity. If you look through Origen's historical lens, it would be impossible to marry Christianity with the military, but in your opinion is it possible to be a soldier while still being a Christian? Would you argue that part of being a Christian in today's world is serving

your country, and therefore fighting for the freedom of its people? How do you make sense of these two opposing views?

Bible passages for further reflection:
Matthew 25:34–36
Luke 14:12–14

PART II: THE CATHEDRAL, MEDIEVAL CHRISTIANITY, 500-1450

CHAPTER 4: CHRISTIANITY AS SPIRITUAL ARCHITECTURE

1. In chapter four, Bass draws parallels between contemporary and medieval society, culminating in a quote from French historian Regine Pernoud, who wrote, "'We are actually closer to medieval times than to those times of the more recent past." Do you agree or disagree with Pernoud's assessment?

2. According to *A People's History,* the actual physical structure of the medieval church was considered holy. Consider your own church. Do you think that that building is treated as "holy geography"? How does your church do well serving as the center point of a community, and how could it do better?

3. Choirs were introduced to the Church in the sixth century, during the rule of Pope Gregory I. What role does music play in your worship services? How would your spiritual life change if music was taken out of our modern worship?

Bible passages for further reflection:
Genesis 3
Luke 10:29–37

CHAPTER 5: DEVOTION: PARADISE RESTORED

1. The idea of a sacred pilgrimage has fallen somewhat to the wayside in most mainline denominations of modern Christianity, but it is still a very important part of other Abrahamic religions today. If you were to plan a holy Christian pilgrimage, where would you go and what would you hope to learn? Would you be influenced more by the Celtic idea of "sacred journeys," where the wandering itself was the destination, or by the ancients, who made pilgrimages to specific physical locations tied to Christ or the saints?

2. Beginning on page 105, Bass addresses the medieval practice of "Praying the Hours." This type of devotion takes discipline and hard work. If you have one, do you find your own prayer practice to be work? Do you find it difficult to fit into your hectic daily schedule? Do you use a prayer book or daily devotional to help make your prayer practice more of a habit? Is it something you enjoy?

3. Beginning on page 109, Bass tells the story of Julian of Norwich. She writes, "To her [Julian], fatherhood represented God's kingship, a kind of distant rule, whereas God's motherhood demonstrated the worldly, sensual, and active property of God." What do you think of this very early Christian interpretation of the divine feminine? Was it as surprising to you as it was to Butler Bass' students on the day of their extra-credit pop quiz?

4. Do you believe that we have something to learn from the medieval people regarding death and the art of dying well? Why do you think that death, the one inevitable and guaranteed life experience, has become an awkward and uncomfortable issue in our post-modern culture?

Bible passages for further reflection:
Isaiah 11:1–11
Revelation 21:1–7

CHAPTER 6: ETHICS: WHO IS MY NEIGHBOR?

1. According to the author, one of the most troubling ethical questions for Christians in the Middle Ages was "who is my neighbor?" Is this still a difficult question for contemporary Christians to answer? Through the lens of your faith, how do you define who your "neighbors" are?

2. Bass writes that in the late thirteenth century "in the pursuit of philosophy, Christians, Jews, and Muslims found common questions of faith and reason—and offered a common critique of corrupt religious authorities" (page 126). Later, she poses a very poignant question: "If we share their problems today, might we too find friendship through *convivencia?*" (page 127). How would you answer this question?

3. Do you agree with Bass's critique of conservative Protestant leaders' actions during October 2002, when the U.S. was headed to war in Iraq? What would you have said to President Bush if he had called you to ask whether or not we should go to war? What advice would you have given him?

4. On page 143, Bass concludes the story of a group of persecuted Christians named the Beguines. She writes that the movement's central spiritual insight was "Love is the Christian way of life, and Jesus's followers are called to enact his way of love." Why, when trying to follow such a simple Christian creed, were these people persecuted? Does this happen still in modern society? Where and how?

   Bible passages for further reflection:
   Isaiah 56:6–8
   Acts 2:1–13
   Revelation 5

PART III: THE WORD: REFORMATION CHRISTIANITY, 1450-1650

CHAPTER 7: CHRISTIANITY AS LIVING WORDS

1. During the Reformation, it is clear that words alone had the power to change things. Do words alone still have the power to change things or have they lost their potency in the cacophony of our modern world? What's a specific example that backs up your opinion?

2. Bass writes, "In recent years, many Christian leaders have called for a new reformation" (page 153). Do you think that the church is in need of another reformation? Is Protestant Christianity, by nature, always in need of reformation, as theologian Frederick Herzog believes? Do you agree with Bass's assessment that "the reform of Christianity appears overdue" or do you think Christianity is doing just fine as it is?

3. The year 1440 saw the invention of the printing press, which ushered in the empowerment of laypeople and the emergence of a new merchant or business class in Europe. What modern invention would you compare to the printing press? How has this modern invention changed the world as a whole and how has it affected Christianity specifically?

Bible passages for further reflection:
John 1:1
James 3:1–10

CHAPTER 8: DEVOTION: SPEAKING OF FAITH

1. Martin Luther's break from Catholicism had "everything do to with words," according to Bass. She writes, "Western Christianity split between the Catholics and the protesters because of a dis-

agreement between an active and passive verb. Words had real consequences. And reading scripture for its transformative power emerged as the primary practice of Protestant piety" (page 165). Is this central tenet of Protestantism still true today? If not, what is the primary practice of Protestant piety today?

2. Johannes Schwöbel, a German reformer, wrote, "The game has been turned completely upside down. Formerly one learned the laws of God from the priests. Now it is necessary to go to school of the laity and learn to read the Bible from them" (page 177). Do you think that this transfer of power to the people made the church less corrupt? Or did this flood of new information simply open the door to misinterpretations and bad translations of the original scripture? Does this reversal continue to play out in your own congregation or denomination?

3. Prayer is one of the practices that have survived throughout Christianity's entire history. Have you ever had a surprise encounter with prayer like Tony Jones, whose story appears on page 177? How important is prayer in your daily Christian life? Do you believe that prayer is truly transformative or is it merely a practice that is required by your faith?

Bible passages for further reflection:

Acts 2:17–18
1 Peter 3:15
Acts 4:31–35

CHAPTER 9: ETHICS: WALKING THE TALK

1. The reformers of the sixteenth century raised the same questions that we face now: "If faith alone saves, then what is the role of works in the Christian life? What is the basis for ethics?" How would you answer these questions today?

2. In many ways and for many Christians both now and in the past, being a Christian is a constant internal battle between selfishness and selflessness. Bass, in boiling down Martin Luther's words, writes, "True Christians demonstrate love through doing good, when 'faith is truly active through love.' People should not care for the neighbor to save their own souls; rather, they do good because faith 'finds expression in works of freest service'" (page 183). Is this one of your struggles as a Christian? If so, how do you deal with the tension? If this is not something you struggle with, has it always been this easy for you or was there a particular experience during your faith journey that illuminated the way?

3. In 1525, the shopkeepers of Memmingen created a political entity called "A Christian Union"; their constitution was based on the practice of social justice and stated that all people had innate rights to things like land, freedom, and wild game. According to Bass, "the impulse for social justice remained a theological cornerstone of Protestant practice" (page 188). How do you define the term social justice? Do you agree that it has remained a cornerstone of Protestantism?

4. A recurring theme in *A People's History of Christianity* is that in each historical period, someone or some group always comes back to the true root of Christianity as love. In 1675, Philipp Jakob Spener, a Lutheran minister, reminded his parishioners that, "It is not enough that we hear the Word with our outward ear, but we must let it penetrate to our heart" (page 205). Do you believe that this central belief is still alive and well in our church communities?

5. If justice is the cornerstone of contemporary faith and love is the true root of Christianity, what is the relationship between love and justice? How do the two interrelate in your congregation, denomination, and the larger church? Do you tend to emphasize one over the other?

Bible passages for further reflection:
Luke 1:46–56
Luke 4:14–21
Matthew 6:9–13

PART IV: THE QUEST: MODERN CHRISTIANITY, 1650–1945

CHAPTER 10: CHRISTIANITY AS A QUEST FOR TRUTH

1. Bass contends that Enlightenment theologians "revolutionized Christianity by making it more rational, irenic, scientific, and liberal" (page 216). How do you think the Enlightenment changed Christianity? Did it change Christianity for better or worse? Did it open the door to more questions and anxiety or did it strengthen faith? Has your faith today encountered any trickle-down effects from this period in history?

2. Bass describes modernity as a time when people "assumed there existed *one* truth about the universe and its various components" (page 218). They saw life as a "quest" to find that one truth. Do you see life as a journey (not focusing on the end result) or as a quest (focusing on the destination)? Do you believe, as the early moderns did, that there is one truth to the universe? What effect does this have on your faith?

Bible passages for further reflection:
Luke 11:5–13

CHAPTER 11: DEVOTION: THE QUEST FOR LIGHT

1. The Quaker focus on the "inner light" is something many people today can relate to. This search for the inner light is part of many

different religions and spiritual practices even outside of Christianity. Do you find that your faith is influenced by sources outside of Christianity? Is the search for the "light within" part of your faith journey? Or are you more traditional and doctrinal?

2. On page 236, Thomas Jefferson is introduced as a spiritual figure. Is this surprising to you? Have you ever thought of Jefferson as a religious leader? Would you have been surprised, as Butler Bass was, to see him depicted in a stained-glass window in a church?

3. This chapter explores the answer to the question "Where is God?" and offers answers from a handful of early modern Christian sources. How would you answer this question? With which group do you most identify?

4. What role has doubt played in your spiritual journey? When has doubt been an obstacle to your religious practice, and when has it, as Emily Dickinson described, kept believing nimble?

   Bible passages for further reflection:
   Genesis 1:1–5
   John 1:1–10
   Matthew 5:14–16
   Ephesians 1:15–23

CHAPTER 12: ETHICS: KINGDOM QUEST

1. One of the most striking aspects of this chapter is the distance we have traveled as a society in the last 150 years. Do you attribute the equalities and freedoms that have come about in those years to Christianity? Or do you see human rights as a political issue, not a spiritual one? What, in your wildest dreams, do you predict will shock Americans 150 years from now?

2. At its core, does Christianity lend itself more to capitalism or socialism? Can either extreme work in a sustainable way with regard to Christian values?

3. On page 266, Bass quotes an elderly gentleman in Pennsylvania as saying, "Without evolution, there is no progressive Christianity." Do you agree or disagree with this statement? What does "progressive Christianity" mean to you? Do you identify yourself as a progressive Christian?

4. Do you believe, in the words of the U.S. Religious Landscape Survey, that "many religions can lead to eternal life" (page 275)? Bass describes the World's Parliament of Religions, the watershed event that introduced pluralism, on a popular level, to Western Christians over 100 years ago. What do you imagine, or what would you like to see, as the role of pluralism in your church 100 years from now?

   Bible passages for further reflection:
   Luke 6:20–23
   Matthew 5:1–11
   Acts 2:41–47

PART V: THE RIVER: CONTEMPORARY CHRISTIANITY, 1945–NOW

CHAPTER 13: THE RIVER

1. Bass writes on page 288, "In the United States it has become commonplace to speak of how divided our society is, a fifty-fifty nation permanently roiled in a culture war of conservatives and liberals." Do you agree with this statement? Is America more divided now than it ever has been in its past or does it just feel that way to those of us living in our current state of turmoil?

2. Do you see Christianity, as the author does, as "a fluid faith"? What does this mean to you? Is change frightening or exciting to you? Do you prefer a comforting faith or new adventure?

3. On page 295, Bass quotes a thirty-something progressive Christian pastor in Washington, DC, who says her congregation communicates to her that "when others know that they are going to church, they always have to qualify it by saying, 'But it's not like that.'" Is this your experience? Has anyone ever made a similar qualification to you?

4. Sociologist Robert Wuthrow found in the 1990s that "Christian spirituality was developing a new orientation toward practice" (page 298). What are your spiritual practices? If you don't have any, which of the practices discussed in chapter thirteen sound appealing to you?

5. Bass writes that she has encountered many Christians who weave other spiritual traditions and practices into their Christian practices. Do you believe that you can still be fully Christian while being open to other religious practices? If not, why? If so, which traditions do you personally find appealing?

   Bible passages for further reflection:
   Psalms 65:9–10
   Isaiah 41:17–20
   Isaiah 43:14–21
   Revelation 22:1–5

EPILOGUE AND FINAL THOUGHTS

1. Were you surprised by the distinction Dr. Livingston made between nostalgia and history? How would you explain the difference between nostalgia and history? Do you think that, as he claimed, nostalgia undermines hope? Are you nostalgic for the

past? Or, do you believe that you have a realistic sense of the Christian past? How has your sense of history changed as a result of reading this book?

2. Bass describes *A People's History of Christianity* as "a history of hope." Do you feel hopeful at the conclusion of this book? What do you see as the greatest cause for hope for present-day Christianity? How can you participate in that promising future, and how can your church community participate?

3. Of all the reformers, thinkers, and ordinary people of faith profiled and cited in this book, who spoke to you most? Make a short list of the three people who most inspired you. Write a single sentence describing what you most admired about this person (or group of people). How can you apply their example, words, and insights to your own life and your community?

4. If Bass were to add a Part VI to her book thirty years from now, what do you think the Devotion chapter would say about the way twenty-first-century Christians interpret the command to love God? What do you think the Ethics chapter would identify as our approach to fostering community and loving our neighbor? That is, in what direction do you see the church, both your own parish and the larger community, developing in the next decades?

5. Is there anyone or any movement in Christian history that you would have liked seen included in *A People's History of Christianity?* In a very real way, no history is ever complete, as it is always open to new stories. Following publication, Diana Butler Bass said she would have liked to also include a story on Pentecostalism focusing on either William Seymour, an African-American preacher who founded the Azusa Street Mission, or Aimee Semple McPherson, the founder of the Four Square Gospel Church. She also would have added a section on indigenous tribes' conversion stories and how native peoples adapted Christianity to their traditional practices. What would you add and why?

6. What does it mean to you to "make history"? Do you think that regular people create history? How do you think your life is contributing to the larger story of the history of Christianity? How would you like to be remembered in relation to your faith, the good you do in the world, and in your congregation or spiritual community?